IMAGES
of Rail

RAILROADING AROUND DOTHAN AND THE WIREGRASS REGION

IMAGES
of Rail

RAILROADING AROUND DOTHAN AND THE WIREGRASS REGION

Dothan Landmarks Foundation

ARCADIA
PUBLISHING

ISBN 978-0-7385-1719-3

Published by Arcadia Publishing
Charleston, South Carolina

Printed in the United States of America

Library of Congress Catalog Card Number: 2004109813

For all general information contact Arcadia Publishing at:
Telephone 843-853-2070
Fax 843-853-0044
E-mail sales@arcadiapublishing.com
For customer service and orders:
Toll-Free 1-888-313-2665

Visit us on the Internet at www.arcadiapublishing.com

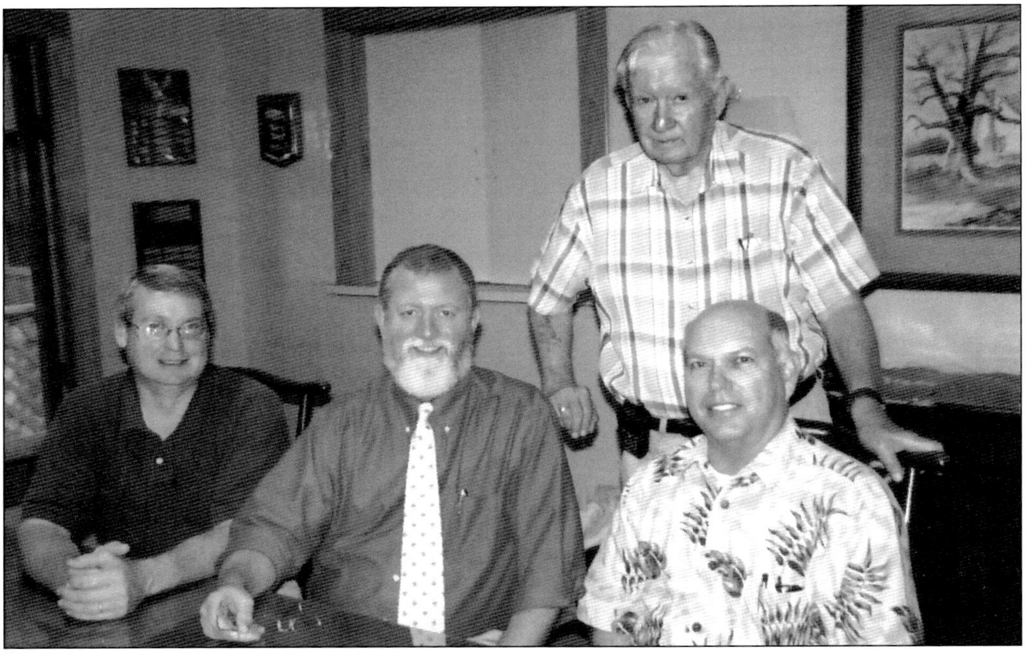

Pictured here, from left to right, is the Historical Preservation Committee of Dothan Landmarks Foundation, Inc.: William Holman, executive director, Dothan Landmarks Foundation, Inc.; Dr. Marty Olliff, director, Archives of Wiregrass History and Culture; Lewis Covington, committee chairman (standing); and T. Larry Smith, Henry County Historical Group. Not pictured is Dr. Larry Brown of Troy University, Dothan Campus. (Courtesy of Dothan Landmarks Foundation, Inc. [DLF].)

Contents

ACKNOWLEDGMENTS

I was a bit surprised (and, of course, flattered) when Katie White of Arcadia Publishing called me several months ago to ask if our organization would consider compiling a book under their *Images of Rail* series.

Our small but energetic historic preservation committee jumped at the opportunity. We were still excited about the success of our recent publication *Houston County: The First 100 Years* through Arcadia's *Images of America* series. Committee members Lewis Covington, T. Larry Smith, Dr. Martin Olliff, and Dr. Larry Brown worked diligently to complete the book you are holding in just a few short months. I feel that a special thank you is in order to Dr. Olliff, director of the Archives of Wiregrass History and Culture (AWHC), for his willingness to share so much of his expertise with historic photographs and computers, as well as for his assistance in writing the captions.

Many of the images found in this book are from the Dothan Landmarks Foundation's (DLF) archives. We selected the bulk of these images from our Tom Solomon Collection. Mr. Solomon was a well-known railroad enthusiast from Headland, Alabama, who not only photographed and collected railroad images, but also was an accomplished painter of railroad scenes. His photograph collection, much of which have never been published until now, was donated to the foundation after his death in 1988.

Many other images found in this book were made available to the committee from a variety of sources. I want to take this opportunity to thank the following individuals, organizations, and institutions for so graciously allowing us to share their photographs with others: Abbeville Public Library, Archives of Wiregrass History and Culture, Theresa Adkison, Ashford Depot Restoration and Preservation Foundation, Bay County Public Library, Rhoda Bell, Billy Benton, Larry Brown, Quinton Bruner, Chattahoochee Industrial Railroad, Clay County Public Library, Paul Dalton, Gordon Dodson, Fred Fischer, Tommy Henderson, Henry County Historical Group, Houston-Love Memorial Library, David Kirkland, Pioneer Museum of Alabama, T. Larry Smith, Reid Smith, the Doug Snellgrove estate, Harry and Leslie Summerford, Troy Public Library, and the Washington County Historical Society.

Unfortunately, due to limited space, many images we wanted to include did not make the final proof. Therefore, this book is not intended to serve as a comprehensive history of railroading in the Wiregrass Region. Instead, we hope it pays tribute to the railroad industry and helps capture the spirit of this important period in our history.

William Holman
Executive Director
Dothan Landmarks Foundation, Inc.
Dothan, Alabama

Introduction

In the 1880s, when railroads first pushed into the Wiregrass Region of southeast Alabama, southwest Georgia, and northwest Florida, the railroad industry was entering its "Golden Age," a time of record expansion and profits for the industry. Only a few years before, the East and West Coasts were connected by the transcontinental railroad, enabling a passenger to travel across the entire country. From 1870 to 1916, total track miles in the United States grew from 53,000 miles to 245,000 miles, an average of over 11 miles per day. During this time, technological improvements such as standard track, more powerful locomotives, air brakes, and larger cars brought uniformity to the industry.

For the Wiregrass Region, the introduction of the railroad meant unprecedented growth. Each train brought potential new settlers, products, merchandise, and a way to ship raw materials such as turpentine, cotton, and other goods to market. Dothan's population exploded with the arrival of the railroad. For example, in 1889, the year the railroad arrived, the town's population was 240. By 1893, only four years later, Dothan had grown to 1,500. By 1900, only 11 years after the first train arrived, the population had grown to 3,875, and by 1920, Dothan's population had already swelled to 10,000 residents.

The pinnacle for rail travel in terms of numbers was 1920, with our nation's trains carrying 1.2 billion passengers. From 1920 to 1941, an expanding network of paved roads, development of the automobile, and the Depression shrank demand for the railroads. Although World War II increased rail traffic, profits continued a downward slide. It was the beginning of the end.

From 1950 to 1992, total track miles decreased 39.2 percent to 136,000 miles. Bankruptcies, mergers, and acquisitions of many railroad companies occurred during this time period due to a continued decrease in passenger travel and freight and mail service. In 1971, the federally subsidized Amtrak was born as a way to help relieve railroads of passenger service deficits.

By 1970, airlines carried 73 percent of all passenger traffic. Railroads carried a mere 7.2 percent. Rail carries even fewer passengers today.

Yet, if you listen, chances are you can still hear the sound of a train whistle in the distance or catch a glimpse of a freight train as it rolls through the countryside toward some unknown destination. The railroad is still a vibrant part of our heritage that we all share. The images in this book help tell the story of *Railroading around Dothan and the Wiregrass Region*.

One

Depots

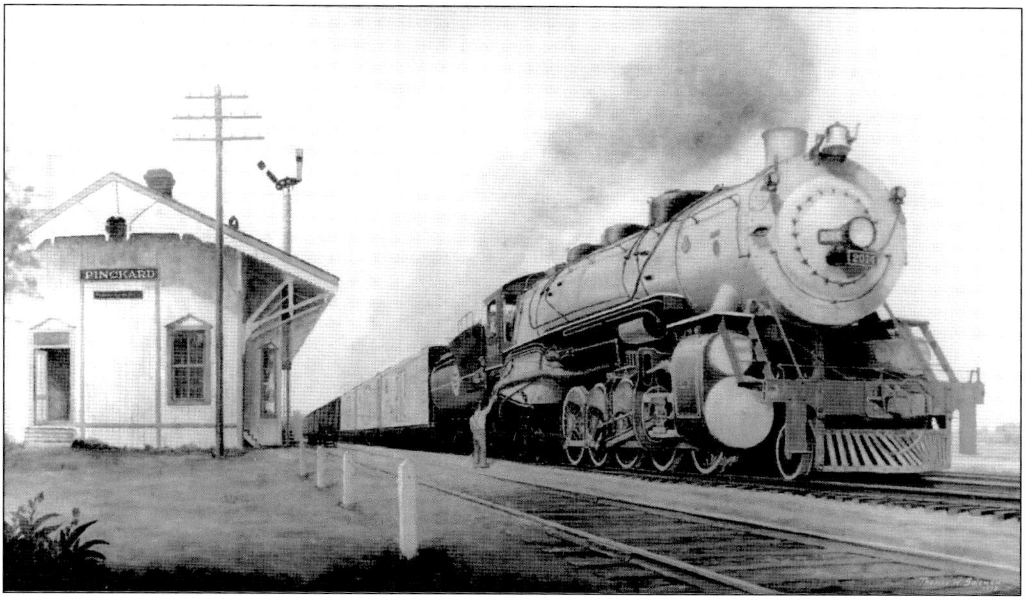

The railroad depot—an icon of the industry—is vividly captured in this painting by the late Tom Solomon of Headland, Alabama. It depicts the passenger station at Pinckard in Dale County, Alabama. (Courtesy of the DLF Dixie Depot Collection, Archives of Wiregrass History and Culture [AWHC].)

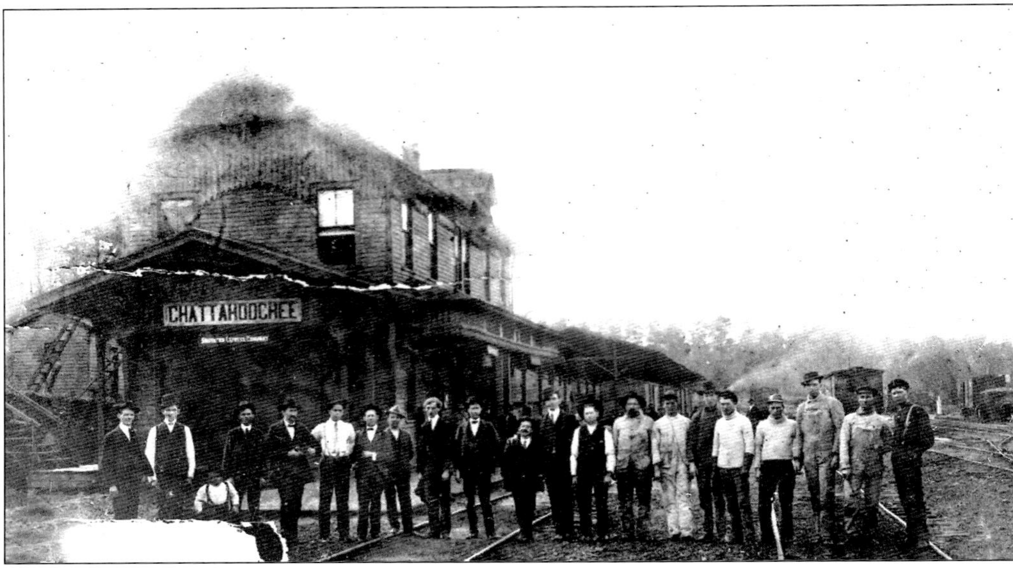

When railroads laid their tracks through the Wiregrass Region in the late 1800s, it marked the beginning of a new era. Here, several townspeople are gathered near the passenger station at Chattahoochee in Gadsden County, Florida. (Courtesy of the Tom Solomon Collection, DLF.)

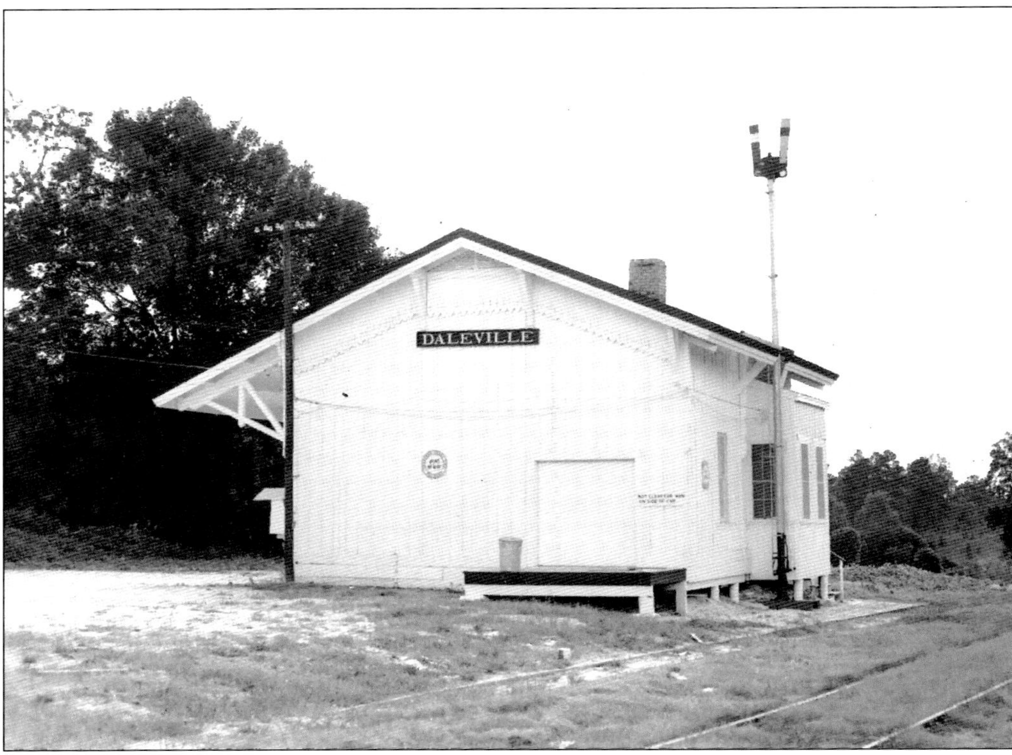

Even the smallest of passenger stations also served as freight depots. This photo of the station at Daleville in Dale County, Alabama, clearly shows the small platform used for loading and unloading freight. (Courtesy of the Ashford Depot Restoration Foundation.)

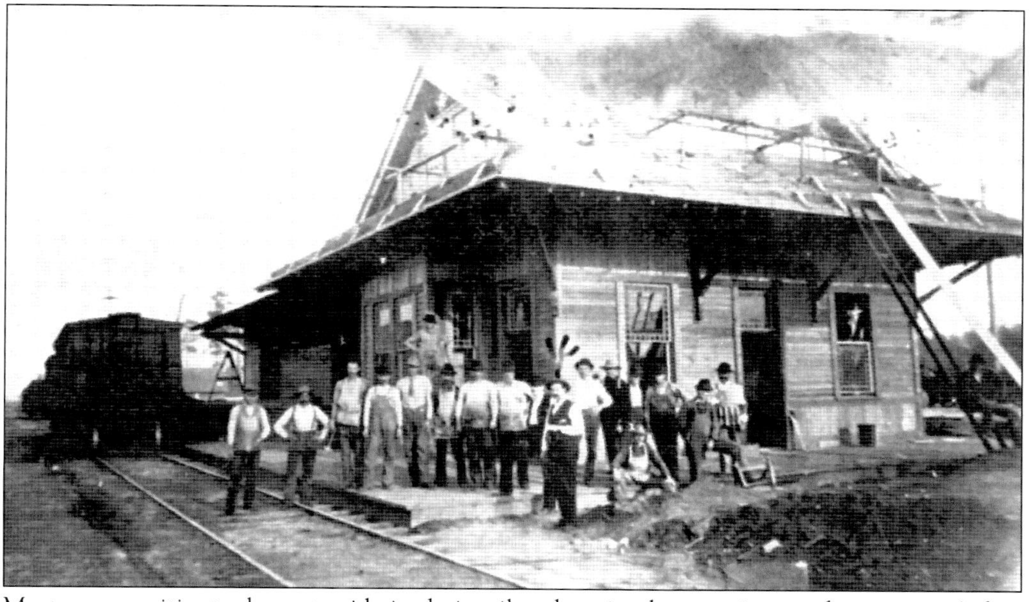

Most communities took great pride in their railroad station because it was often a visitor's first impression of their town. Pictured is the construction in 1896 of the station at Chipley in Washington County, Florida. (Courtesy of Washington Company Historical Society.)

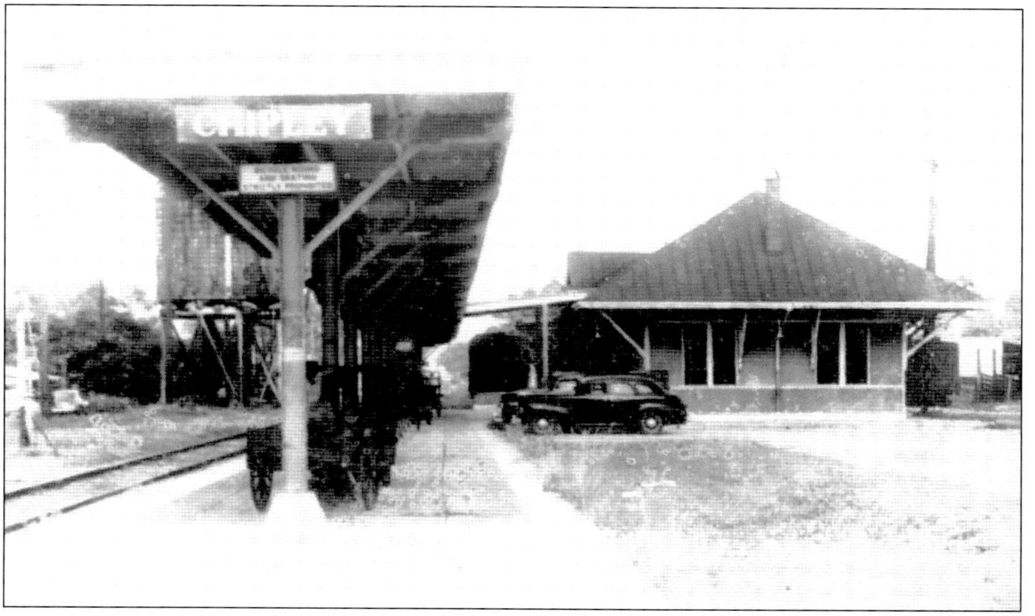

William D. Chipley, a Florida railroad baron, is responsible for developing the Pensacola & Atlantic Railroad in the 1870s that passed through the Florida town now bearing his name. This railroad later became part of the Louisville & Nashville (L & N). (Courtesy of Washington Company [Florida] Historical Society.)

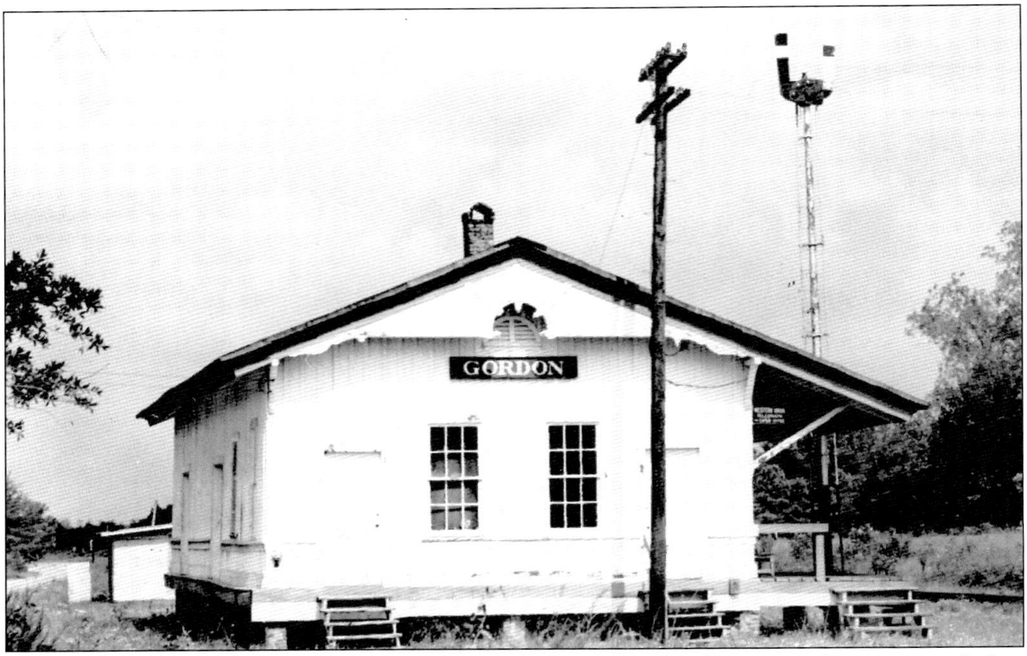

One common architectural feature of railroad depots is the large, overhanging roof that protected waiting passengers from the elements. The overhang is clearly seen in this photo of the Gordon station in southern Houston County, Alabama. (Courtesy of the Tom Solomon Collection, DLF.)

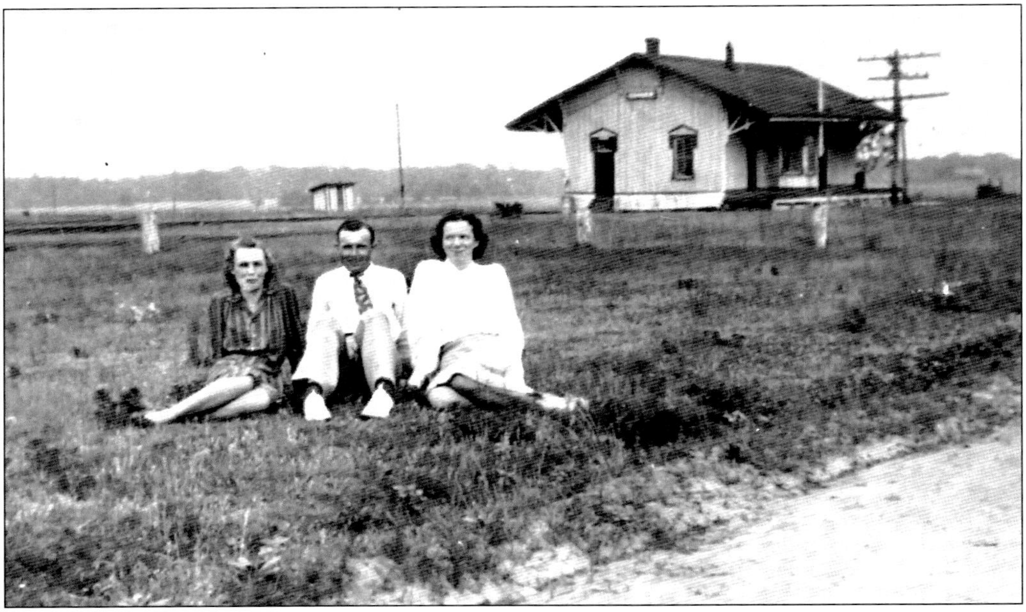

Once the railroads became established, depots literally dotted the landscape and were found every few miles along most tracks. In March of 1942, these unidentified people posed for their photo near the Grimes station in Dale County, Alabama. (Courtesy of the Tom Solomon Collection, DLF.)

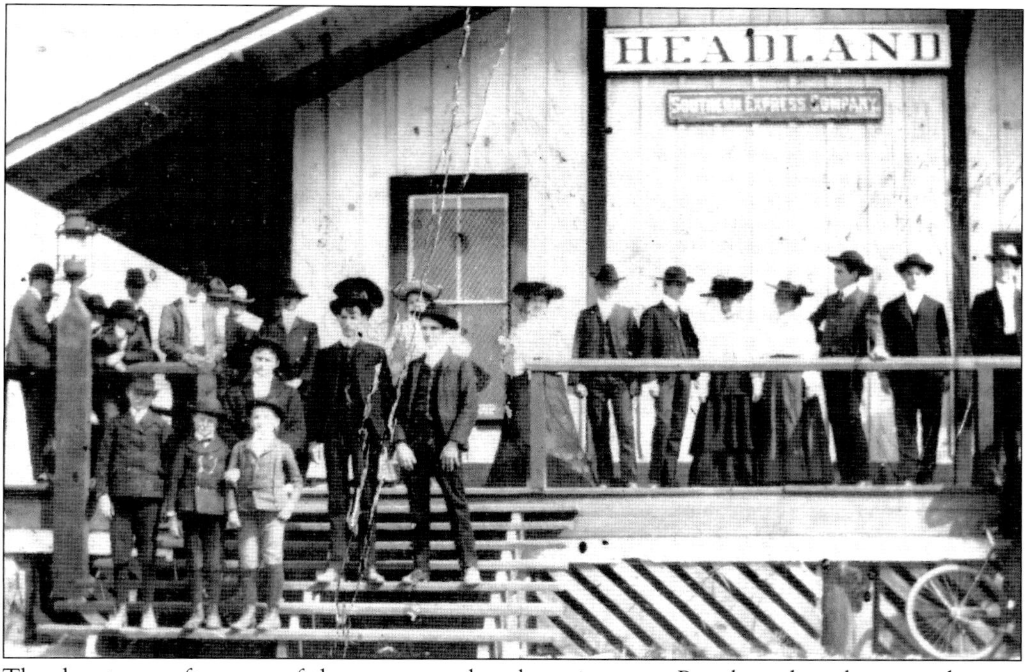

The depot was often one of the most popular places in town. People gathered to see who was getting on or off the train or to see what new products or merchandise had arrived. This 1903 photo is of the Headland depot in Henry County, Alabama. (Courtesy of the Henry County Historical Group.)

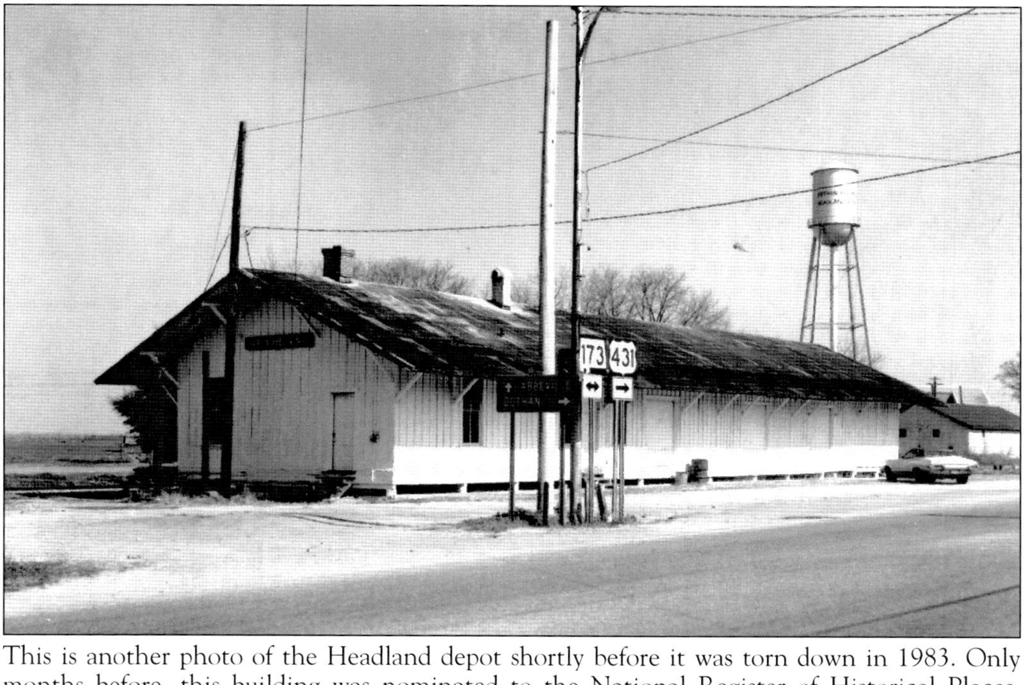

This is another photo of the Headland depot shortly before it was torn down in 1983. Only months before, this building was nominated to the National Register of Historical Places. (Courtesy of the Henry County Historical Group.)

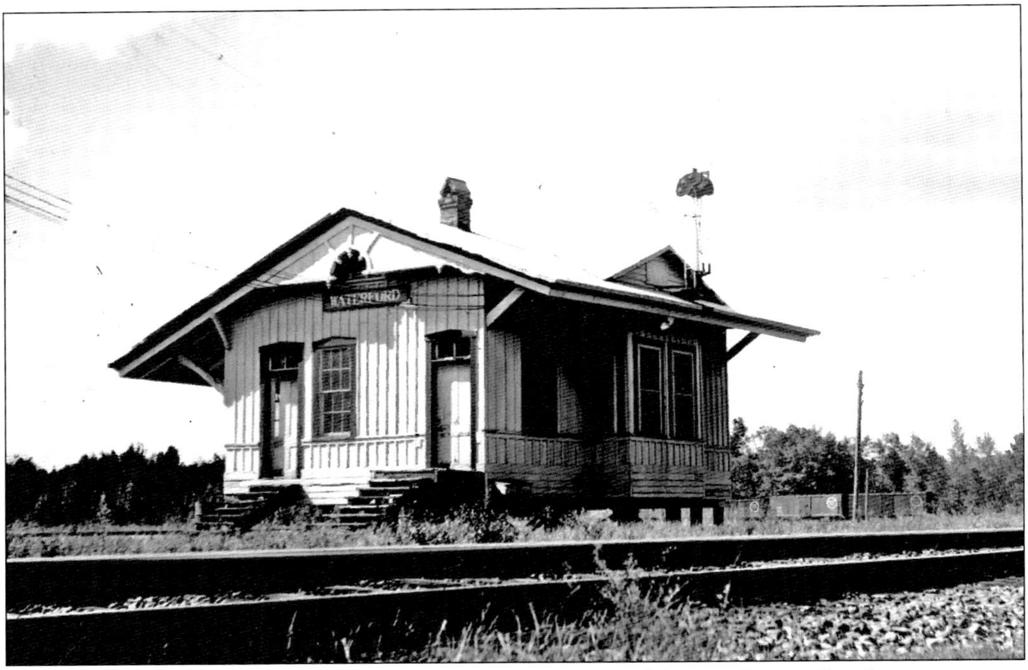

This image is of the depot at Waterford in Dale County, Alabama. Originally, the community was known as Demmick, but it was changed to Waterford in 1907 because of the large water tank adjacent to the tracks where steam engines stopped to refill. (Courtesy of the Tom Solomon Collection, DLF.)

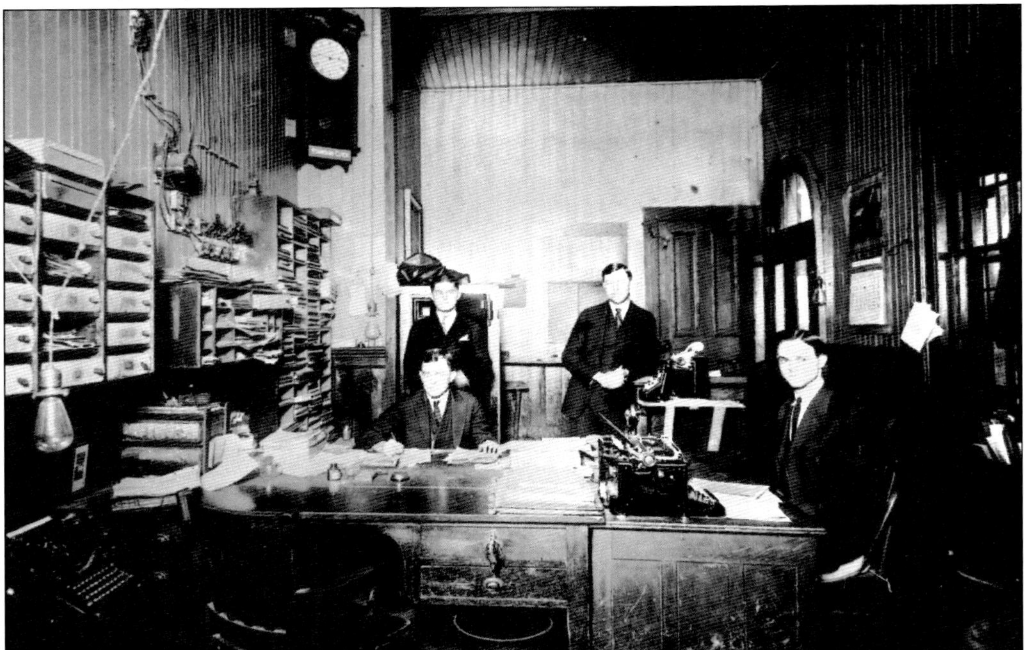

These employees of the Central of Georgia Railway took a break from their duties to pose for a picture inside the office of the Central of Georgia depot in Dothan. (Courtesy of DLF.)

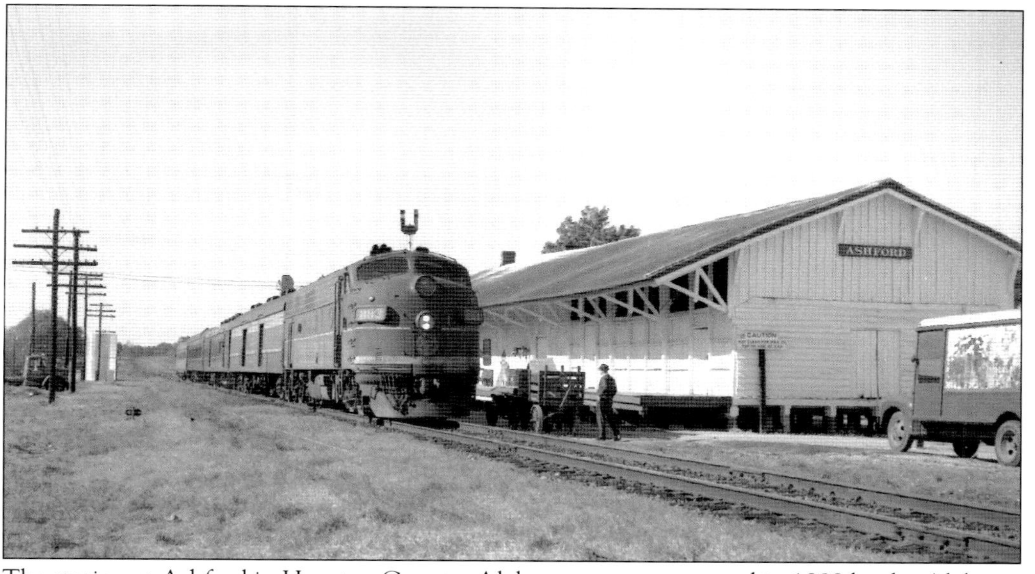

The station at Ashford in Houston County, Alabama, was constructed in 1888 by the Alabama Midland Railway at a cost of $4,500. This photo of the combination passenger and freight station was taken in December of 1963. (Courtesy of the Tom Solomon Collection, DLF.)

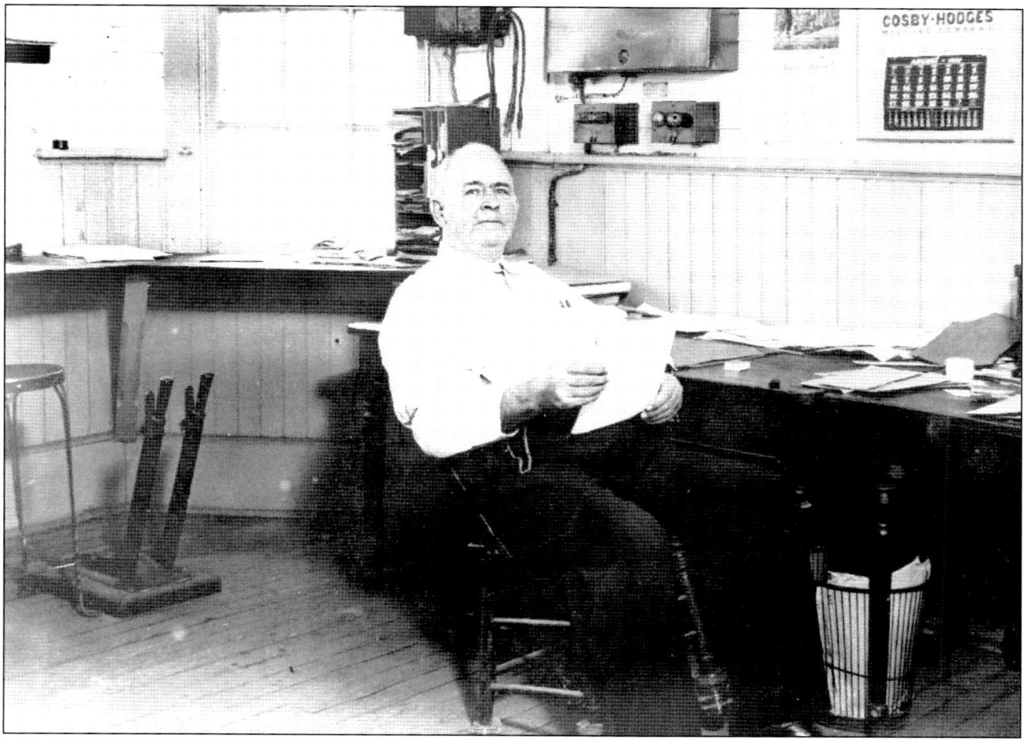

J.C. Allgood, station master at the Ashford station in Houston County, Alabama, posed for this picture in 1937. Notice the two levers behind him. These levers controlled the semaphore pole erected outside the station. (Courtesy of the Ashford Depot Restoration Foundation.)

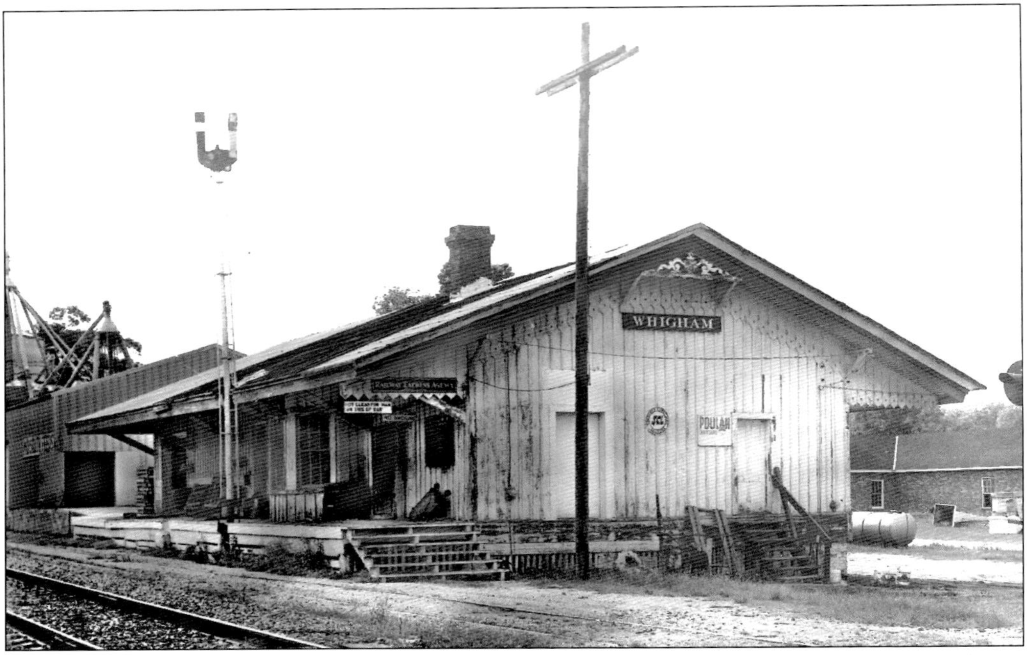

This photo depicts the station at Whigham in Decatur County, Georgia. Notice the two doors. Early depots were built when travel was racially segregated and stations had separate waiting rooms for blacks and whites. (Courtesy of the Tom Solomon Collection, DLF.)

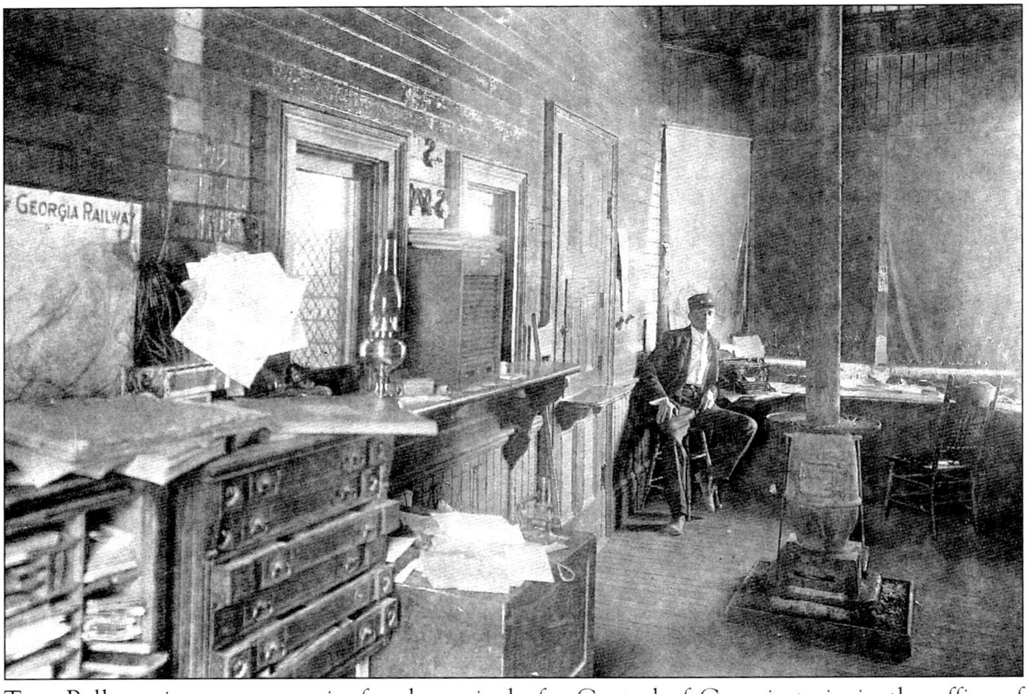

Tom Bell, station master, waits for the arrival of a Central of Georgia train in the office of the station at Slocomb in Geneva County, Alabama, c. 1900. (Courtesy of Rhoda Bell and Paul Dalton.)

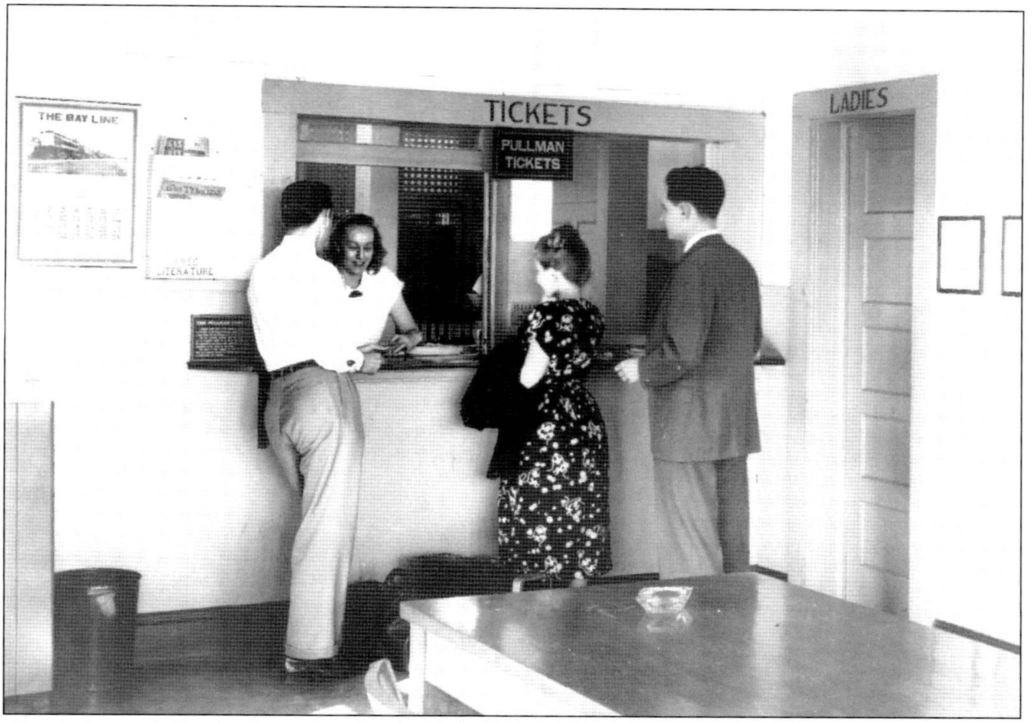

The Atlanta & St. Andrews Bay Railway, known as the Bay Line, was popular for its excursion trains to Panama City, Florida. In this 1948 photo, several people are shown purchasing tickets at the station in Panama City, Florida. (Courtesy of David Kirkland.)

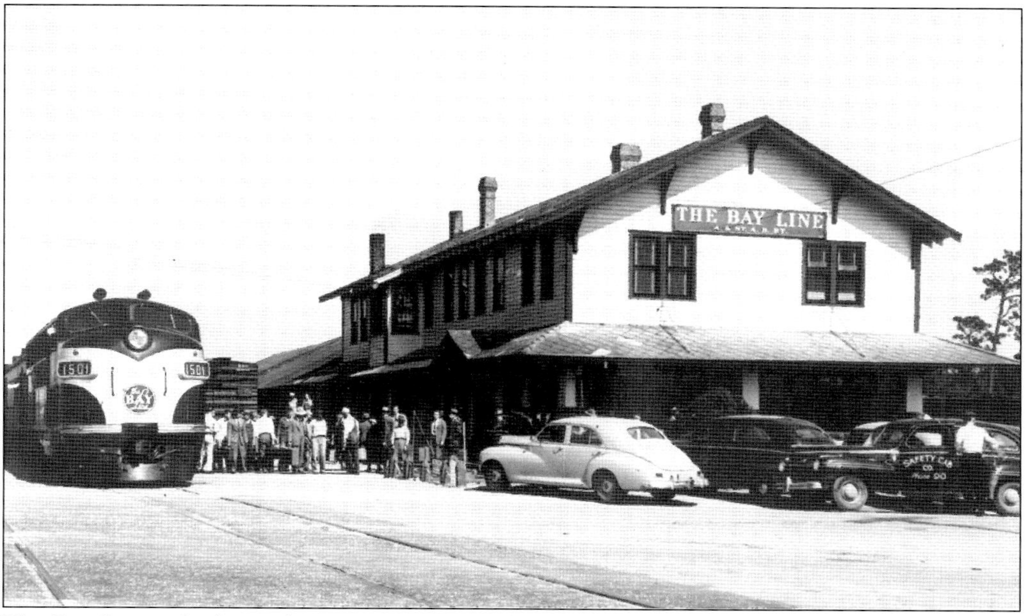

The Bay Line, which ran from Panama City, Florida, to Dothan, Alabama, became one of the premier short line railroads in the country. This 1950s photo depicts the Bay Line station in Panama City, Florida. (Courtesy of David Kirkland.)

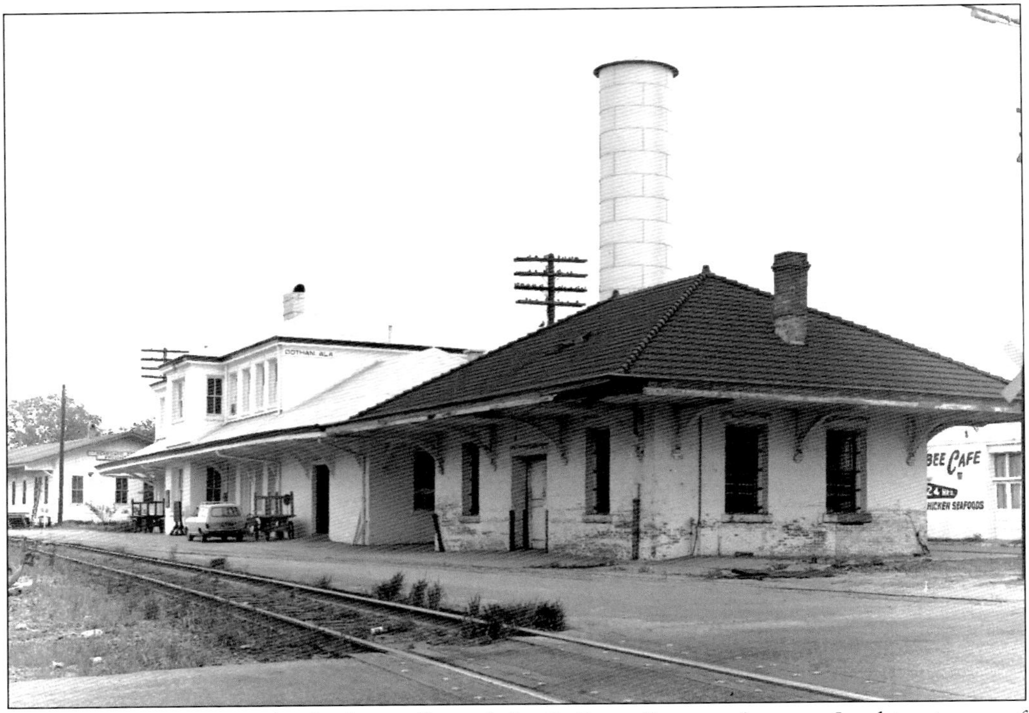

Many railway stations also had an office of the Railway Express Agency. In this picture of the Atlantic Coast Line (ACL) station in Dothan, Alabama, the Railway Express Agency was located in the adjacent building with the tile roof. (Courtesy of the Doug Snellgrove Estate.)

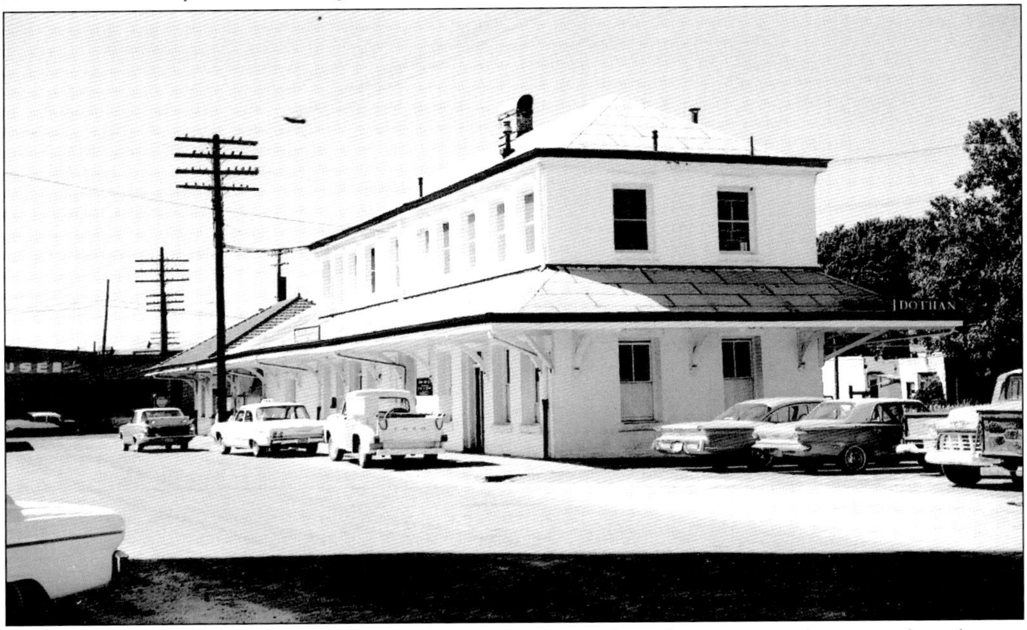

The Atlantic Coast Line station in Dothan was located in the section of town referred to as "Dixie." Built in 1907, the station is now listed on the National Register of Historic Places. (Courtesy of the Tom Solomon Collection, DLF.)

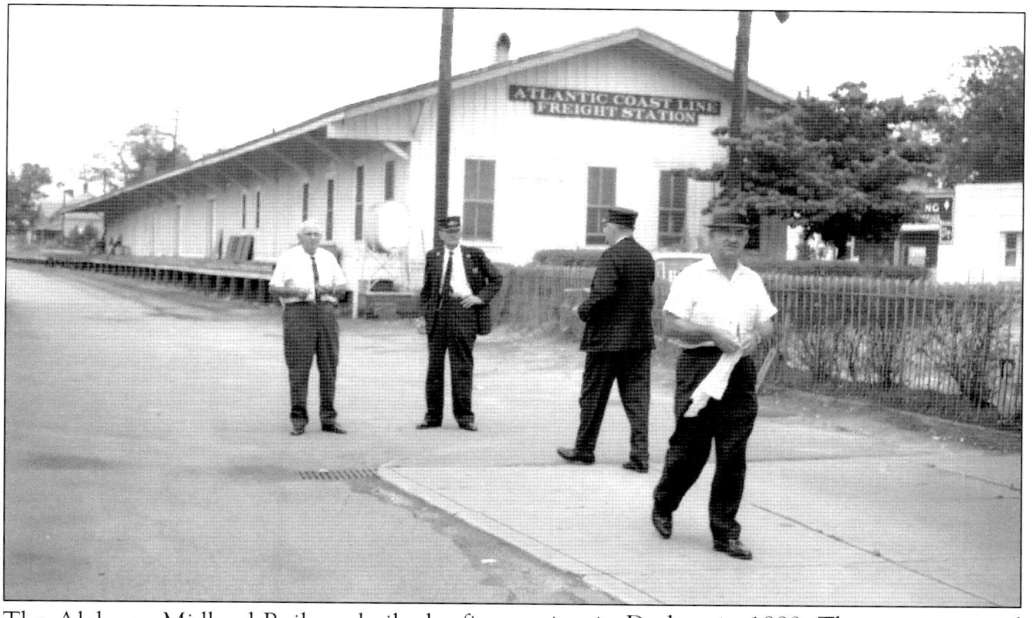

The Alabama Midland Railway built the first station in Dothan in 1889. The passenger and freight station can be seen in the background of this 1964 photo. Pictured from left to right are ? Clements, C.H. Quinn, D.W. Davidson, and J.M. Garner. (Courtesy of the Tom Solomon Collection, DLF.)

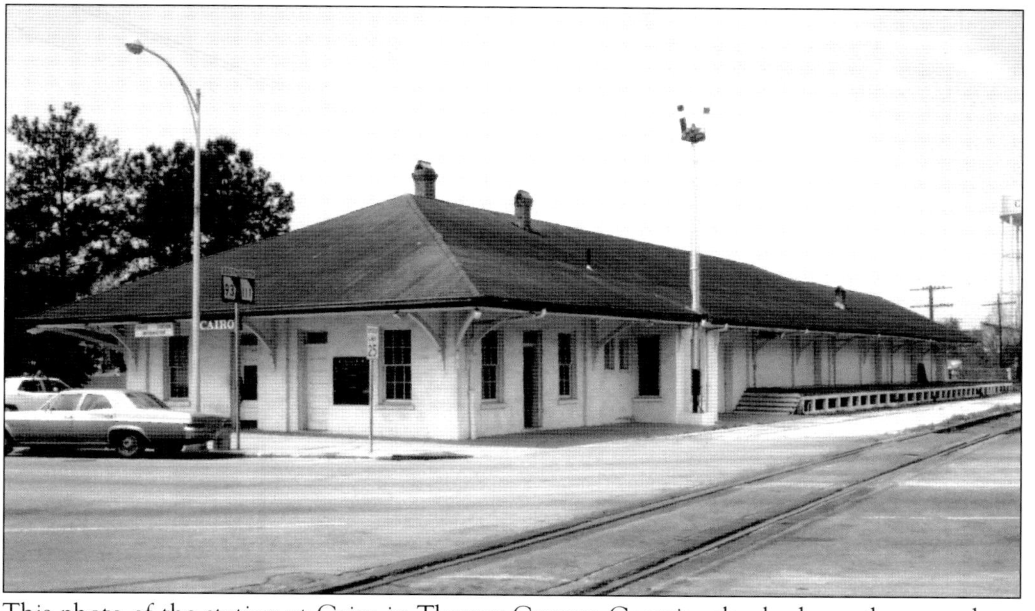

This photo of the station at Cairo in Thomas County, Georgia, clearly shows the semaphore pole protruding through the roof of the building. These poles were used to signal to the engineers when it was safe to proceed. (Courtesy of the Tom Solomon Collection, DLF.)

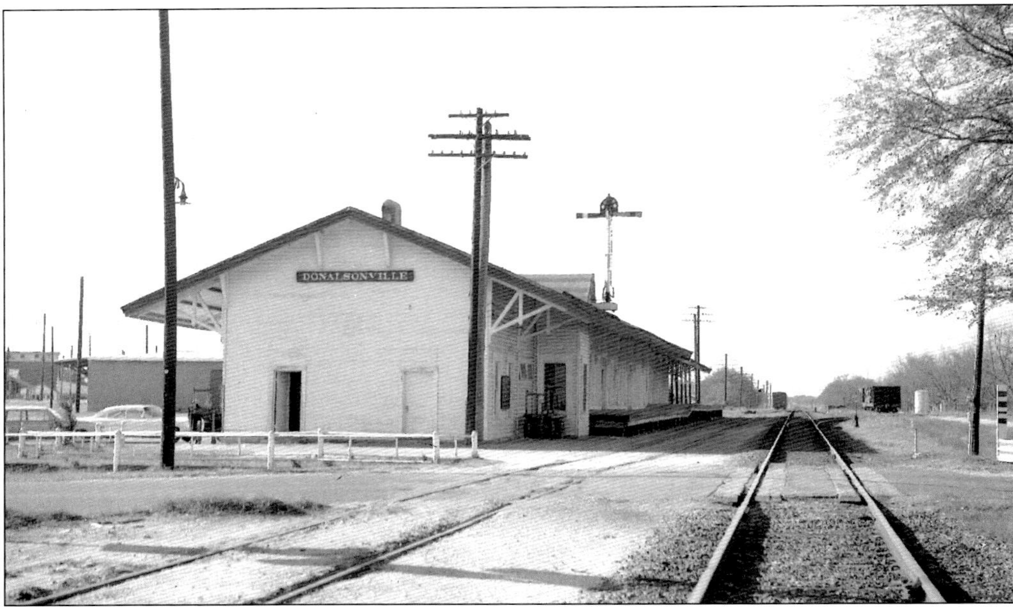

As shown in this November 30, 1963 photograph, the Donalsonville, Georgia depot was typical of those built by the Alabama Midland Railway (and later the Atlantic Coast Line) for passengers and freight. The office and racially segregated waiting rooms were behind the bay window, and the freight section adjoined the dock. (Courtesy of the Tom Solomon Collection, DLF.)

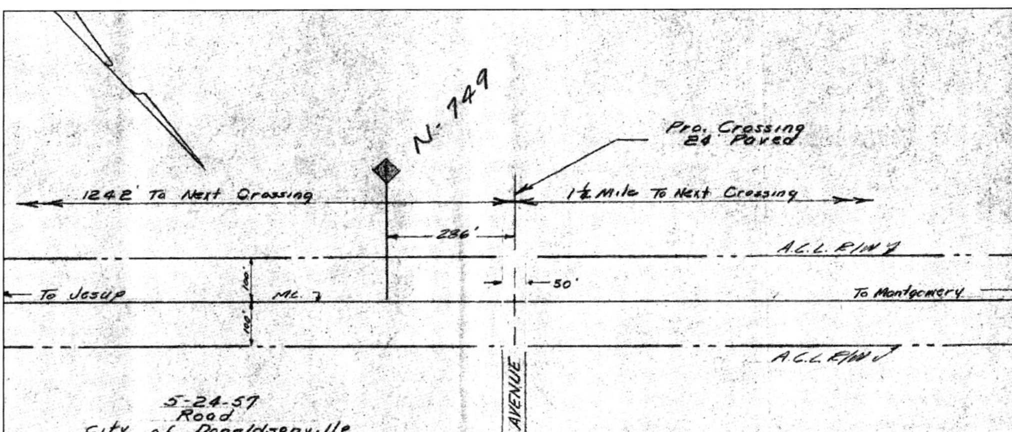

Every crossing, every easement, and every physical change in railroad property was subject to negotiation and formalized in contracts. This 1957 contract drawing concerns the extension of Broome Avenue on the west end of Donalsonville, Georgia, across the Atlantic Coast Line (ACL) right of way. (Courtesy of the DLF Dixie Depot Collection, AWHC.)

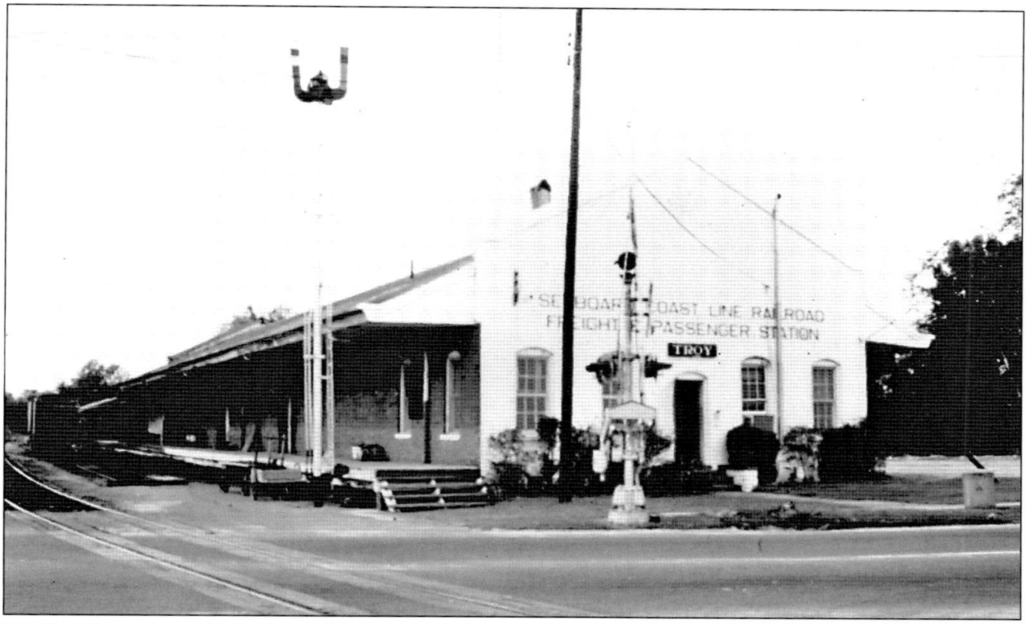

Unlike Donalsonville, Troy, Alabama, had enough rail traffic to justify separating the freight and passenger stations. This modern Seaboard Coast Line (SCL) freight station featured brick veneer; a tall, sturdy semaphore signal pole; and a gated crossing. (Courtesy of the Tom Solomon Collection, DLF.)

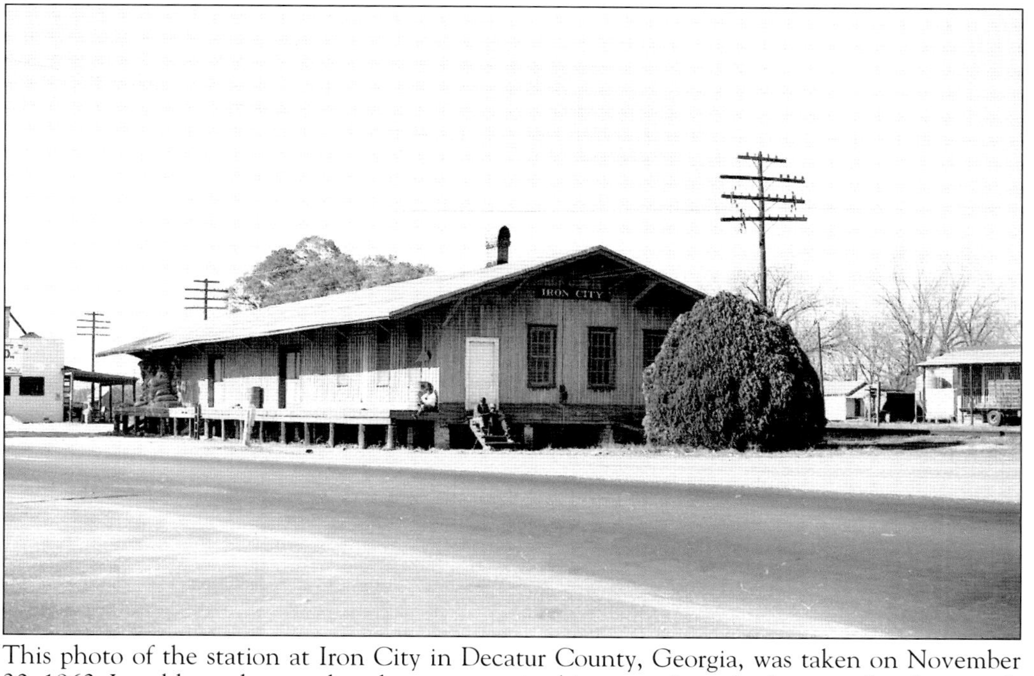

This photo of the station at Iron City in Decatur County, Georgia, was taken on November 30, 1963. Local legend states that the town received its name from the large stacks of iron rails that were once stored there during construction of the railroad. (Courtesy of the Tom Solomon Collection, DLF.)

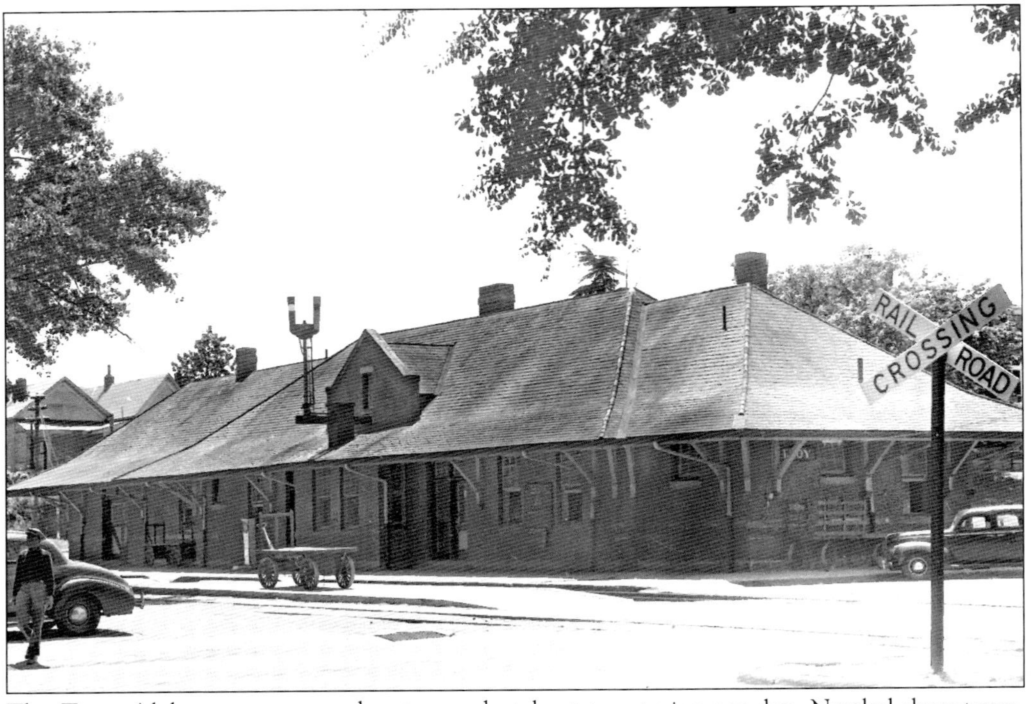

The Troy, Alabama passenger depot served at least two trains per day. Nestled downtown, the depot is one of the more substantial buildings on the old ACL/SCL route. It was built of brick and was dedicated to passenger service. The cart at trackside was used to unload baggage. (Courtesy of the Henry County Historical Group.)

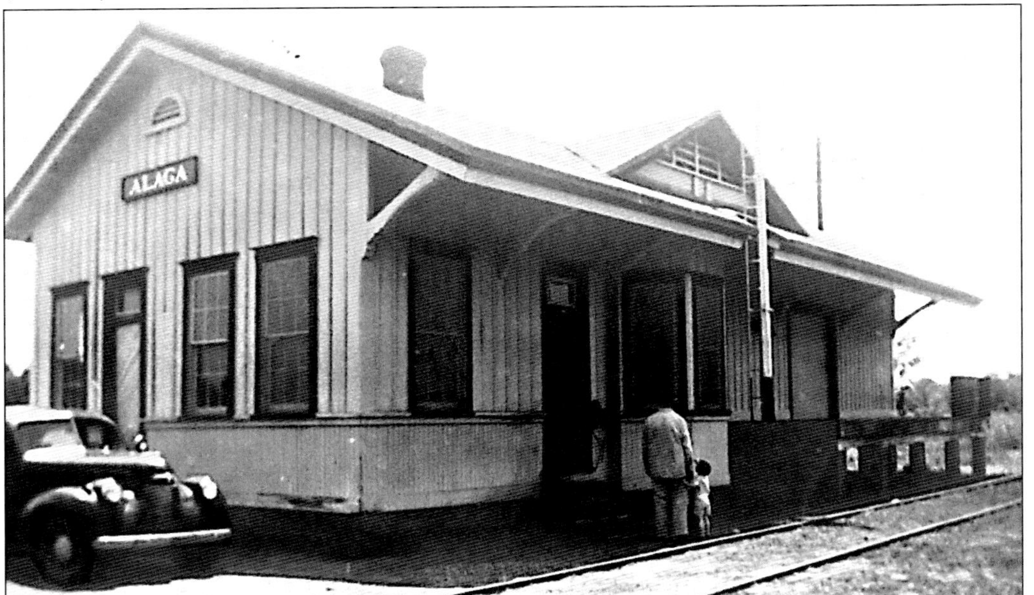

Alaga, abutting the Chattahoochee River in Houston County, Alabama, was a tiny town that no longer exists. Its passenger-freight station is an even smaller version of those in the small towns of Ashford, Alabama, and Donalsonville, Georgia. (Courtesy of DLF.)

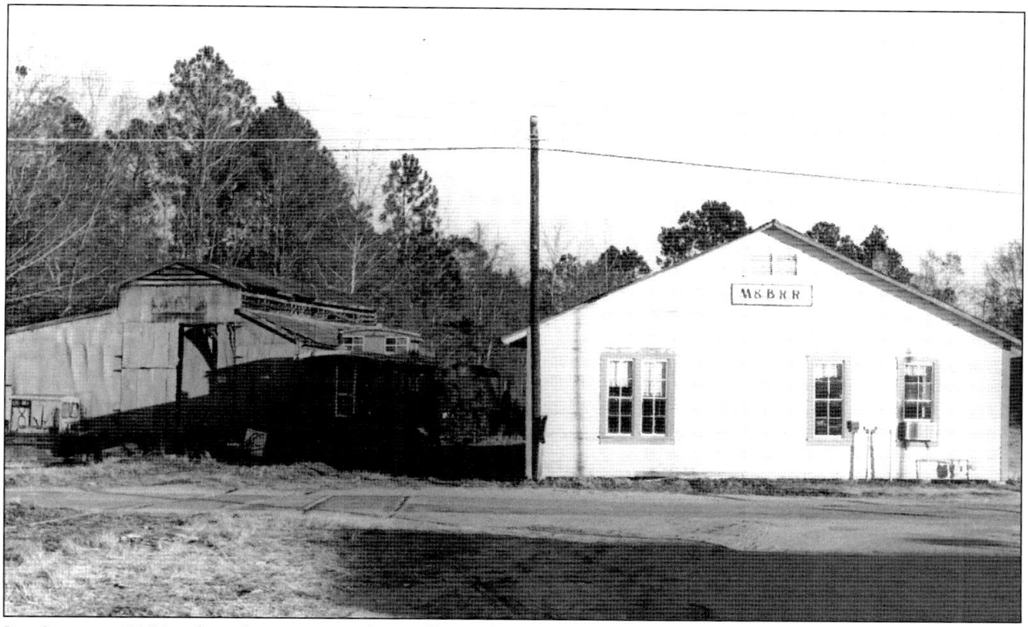

In August 1971, this depot served as offices for the dying Marianna & Blountstown Railroad. The line was the shortest in Florida, and began life in 1909 as a logging road. For its first 20 years, it offered passenger service, and it then ran freight until it expired in 1972. (Courtesy of David Kirkland.)

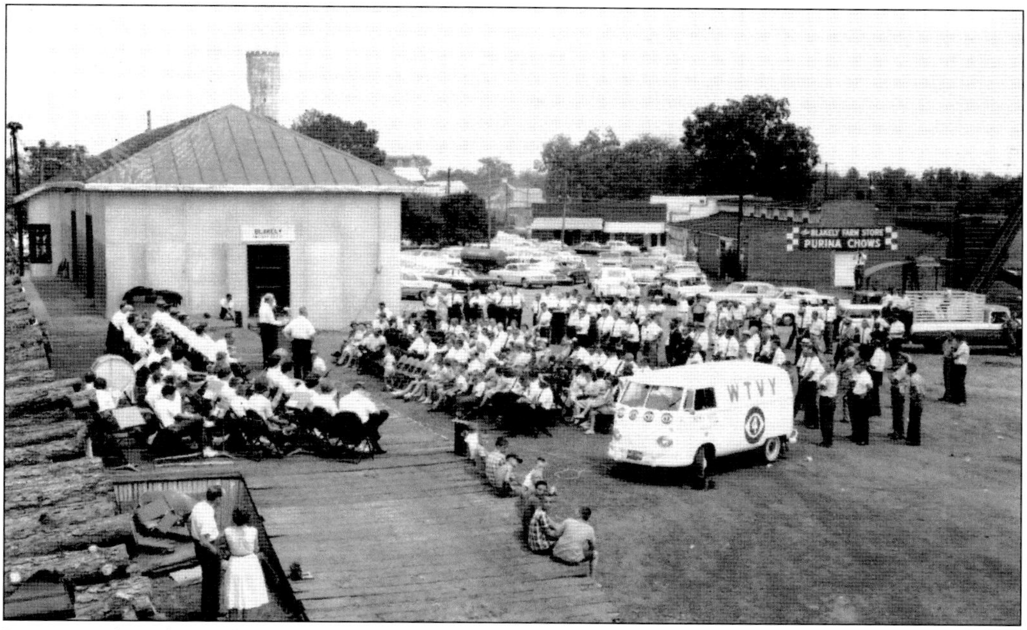

In towns that depended on railroads, the depot frequently had roles to play in civic events. In August 1963, Blakeley, Georgia, kicked off "Operation Silver Dollar" at its Central of Georgia/Chattahoochee Industrial Railroad depot. WTVY-TV of Dothan, Alabama, covered the festivities that marked the opening of the giant paper mill only a few miles away. (Courtesy of the Chattahoochee Industrial Railroad.)

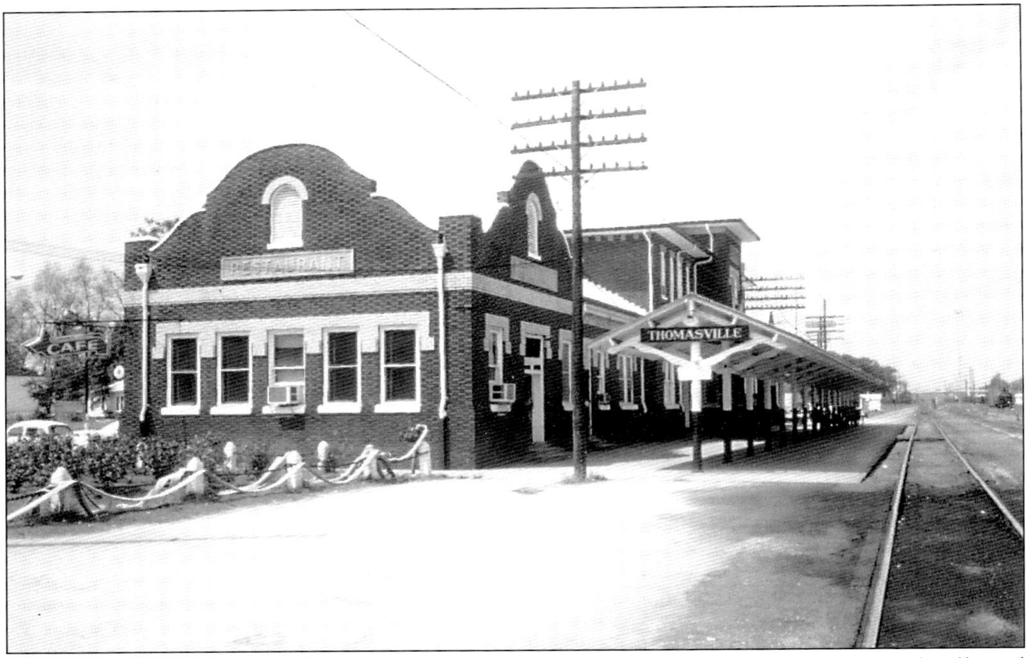

The Thomasville, Georgia depot is a remarkable architectural piece built *c.* 1915 and still used today. The unusual café/restaurant appeals to tourists who stop in this picturesque town and to locals looking for a place to dine. (Courtesy of the Tom Solomon Collection, DLF.)

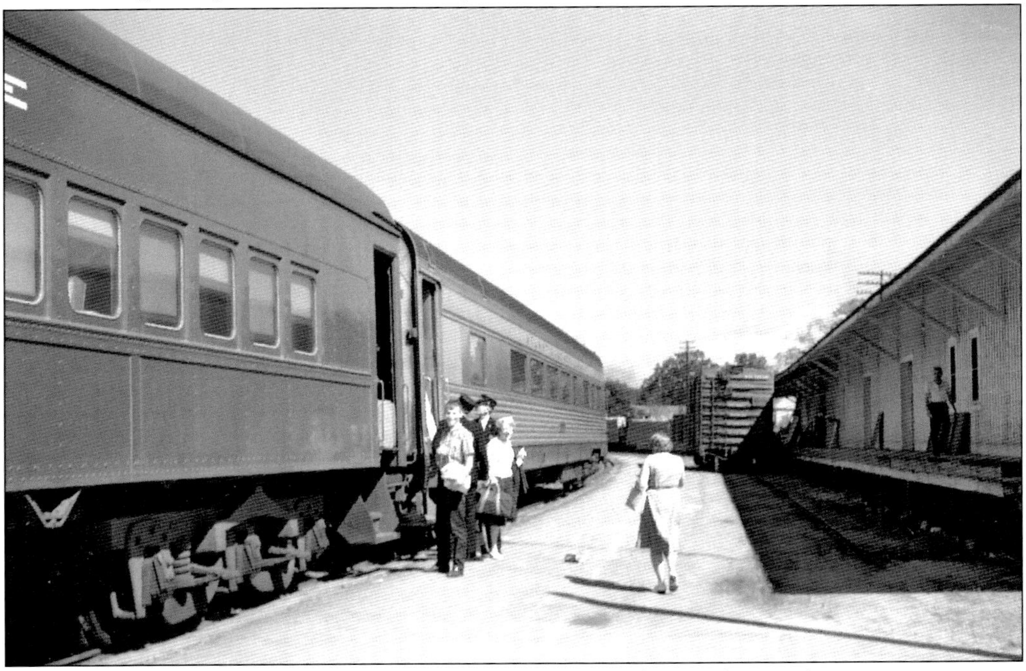

The ACL passenger depot in Dothan sits next to its freight depot. This configuration sometimes meant that passengers crossed freight tracks to board or detrain. (Courtesy of the Tom Solomon Collection, DLF.)

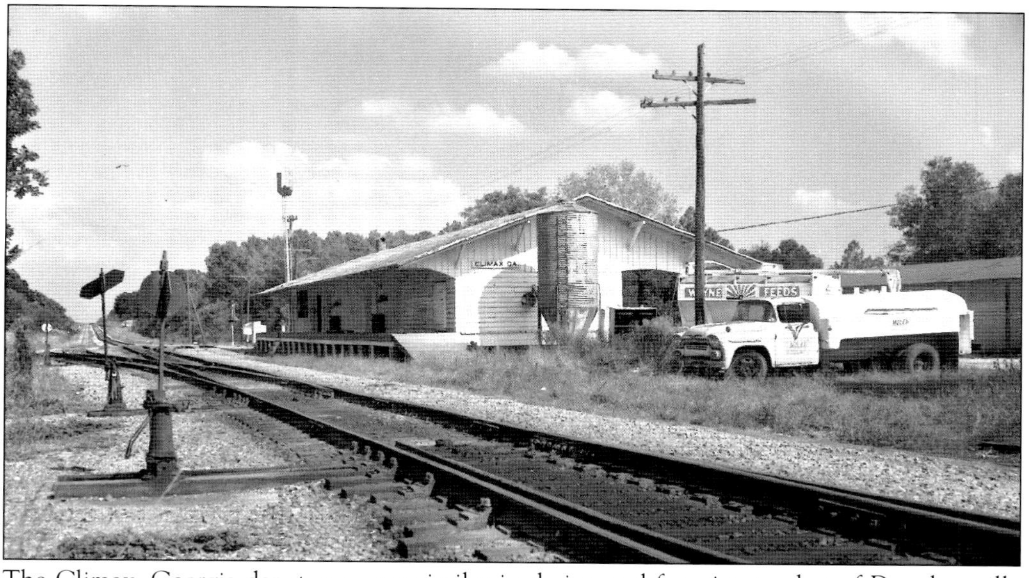

The Climax, Georgia depot was very similar in design and function to that of Donalsonville and even Ashford, Alabama. This 1973 view shows the freight area with the passenger waiting rooms at the far end. Note the three different switches on the left side of the tracks. (Courtesy of the Tom Solomon Collection, DLF.)

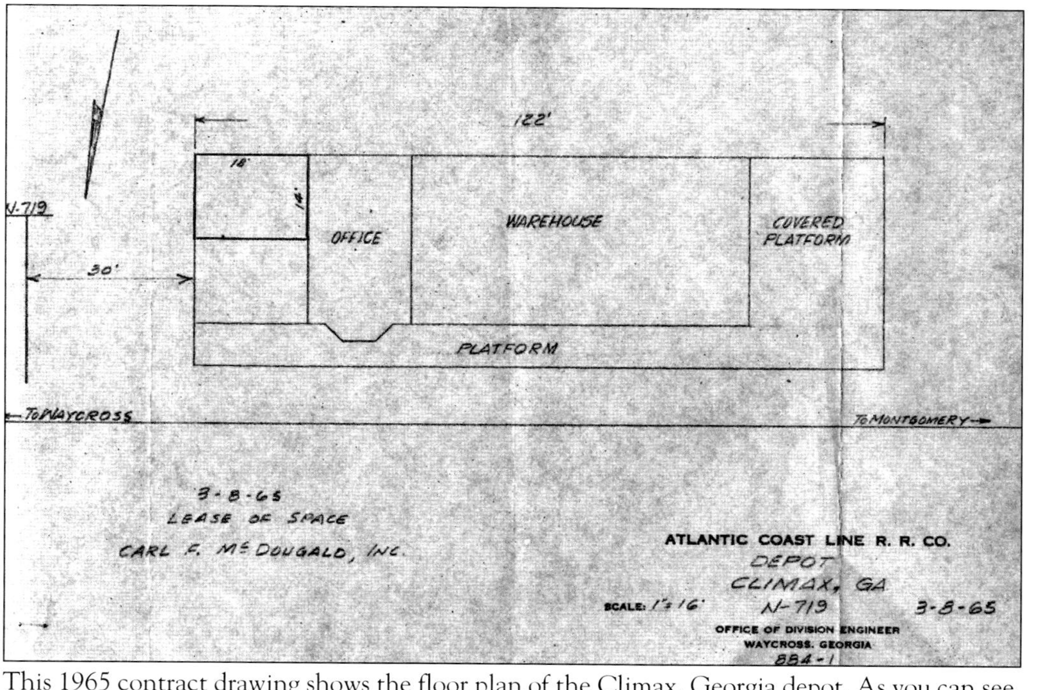

This 1965 contract drawing shows the floor plan of the Climax, Georgia depot. As you can see, Carl F. McDougald, Inc., has contracted to rent the 18- by 14-foot "colored waiting room" at the upper left corner of the building. (Courtesy of the DLF Dixie Depot Collection, AWHC.)

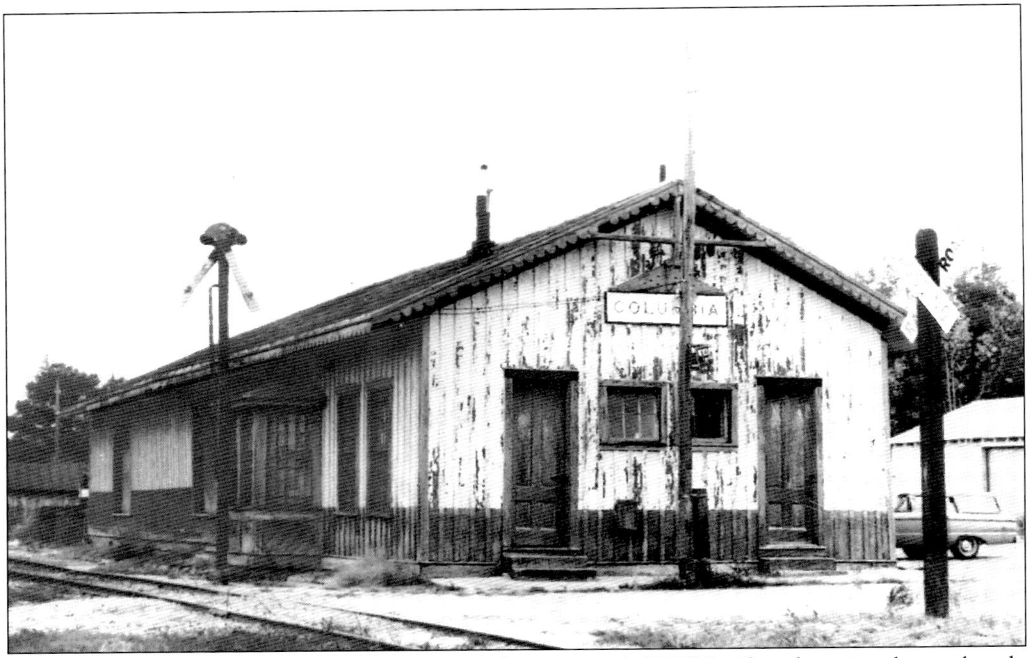

Unfortunately, an estimated 75 to 85 percent of our nation's 80,000 railroad stations have already been destroyed. One such station used to stand at Columbia in Houston County, Alabama. (Courtesy of DLF.)

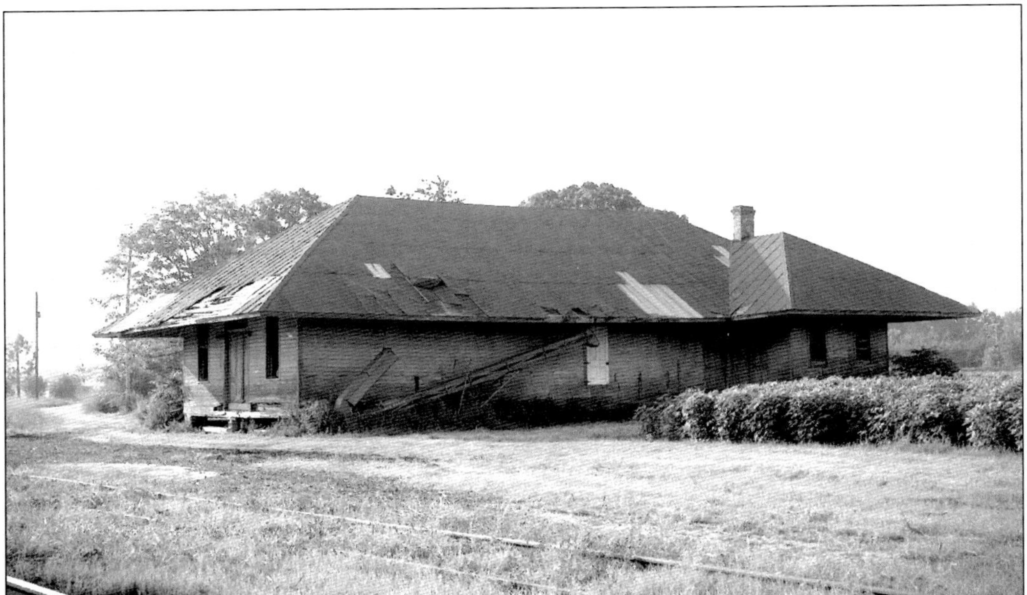

According to an elderly resident of Jakin, Georgia, this building was the commissary of the Blakely-Southern Railway, a 22-mile line built in 1911 and abandoned in 1915. Its rolling stock consisted of a single engine, passenger car, and freight car. (Courtesy of the Tom Solomon Collection, DLF.)

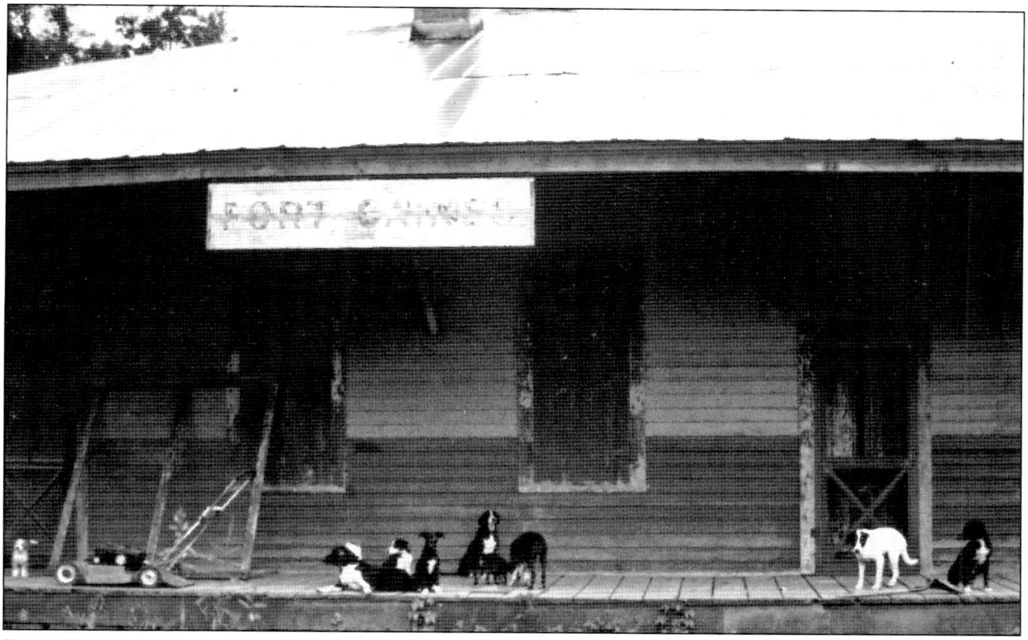

Fort Gaines, Georgia, was founded in 1814 where Cemocheechobee Creek joins the Chattahoochee River. The Southwestern Railroad came to Fort Gaines in 1858, followed by the Central of Georgia, which built this depot. This 1979 photo shows the station abandoned except by the neighborhood dogs. It later burned. (Courtesy of the Clay County [Georgia] Public Library.)

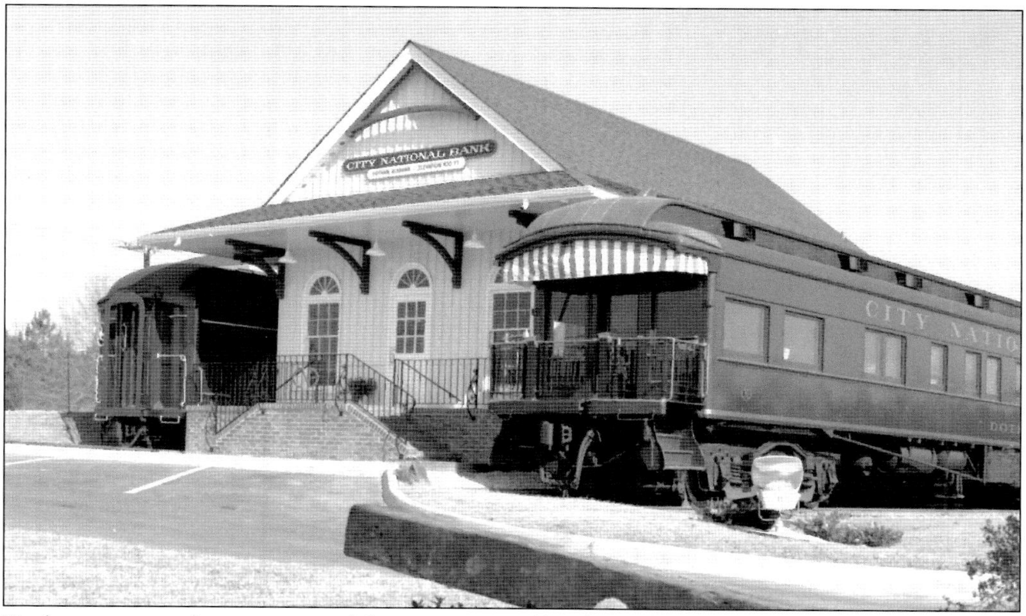

Dothan was once home to one of the most unusual banks in the country. Known as the "railroad branch" of City National Bank, the reconstructed depot building featured two rail cars as well as railroad artifacts from throughout the Wiregrass Region. The railroad branch was torn down in the late 1980s. (Courtesy of the Doug Snellgrove Estate.)

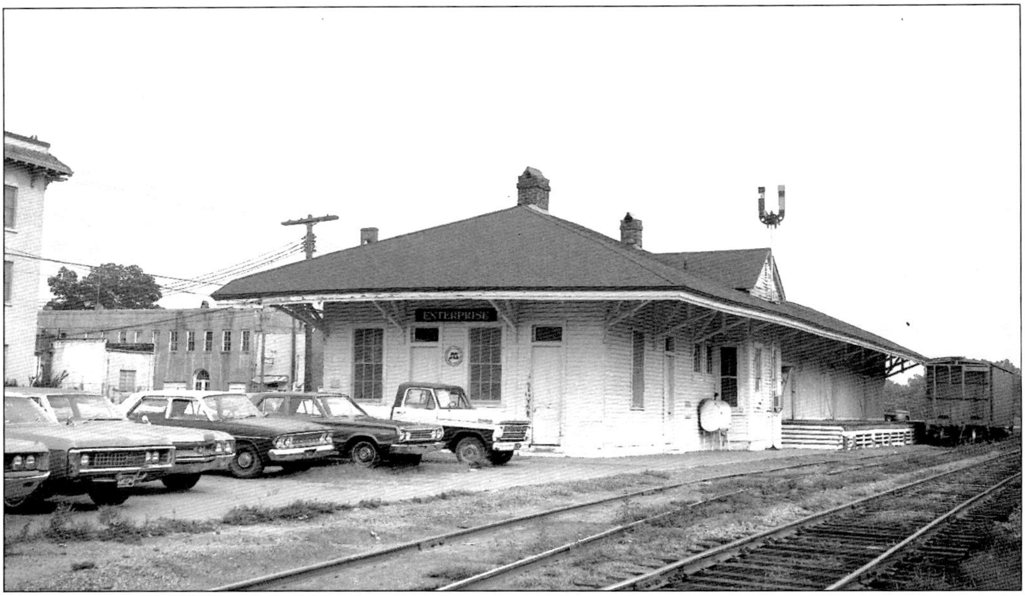

This railroad depot at Enterprise in Coffee County, Alabama, is one of the few depots remaining in the Wiregrass Region. It was constructed in 1903, was used by the Atlantic Coast Line, and currently houses the Pea River Historical Society. (Courtesy of the Tom Solomon Collection, DLF.)

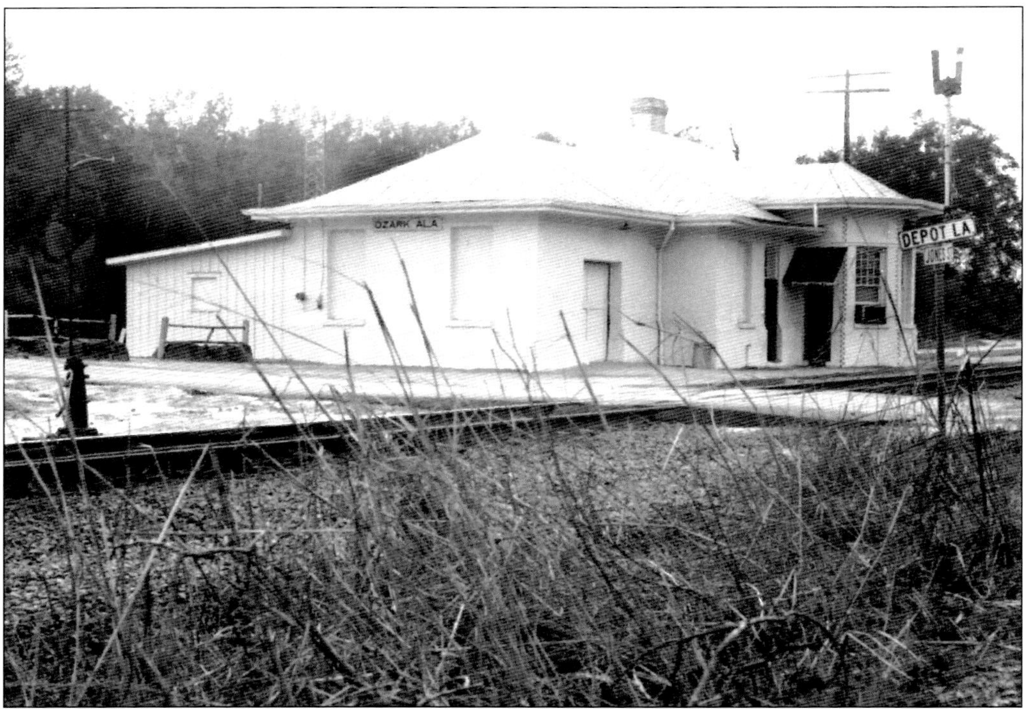

Another railroad station that will gain a new lease on life is located in Ozark in Dale County, Alabama. In 2004, the City of Ozark acquired the structure and is developing plans to relocate and restore the building. (Courtesy of Gordon Dodson.)

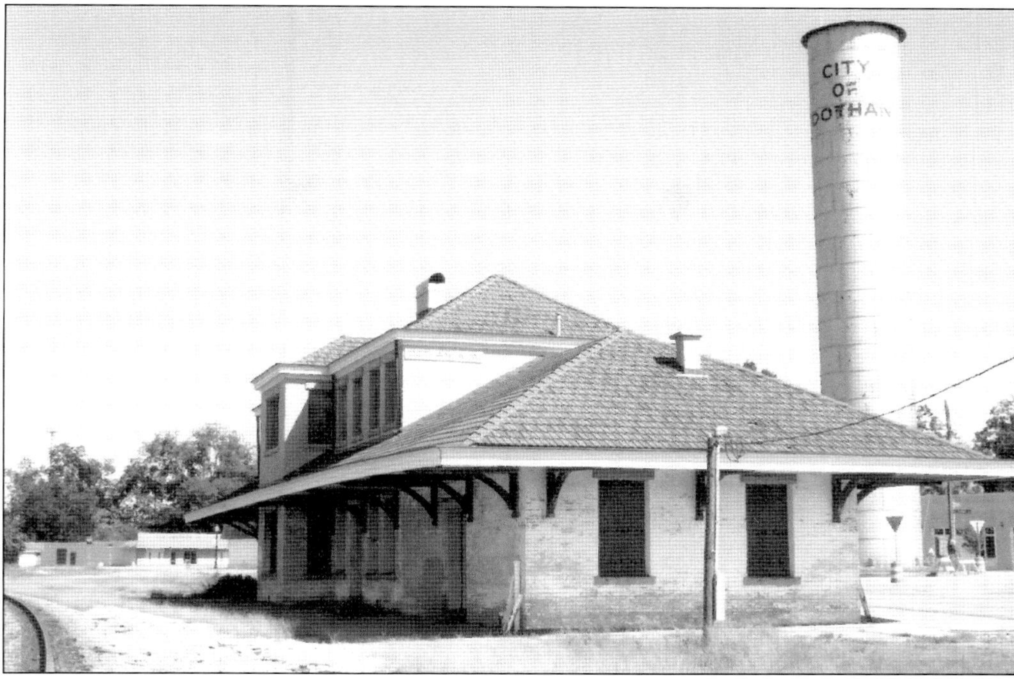

Dothan is fortunate in that all three railroad stations are still standing. Pictured is the Atlantic Coast Line station in downtown Dothan's "Dixie" area. Constructed in 1907, this building will soon be renovated by the Wiregrass Transit Authority for use as office space and a transportation center. (Courtesy of DLF.)

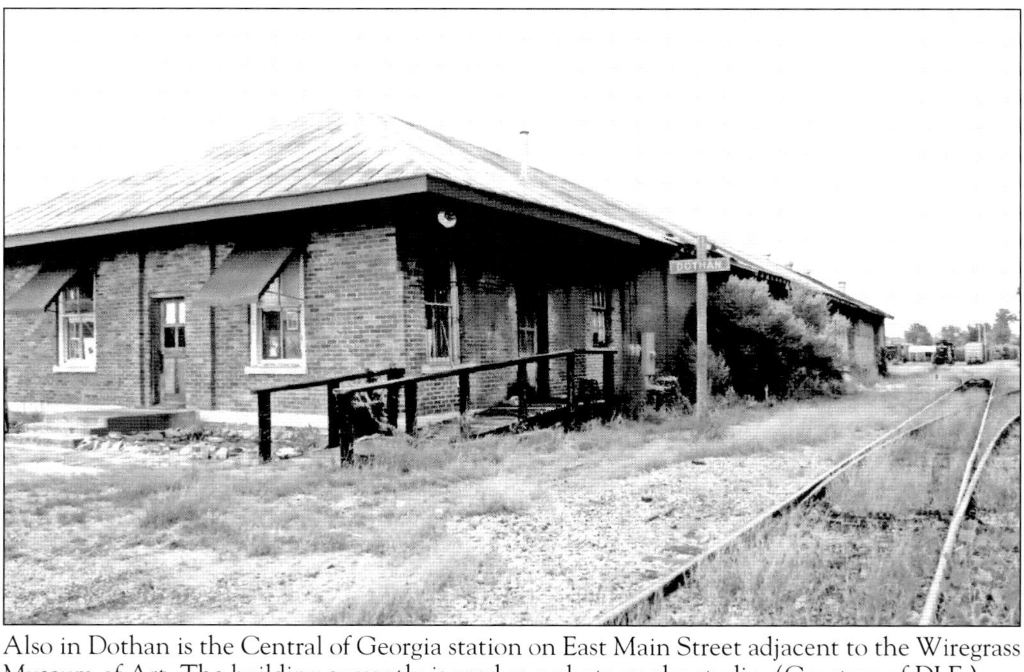

Also in Dothan is the Central of Georgia station on East Main Street adjacent to the Wiregrass Museum of Art. The building currently is used as a photography studio. (Courtesy of DLF.)

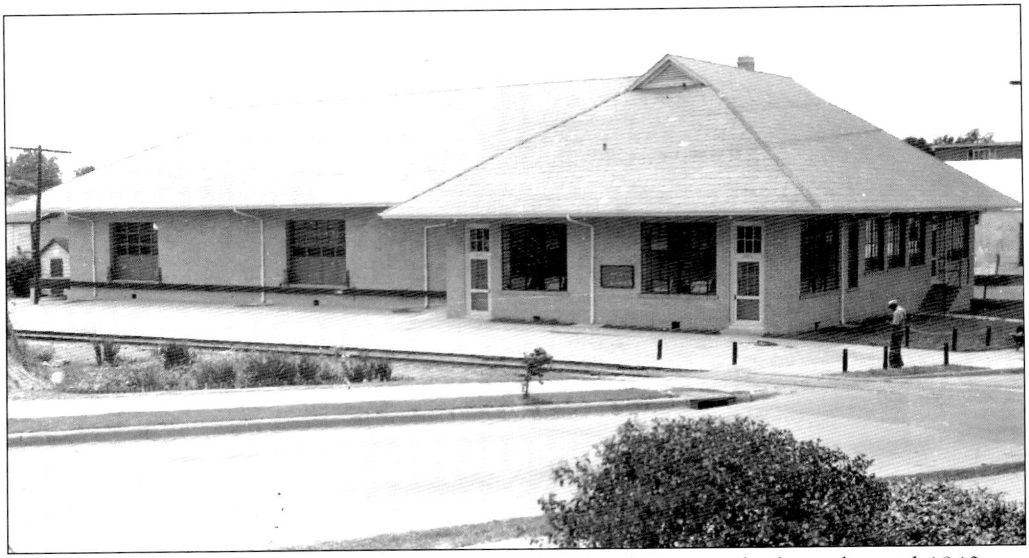

This photo depicts the "new" Bay Line station shortly after it was built in the mid-1940s on East Main Street in Dothan. It replaced the wooden structure that was located on the same site. (Courtesy of Quinton Bruner.)

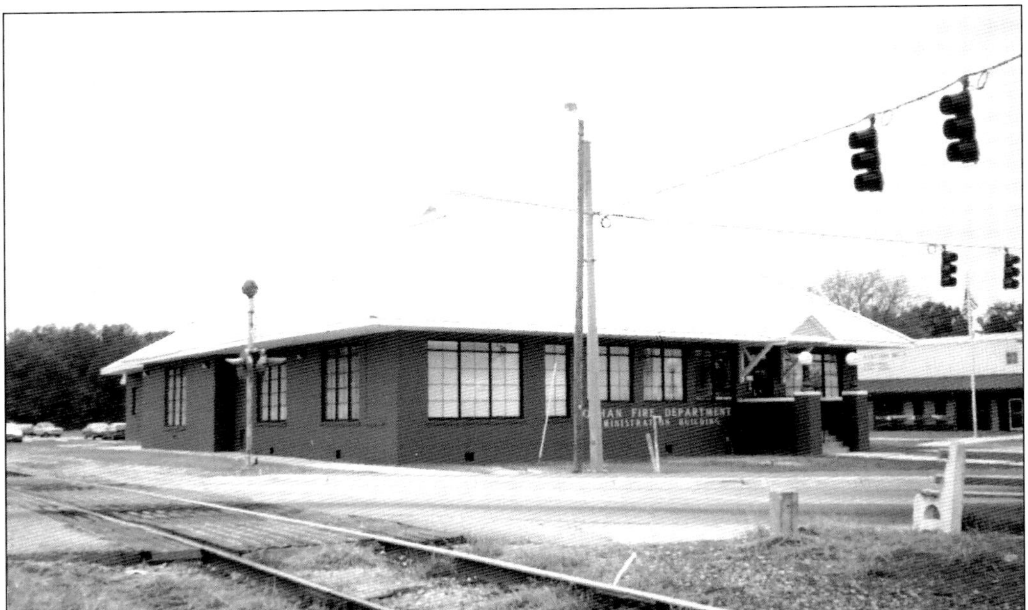

In 1997, the owner of the Bay Line, Mr. Earl Durden, donated that same depot with six acres of surrounding property to the City of Dothan. The building now houses the city's Central Fire Station. (Courtesy of David Kirkland.)

Two

Riding the Rails

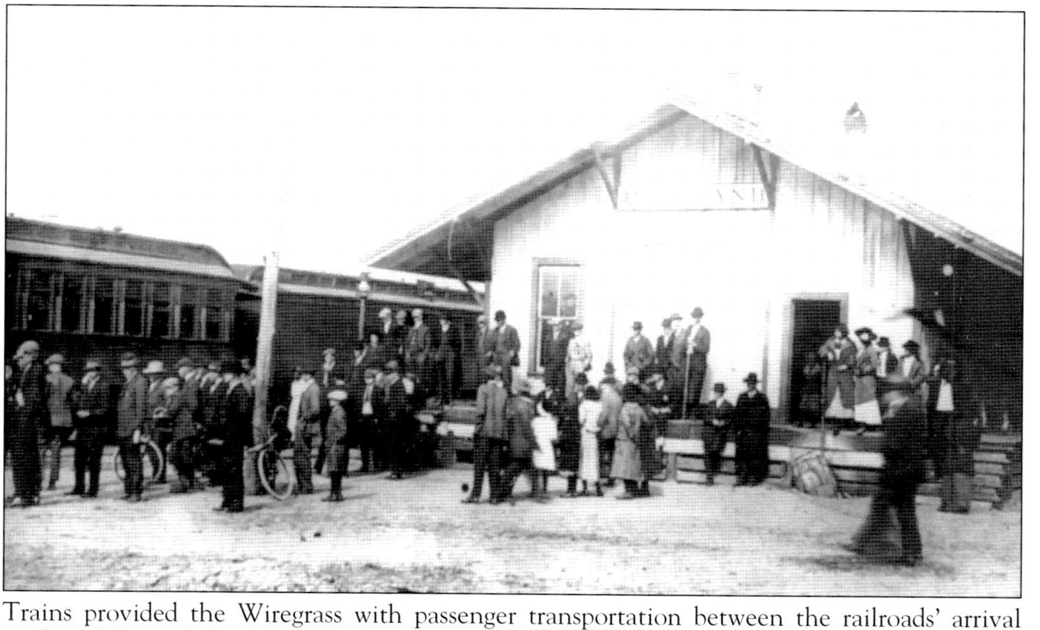

Trains provided the Wiregrass with passenger transportation between the railroads' arrival in the 1880s and the federal highway programs of the 1950s–1970s. In Headland, Alabama, passengers and friends meet the train in February 1913. Included in this group were Curt Solomon, Rob Parrish, Mrs. Gera Mitchell, and John Davis. (Courtesy of the Abbeville [Alabama] Memorial Library.)

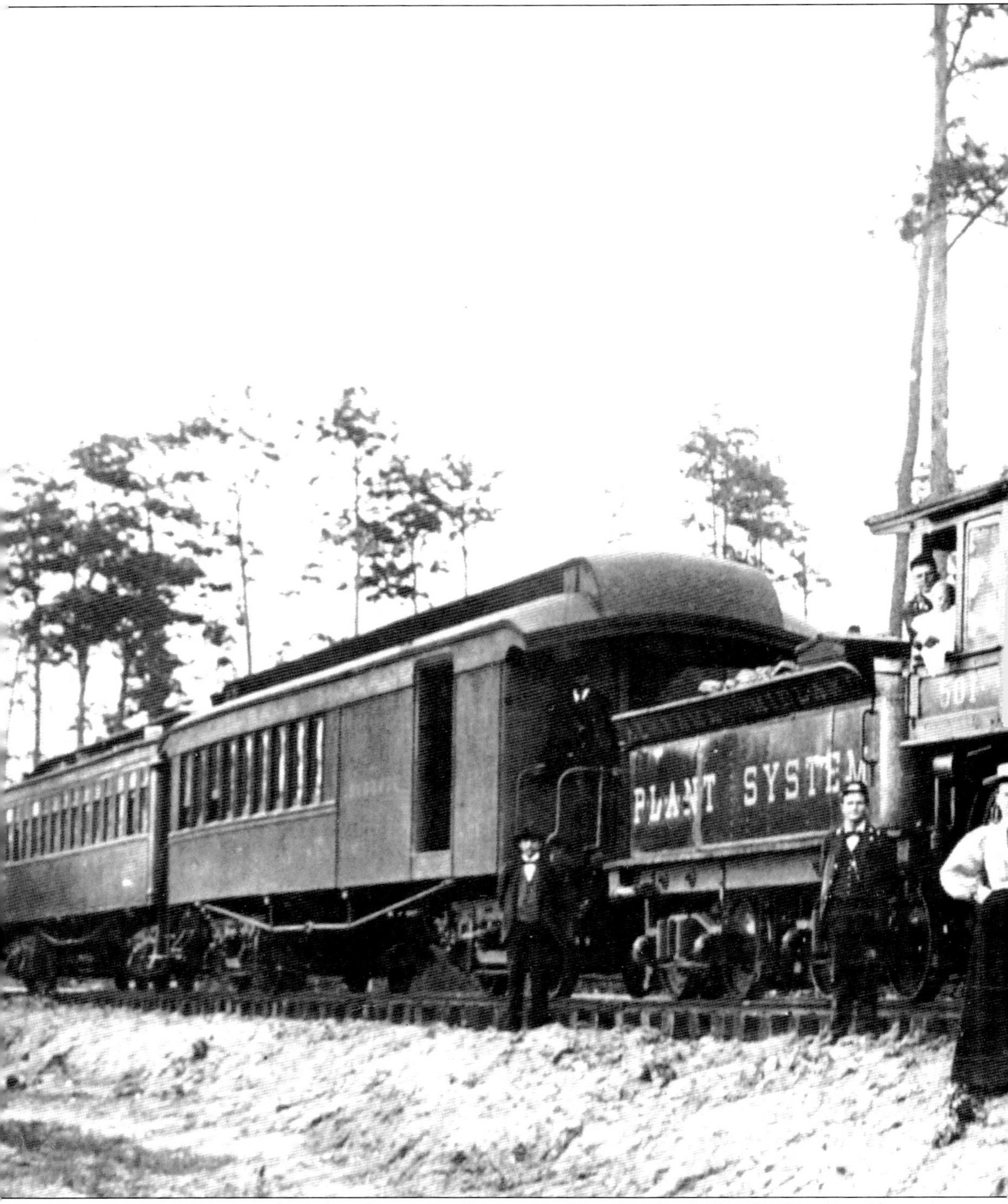

In the era of poor roads, railroads cut travel time significantly. The Abbeville-Headland branch line of the Alabama Midland Railway (later purchased by Henry Plant) made the trip from Dothan to the county seat much shorter. On this 1893 train into Abbeville are, from left to

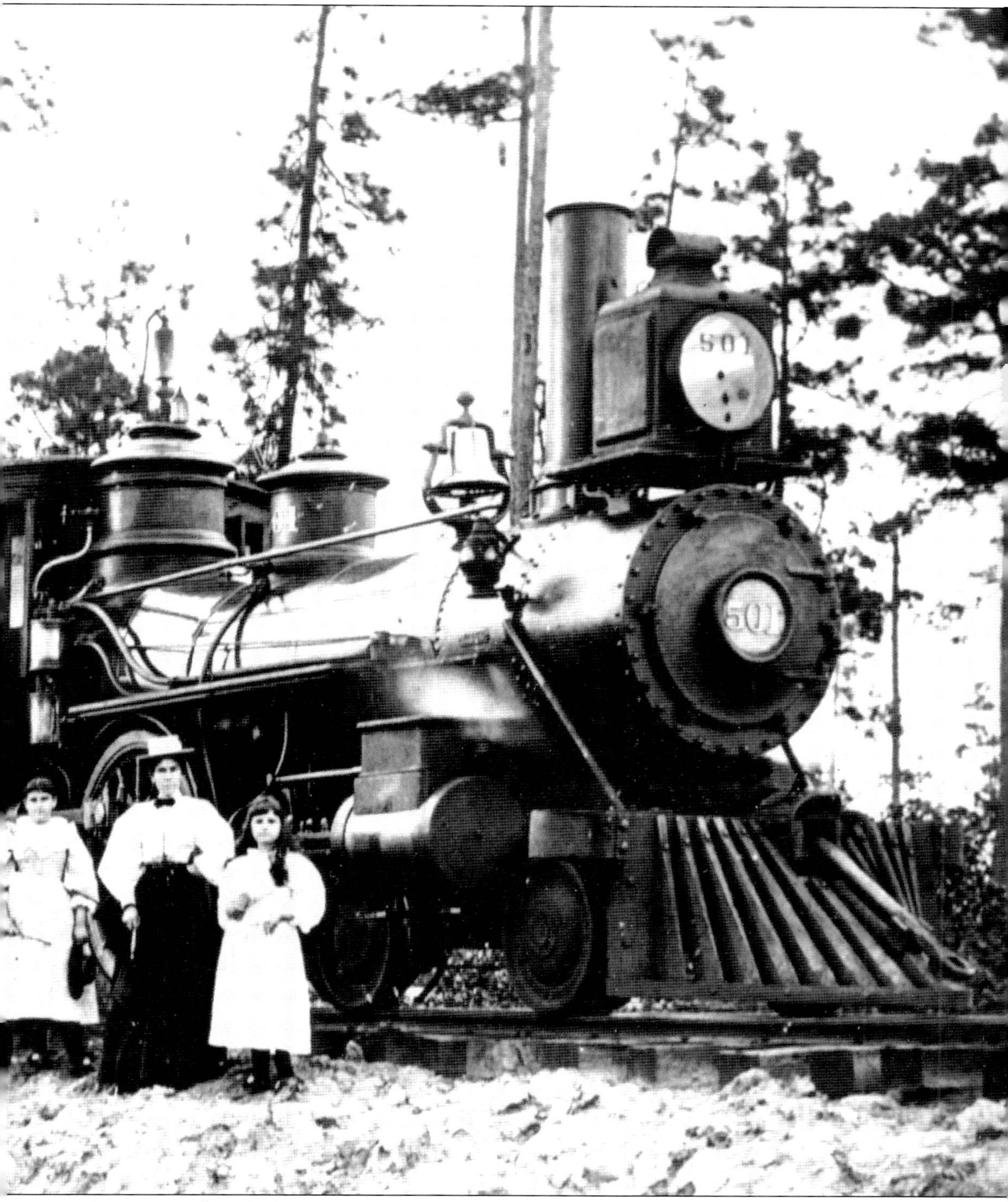

right, two unidentified, conductor Jim Bowdoin, engineer George Weatherford holding Nell Bowdoin, Mrs. ? Bowdoin, ? Terry, Mrs. ? Weatherford, and ? Terry.

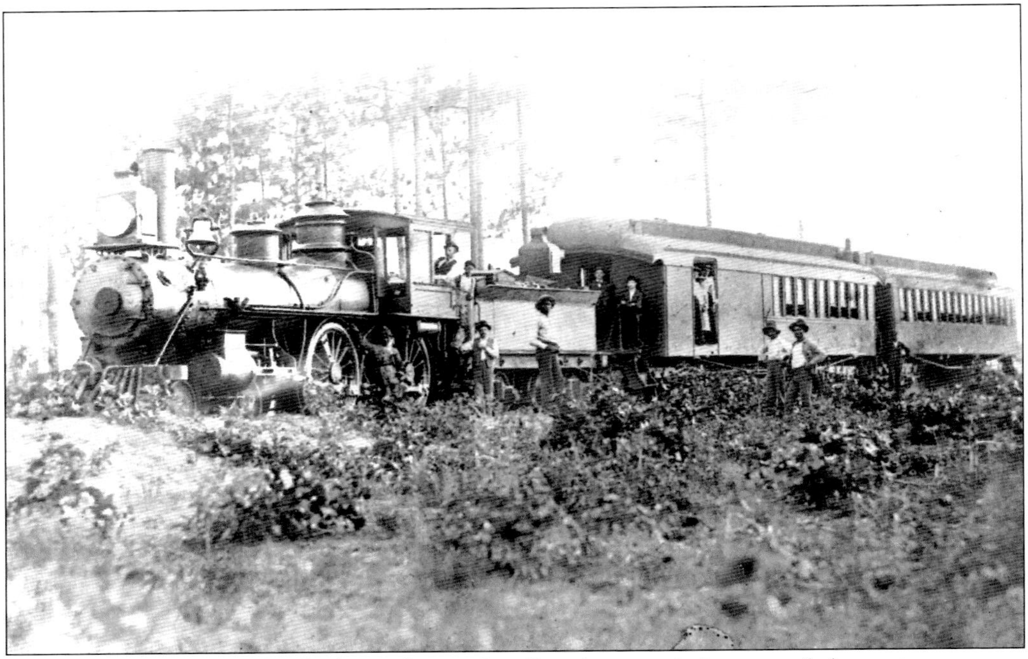

Engineer George Weatherford, conductor Jim Bowdoin, and the rest of the train crew are shown on the first run on the Abbeville-Headland branch line in 1893. This train—small engine, tender, combination baggage-passenger car, and one full coach—is typical on the short runs that dominated Wiregrass passenger service. (Courtesy of the Tom Solomon Collection, DLF.)

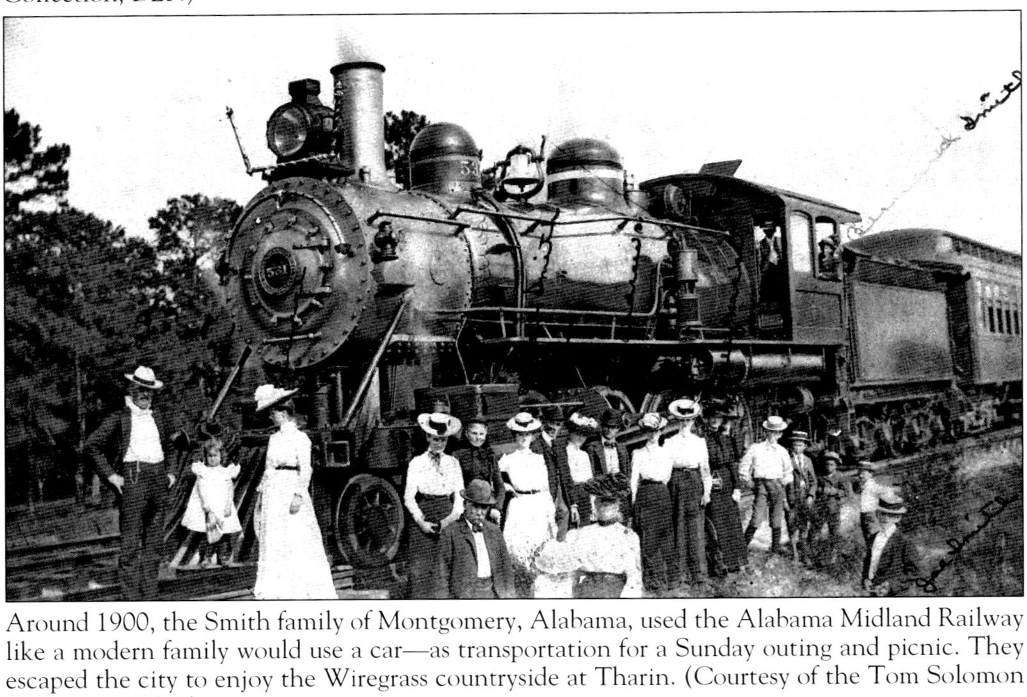

Around 1900, the Smith family of Montgomery, Alabama, used the Alabama Midland Railway like a modern family would use a car—as transportation for a Sunday outing and picnic. They escaped the city to enjoy the Wiregrass countryside at Tharin. (Courtesy of the Tom Solomon Collection, DLF.)

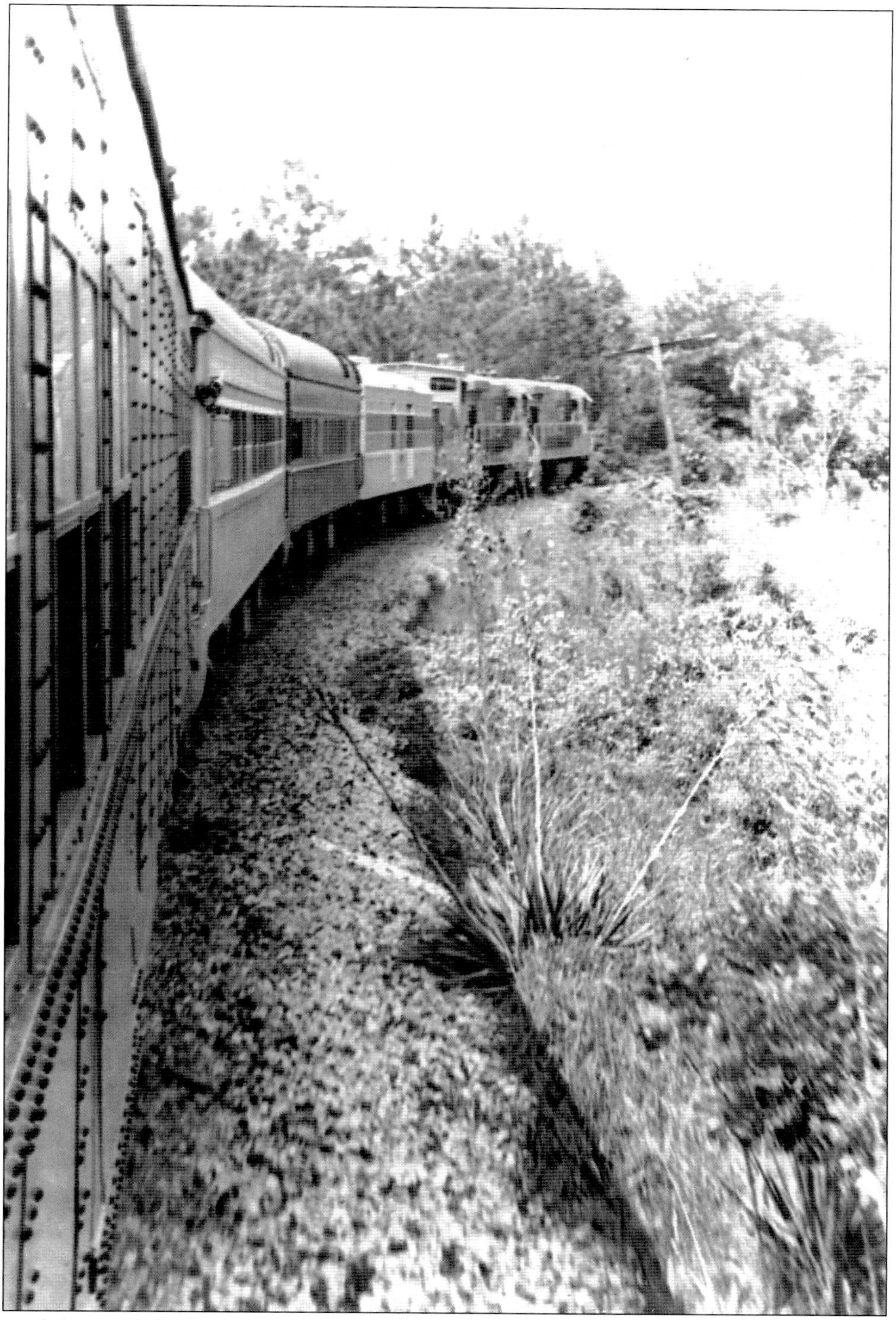

One of the joys of riding passenger trains is the view. In this 1970s photograph, the camera captures the drama of a ride on a Louisville & Nashville train as it passed a Spanish Bayonet plant in north Florida. (Courtesy of the Washington County [Florida] Historical Society.)

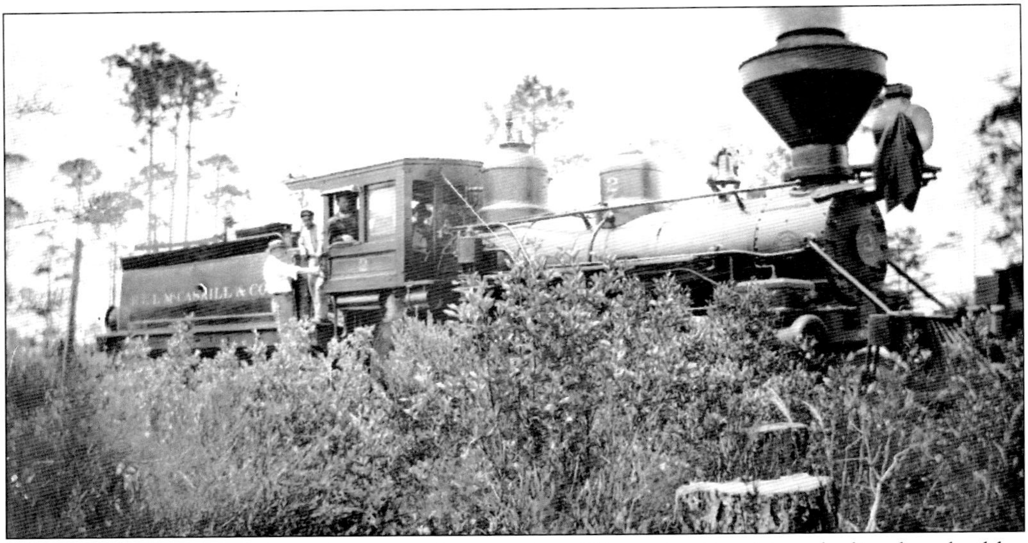

Railroads brought people, industry, and prosperity. When the Bay Line declined to build a branch into Lynn Haven, Florida, residents hired a contractor to put in the tracks. Here, the McCaskill & Company locomotive tries out the Lynn Haven route for the first time. (Courtesy of David Kirkland.)

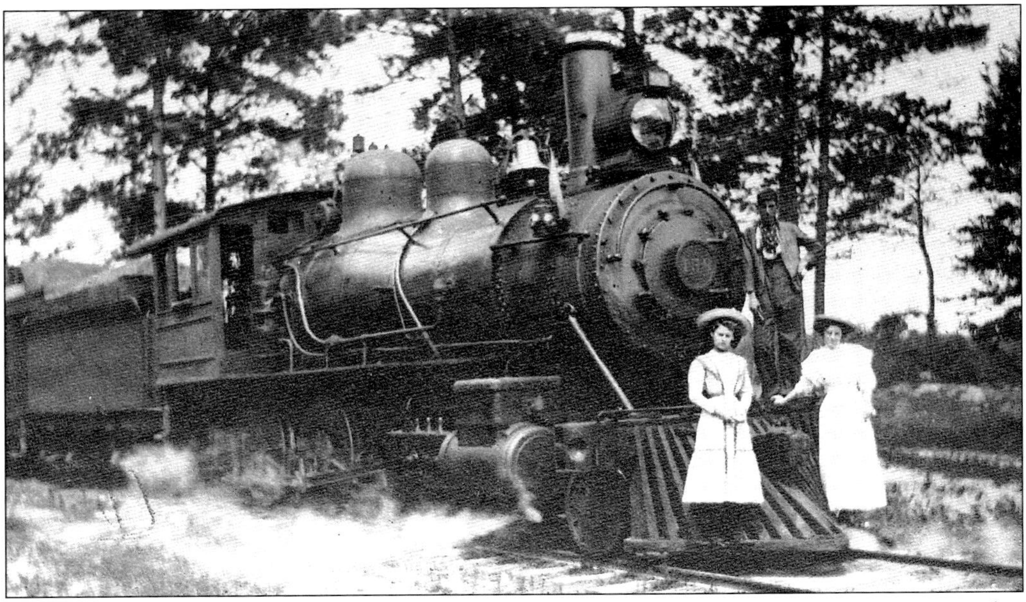

The engineer of Engine No. 158 takes time to pose with these two attractive women in this unidentified and undated photograph. Picture collections from this era show that everyone was thrilled to pose with the latest technology. Obviously, photographers made a good business from passengers and crews alike. (Courtesy of the Tom Solomon Collection, DLF.)

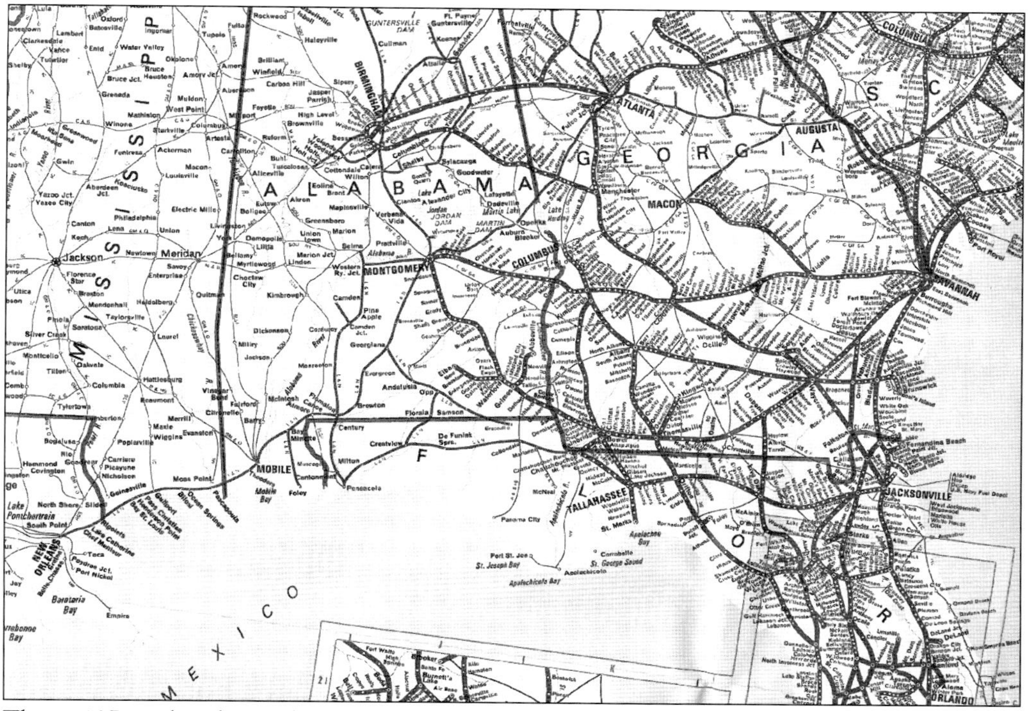

This c. 1971 railroad map shows how well railroads covered the Wiregrass. The Seaboard Coast Line routes are bold, with feeder and allied routes in light lines. (Courtesy of the DLF Dixie Depot Collection, AWHC.)

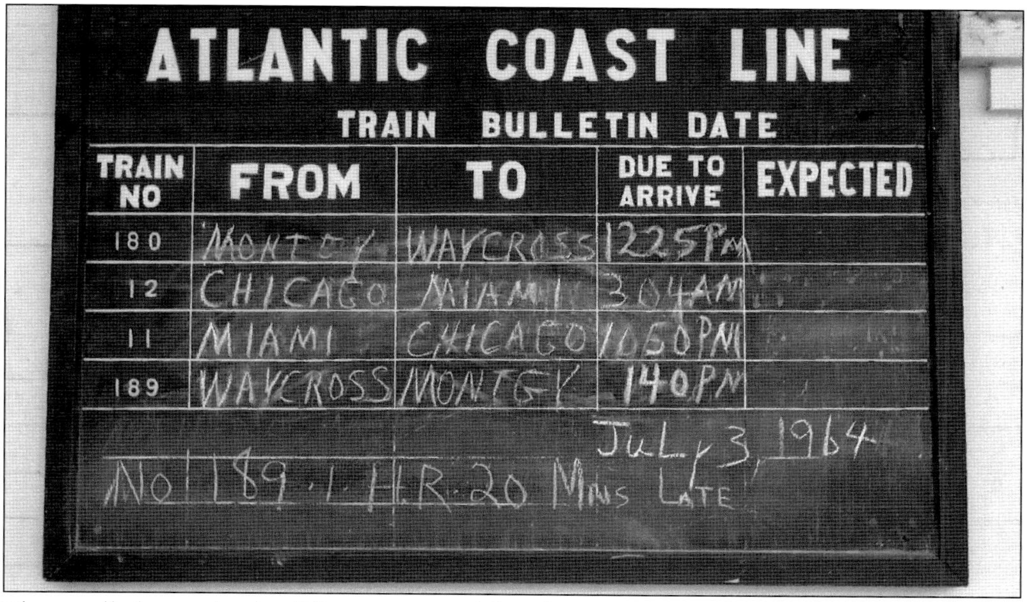

The small depots in the Wiregrass posted hand-written train notices on chalk boards to keep passengers informed, as with this ACL announcement board in Dothan on July 3, 1964. Things rarely change—even then the train was quite late. (Courtesy of the Tom Solomon Collection, DLF.)

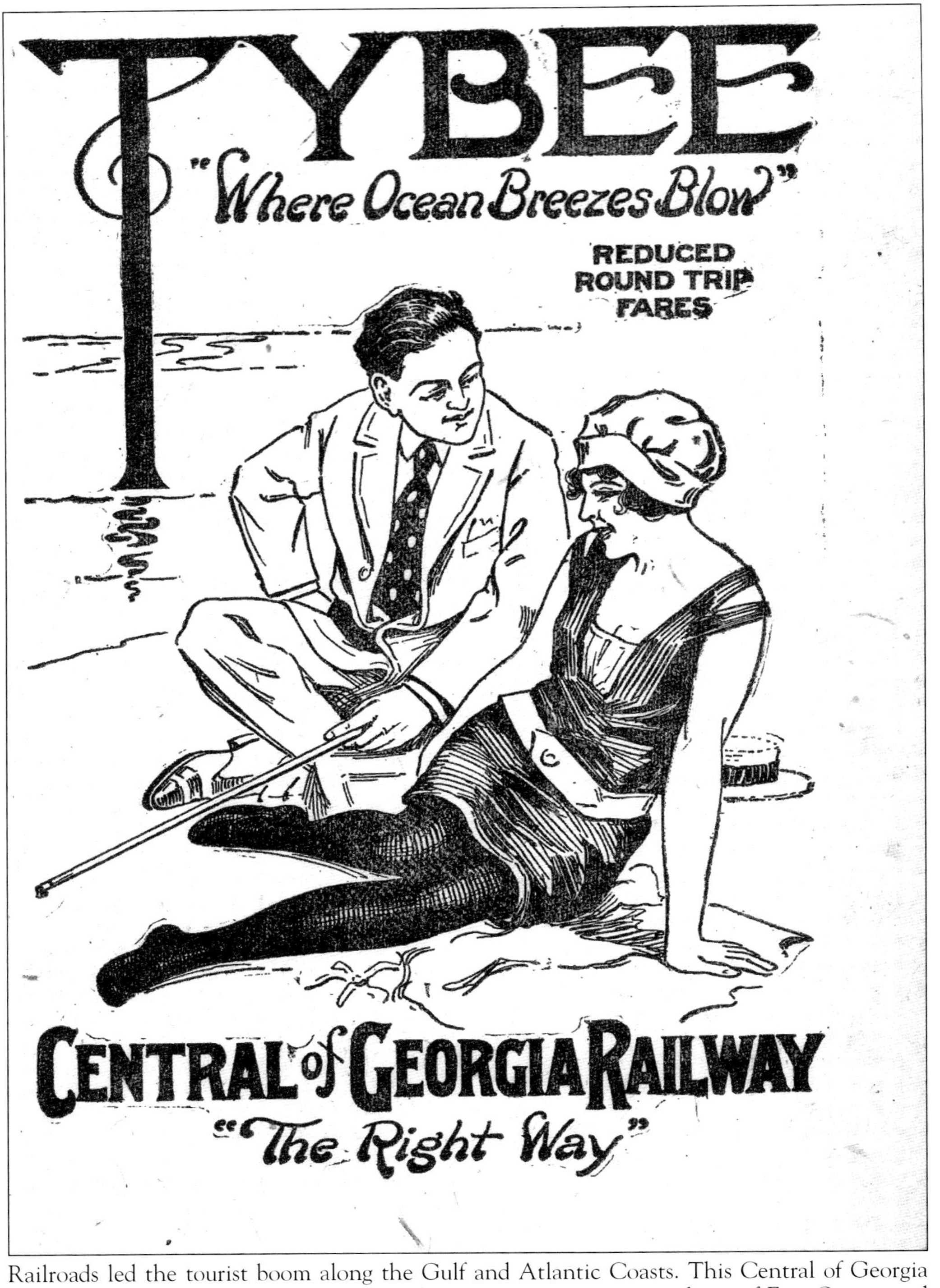

Railroads led the tourist boom along the Gulf and Atlantic Coasts. This Central of Georgia advertisement from the July 7, 1924 *Southwest Georgian* entices residents of Fort Gaines and vicinity to vacation on Tybee Island, near Savannah. (Courtesy of the Clay County [Georgia] Public Library.)

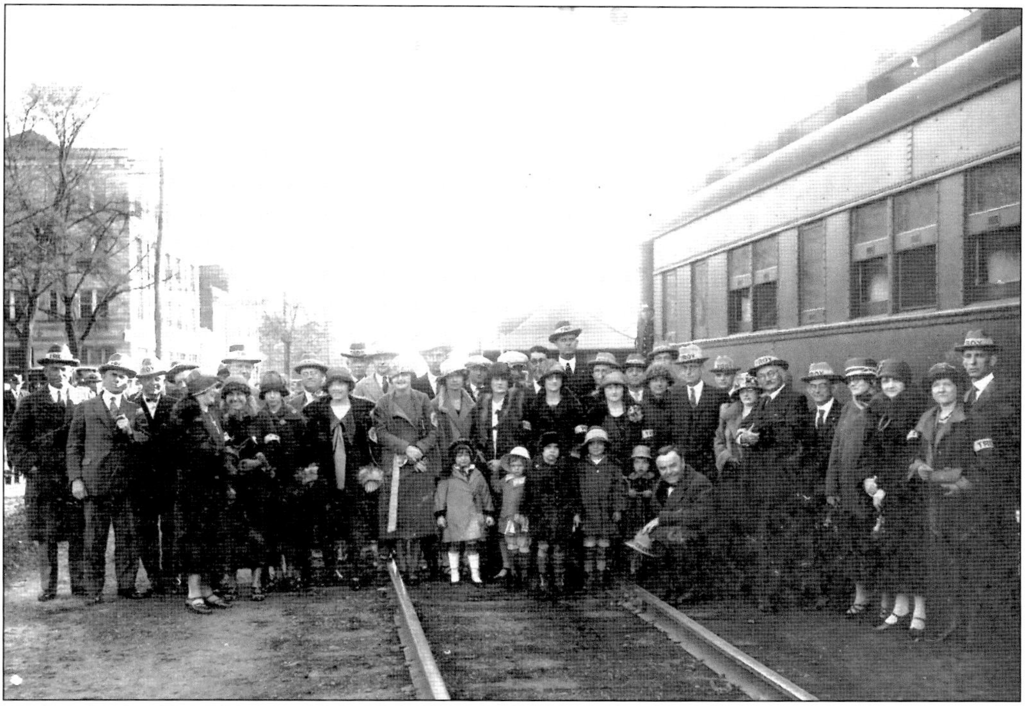

Railroads also brought tourists into the heart of the Wiregrass. During the early 1920s, Rotary Club members from around the world traveled by rail to Troy, Alabama, at the invitation of Alabama's former governor Charles Henderson, also Troy's favorite son. He is pictured sixth from the right in this photograph of the club's local delegation. (Courtesy of the Pioneer Museum of Alabama.)

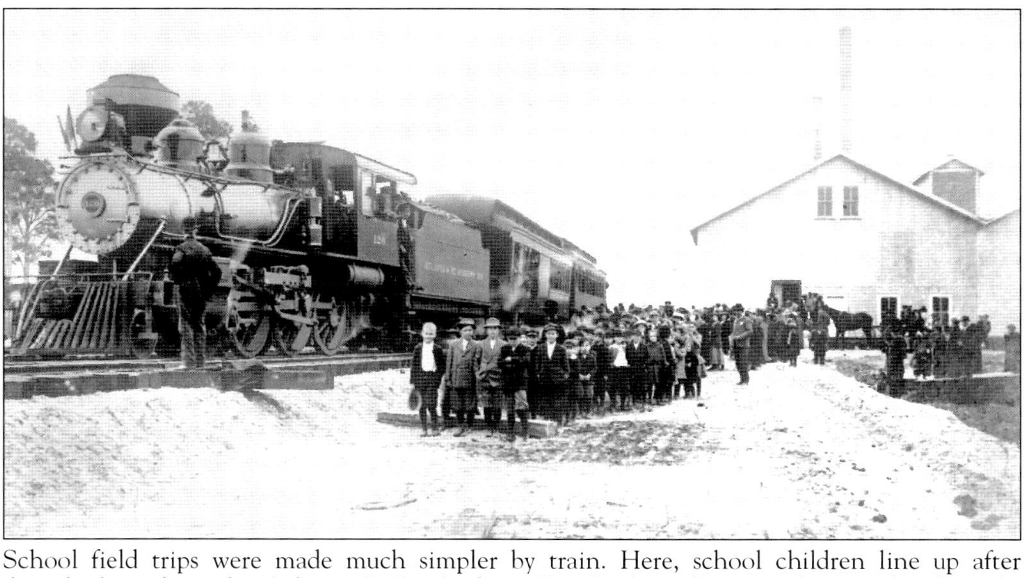

School field trips were made much simpler by train. Here, school children line up after disembarking from the Atlanta & St. Andrews Bay Railway (Bay Line) train that brought them to the Panama City, Florida depot on an excursion. (Courtesy of the Tom Solomon Collection, DLF.)

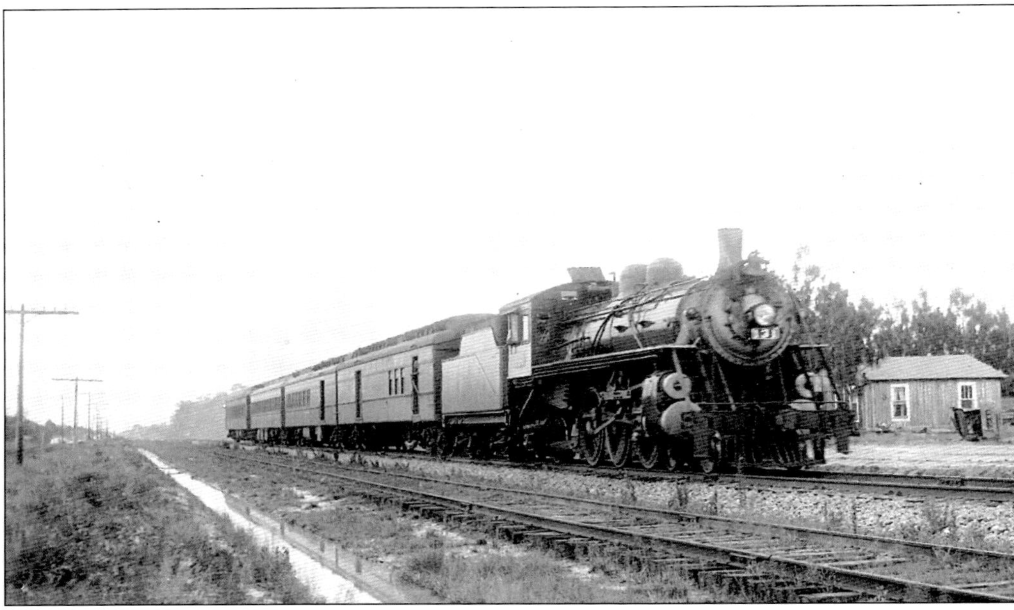

In this undated photograph, the Atlanta & St. Andrews Bay Railway Engine No. 131 pulls three passenger cars and a baggage car past section houses on its way from Dothan to Panama City. (Courtesy of the Tom Solomon Collection, DLF.)

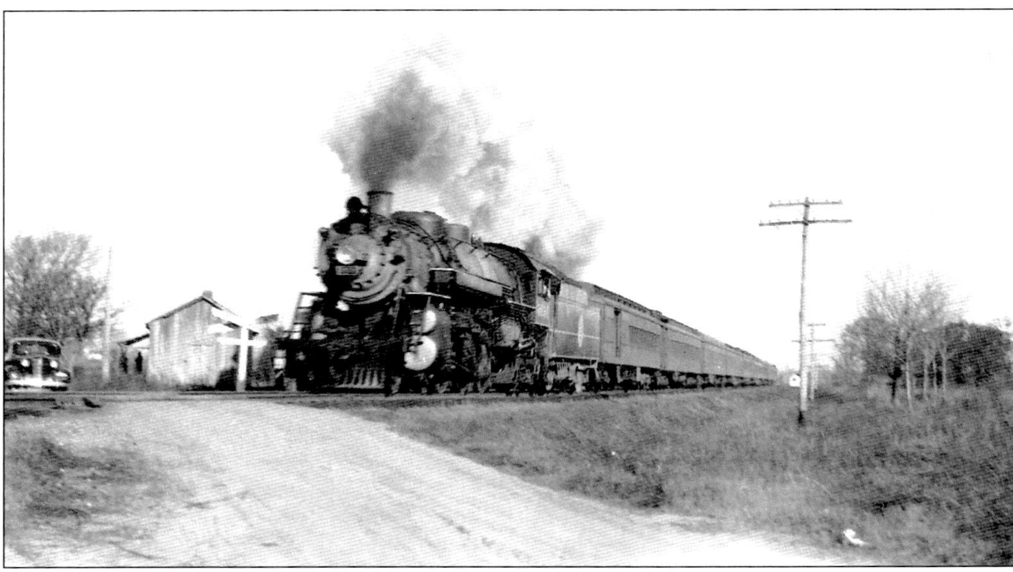

Heavyweight flyers (long-distance express trains) like this, the Louisville & Nashville's *Florida Arrow*, brought business passengers, private travelers, and tourists from Chicago through the Wiregrass to Florida. In this 1940s photograph, the ACL No. 1696 pulls the *Florida Arrow* through a small town. (Courtesy of the Tom Solomon Collection, DLF.)

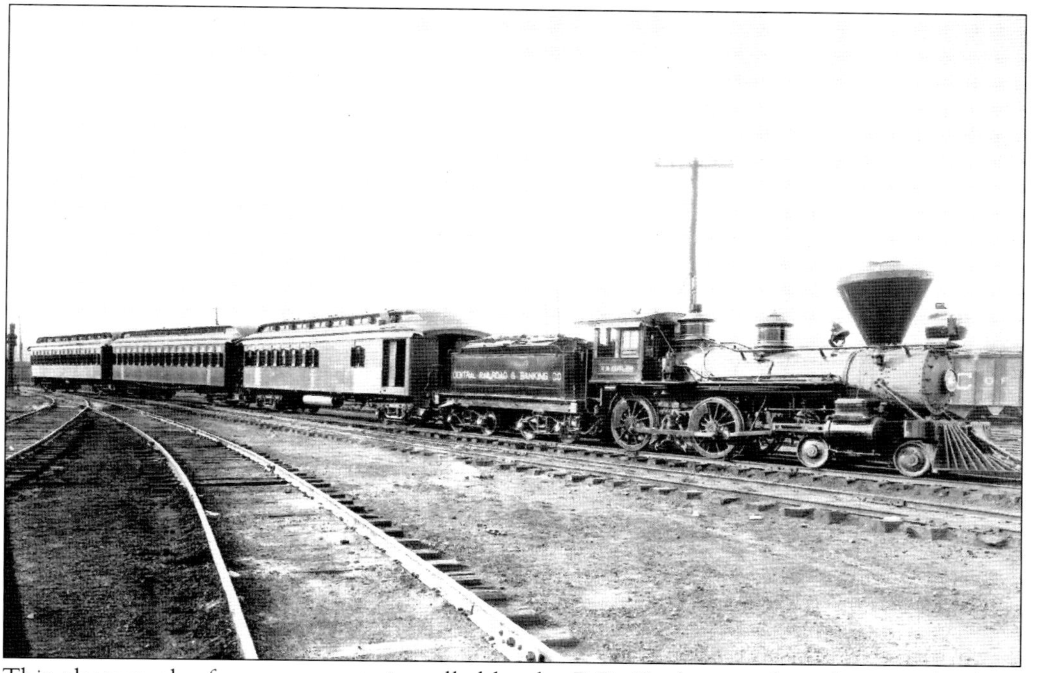

This photograph of a passenger train pulled by the *R.R. Cuyler* must have been made about 1895, when the Central Railroad & Banking Company became the Central of Georgia Railway. (Courtesy of the Houston-Love Memorial Library, Dothan, Alabama.)

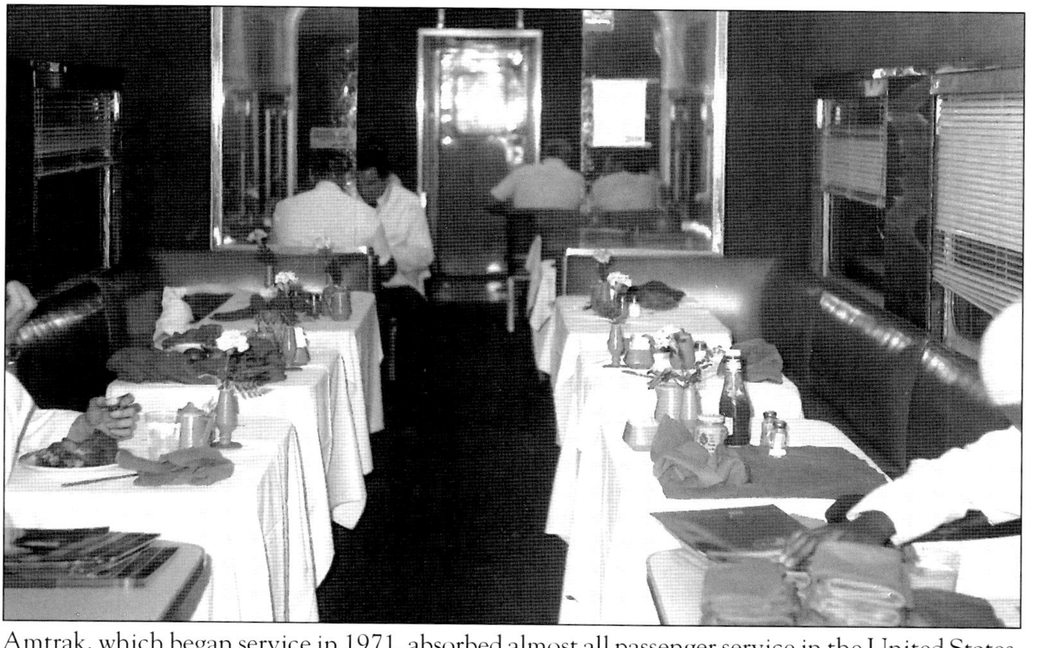

Amtrak, which began service in 1971, absorbed almost all passenger service in the United States. Its *Floridian*, replacing the old *Florida Arrow* from Chicago to Miami, sported a comfortable and modern dining car, shown here on the leg from Montgomery to Dothan, Alabama. (Courtesy of the Tom Solomon Collection, DLF.)

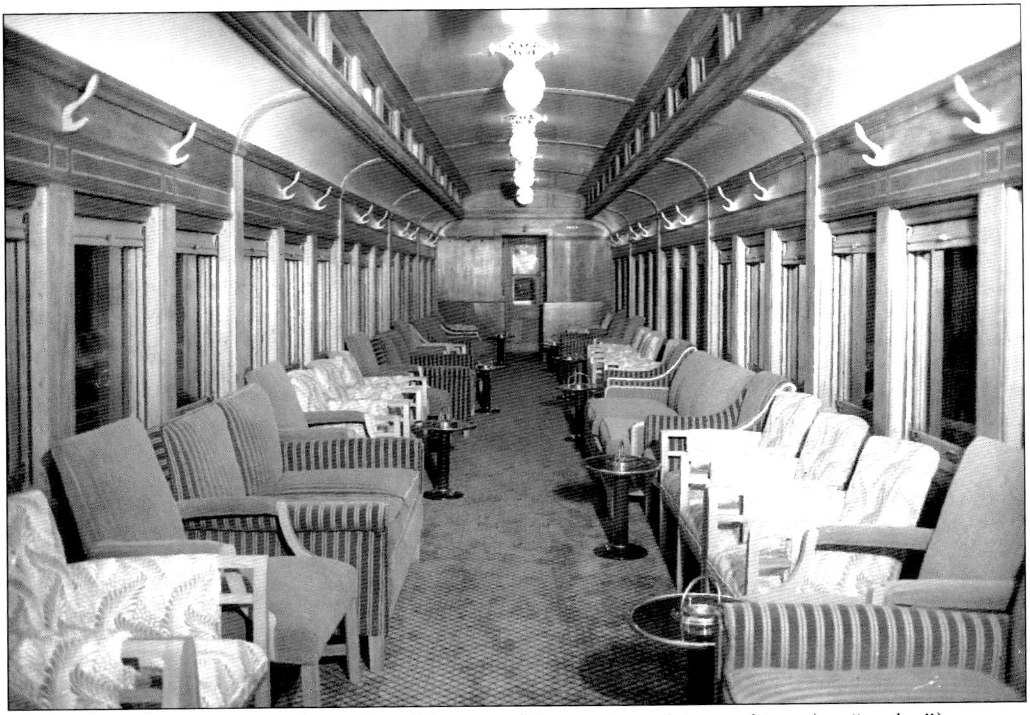

With its rich paneling and comfortable, movable seating, this smoking (or "parlor") car on the Bay Line's *Beach Special* encouraged passengers to relax and enjoy the ride to the Gulf of Mexico. (Courtesy of Quinton Bruner.)

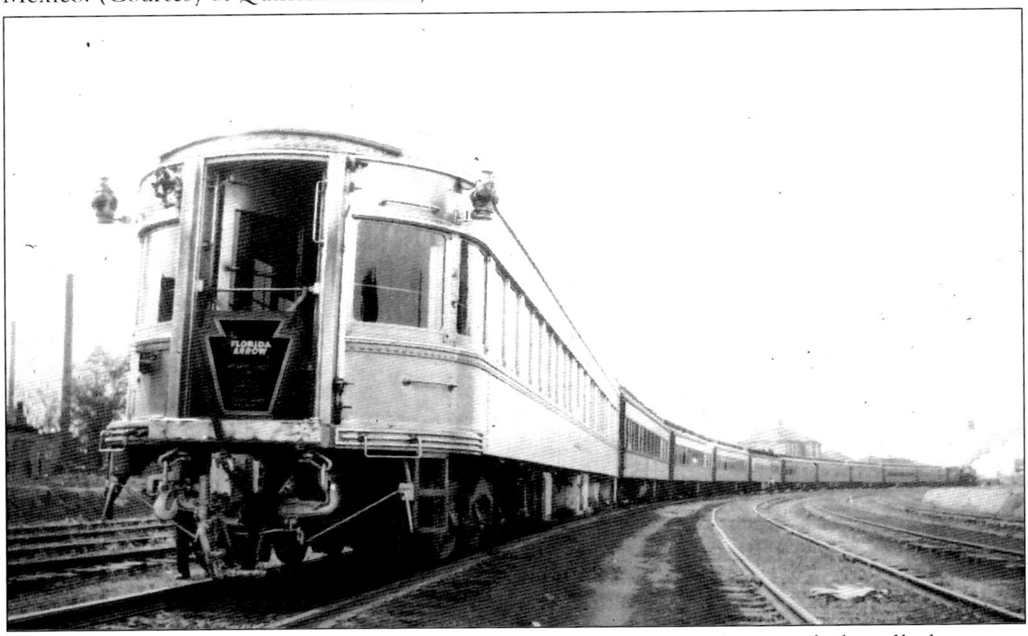

The *Florida Arrow*, leaving Dothan, Alabama, in January 1936, carried the all-aluminum observation-lounge car, the *George M. Pullman*. The Pullman Company pioneered the classic sleeper car for long-distance rail travel. (Courtesy of the Tom Solomon Collection, DLF.)

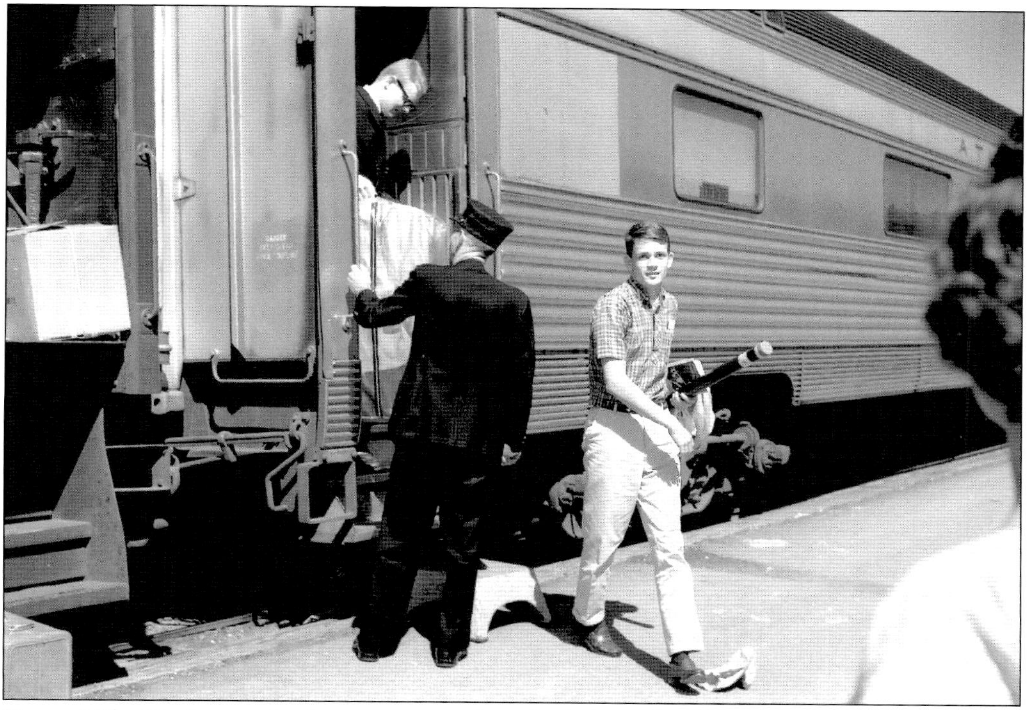

Young Mike Bledsoe and other passengers disembark from the Atlantic Coast Line Passenger Train No. 189 at Dothan, Alabama, on September 2, 1964. For years, the No. 189 crossed the Wiregrass from Waycross, Georgia, to Montgomery, Alabama. (Courtesy of the Tom Solomon Collection, DLF.)

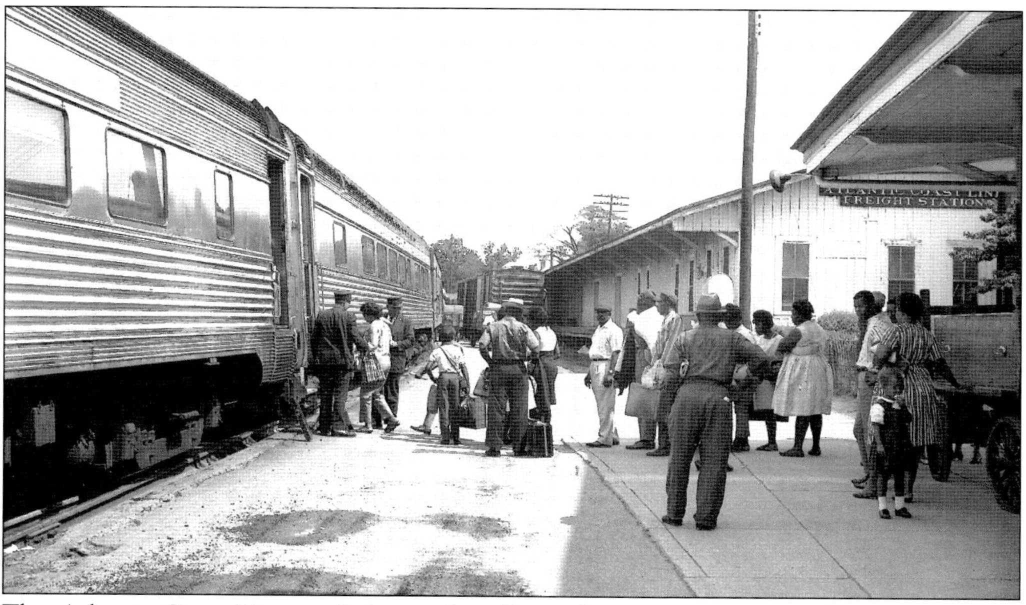

The Atlantic Coast Line used the modern Streamliner passenger cars after 1955. In this September 3, 1965 image, passengers board Train No. 189 from Dothan to Montgomery. (Courtesy of the Tom Solomon Collection, DLF.)

ONE-WAY ADULT FARES IN CENTS

GOOD FOR TRANSPORTATION IN PARLOR OR SLEEPING CARS

Index No.	Between / And	1 Dothan, Ala.	2 Keytons, Ala.	3 Hodgesville, Ala.	4 Madrid, Ala.	5 Campbellton, Fla.	6 Jacobs, Fla.	7 Cottondale, Fla.	8 Alford, Fla.	9 Compass Lake, Fla.	10 Fountain, Fla.	11 Youngstown, Fla.	12 Panama City, Fla.
1	Dothan, Ala.	------											
2	Keytons, Ala.	30	------										
3	Hodgesville, Ala.	35	30	------									
4	Madrid, Ala.	45	30	30	------								
5	Campbellton, Fla.	65	40	35	30	------							
6	Jacobs, Fla.	80	50	45	35	30	------						
7	Cottondale, Fla.	100	75	75	55	40	30	------					
8	Alford, Fla.	125	95	95	80	65	50	30	------				
9	Compass Lake, Fla.	150	125	120	105	85	75	50	30	------			
10	Fountain, Fla.	180	150	145	135	110	100	80	55	30	------		
11	Youngstown, Fla.	205	180	175	155	140	130	100	80	55	30	------	
12	Panama City, Fla.	270	245	240	230	205	195	175	145	125	95	80	------

♦ROUND-TRIP ADULT FARES IN CENTS

GOOD FOR TRANSPORTATION IN PARLOR OR SLEEPING CARS.

Index No.	Between / And	1 Dothan, Ala.	2 Keytons, Ala.	3 Hodgesville, Ala.	4 Madrid, Ala.	5 Campbellton, Fla.	6 Jacobs, Fla.	7 Cottondale, Fla.	8 Alford, Fla.	9 Compass Lake, Fla.	10 Fountain, Fla.	11 Youngstown, Fla.	12 Panama City, Fla.
1	Dothan, Ala.	------											
2	Keytons, Ala.	45	------										
3	Hodgesville, Ala.	55	45	------									
4	Madrid, Ala.	70	45	45	------								
5	Campbellton, Fla.	100	60	55	45	------							
6	Jacobs, Fla.	120	75	70	55	45	------						
7	Cottondale, Fla.	150	115	115	85	60	45	------					
8	Alford, Fla.	190	145	145	120	100	75	45	------				
9	Compass Lake, Fla.	225	190	180	160	130	115	75	45	------			
10	Fountain, Fla.	270	225	220	205	165	150	120	85	45	------		
11	Youngstown, Fla.	310	270	265	235	210	195	150	120	85	45	------	
12	Panama City, Fla.	405	370	360	345	310	295	265	220	190	145	120	------

♦Denotes reduction.

2

According to this tariff—or published rate sheet—effective May 20, 1950, an adult could make a round trip from Dothan, Alabama, to Panama City, Florida, in a Bay Line luxury parlor car or Pullman sleeper for $4.05. Adjusted for inflation, that trip would have cost $29.88 in 2003. Unfortunately, the Bay Line has long since ceased its passenger service. (Courtesy of Quinton Bruner.)

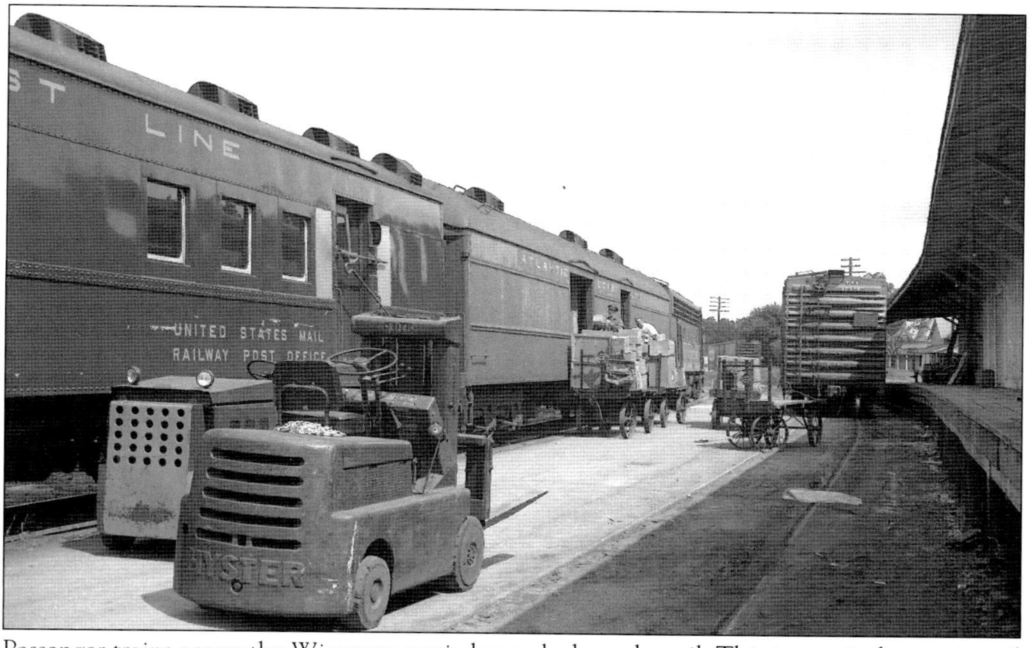

Passenger trains across the Wiregrass carried parcels through mail. This is a typical scene in rail yards across the region—handlers transfer parcels from ACL Train No. 180 to baggage wagons next to the freight station. It was taken on September 3, 1965, in Dothan. (Courtesy of the Tom Solomon Collection, DLF.)

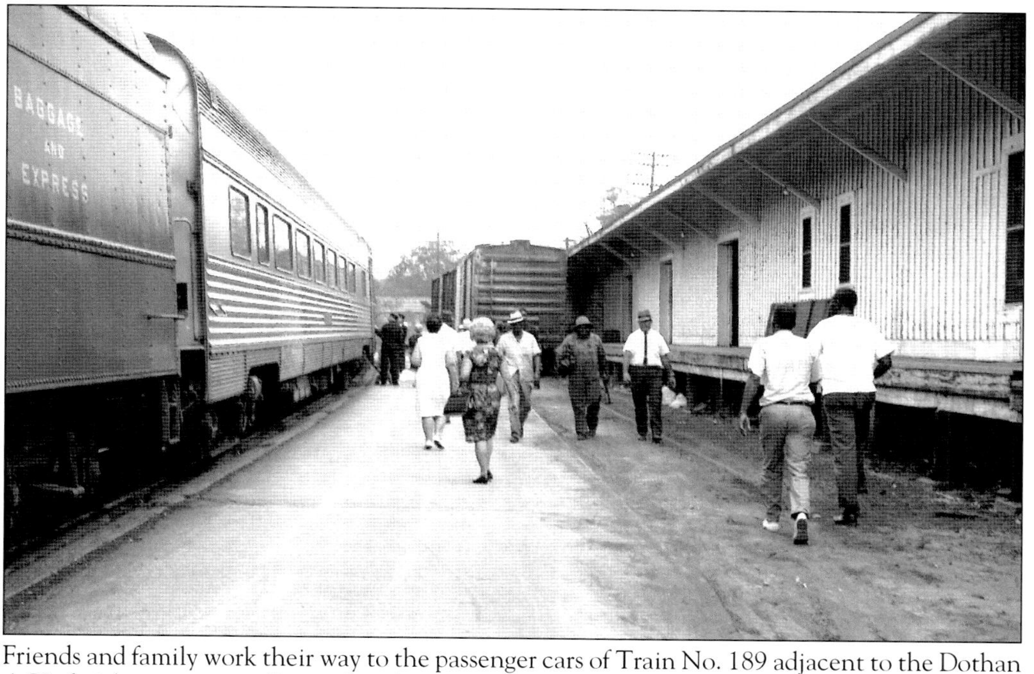

Friends and family work their way to the passenger cars of Train No. 189 adjacent to the Dothan ACL freight station on September 3, 1965. Because the No. 189 and the No. 180 were late, they arrived at the depot simultaneously, forcing crews to scramble and passengers to board and detrain in the freight area. (Courtesy of the Tom Solomon Collection, DLF.)

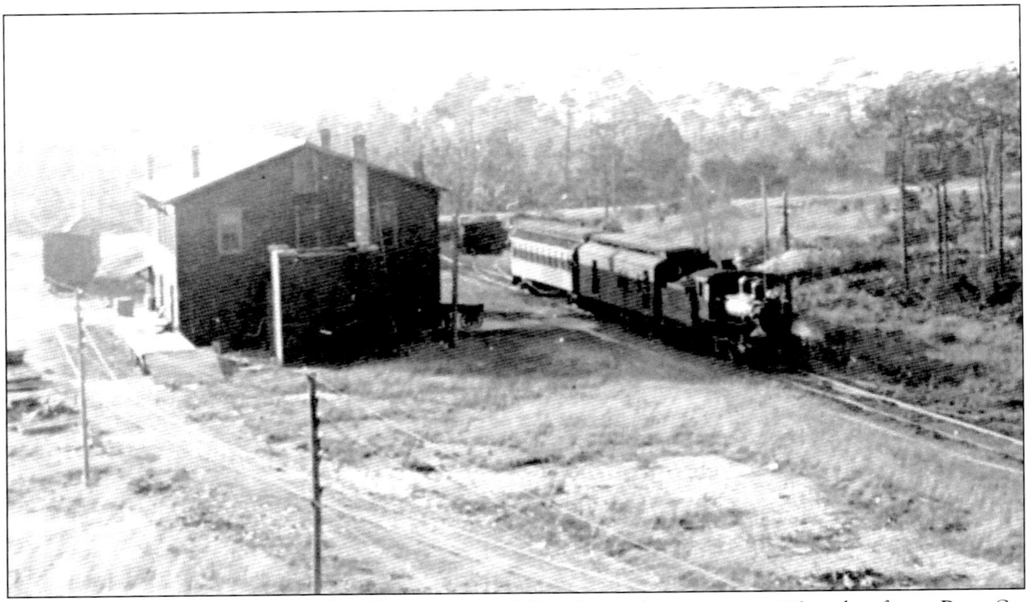

The Apalachicola Northern (AN) transported freight and passengers 96 miles from Port St. Joe to the Louisville & Nashville (later CSX) line at River Junction (Chattahoochee), Florida. Chartered by the state in 1903, the AN began construction in 1905 and ran its first train in 1907. From 1937 to 1999, St. Joe Paper Company owned the line. Rail Management Corporation acquired the line in 2002. (Courtesy of the Tom Solomon Collection, DLF.)

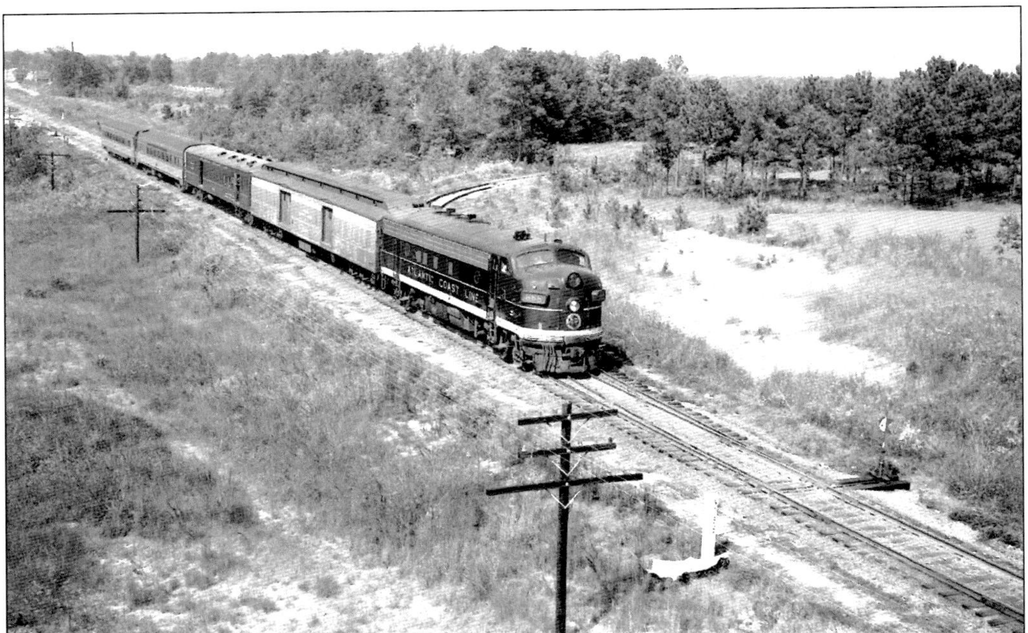

This is an excellent view of the ACL No. 189—with streamliner engine, baggage car, mail car, and two passenger cars—traversing the Wiregrass from Waycross to Montgomery in the 1960s. ACL halted passenger service in the 1970s. (Courtesy of the Tom Solomon Collection, DLF.)

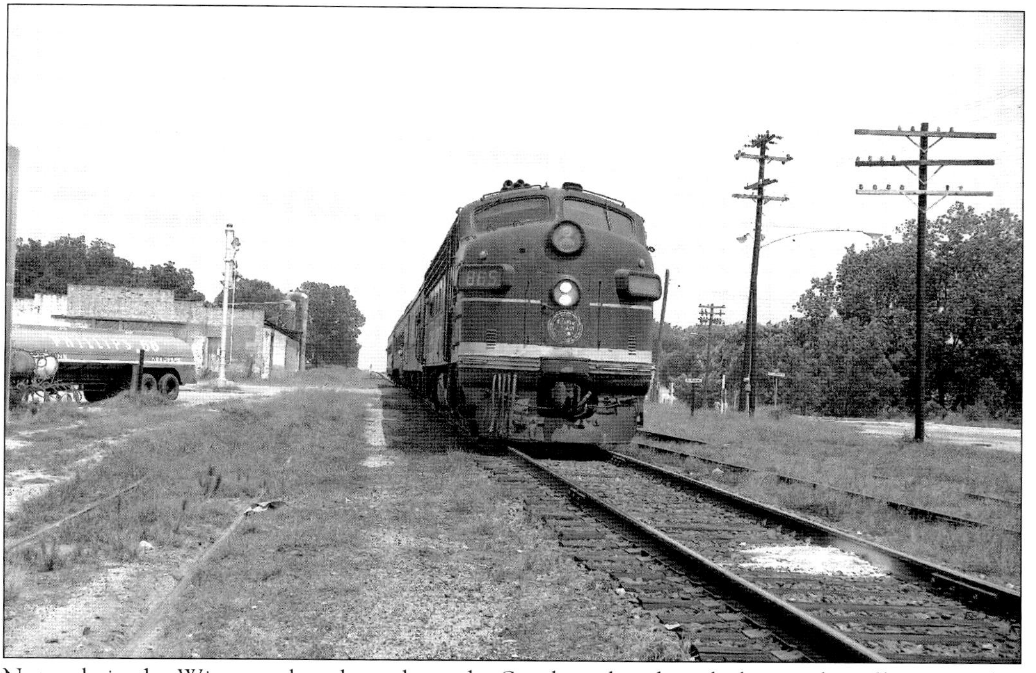

Not only in the Wiregrass but throughout the South, railroad tracks bisected small towns. This ACL train cuts through the middle of sleepy Ashford, Alabama, in June 1964, manned by engineer B.C. Rowell, conductor D.W. Davidson, and flagman C.H. Quinn. (Courtesy of the Tom Solomon Collection, DLF.)

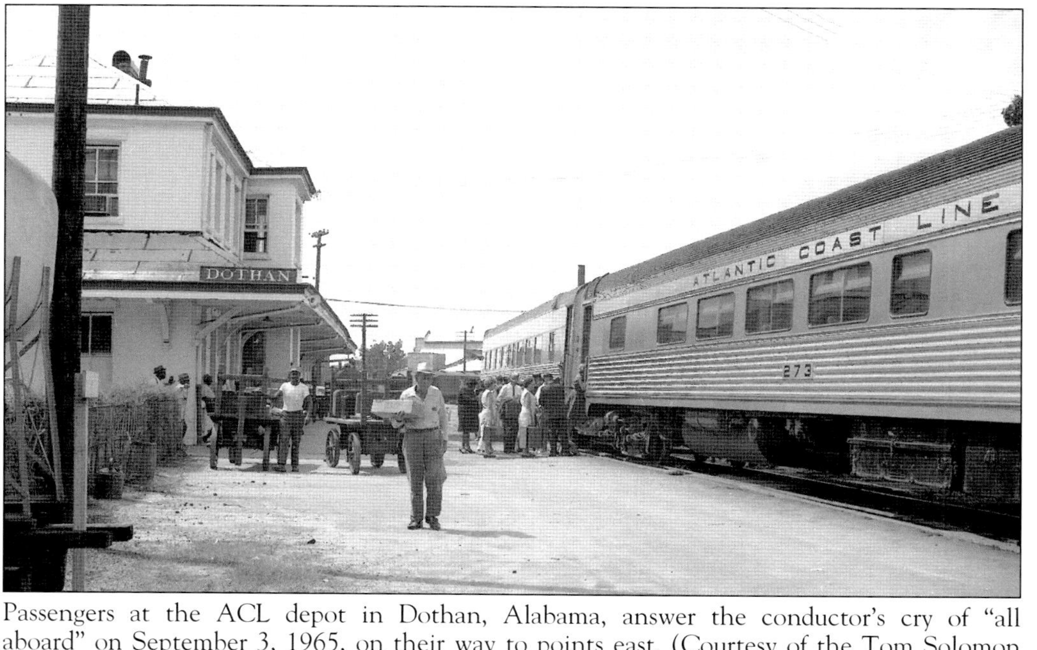

Passengers at the ACL depot in Dothan, Alabama, answer the conductor's cry of "all aboard" on September 3, 1965, on their way to points east. (Courtesy of the Tom Solomon Collection, DLF.)

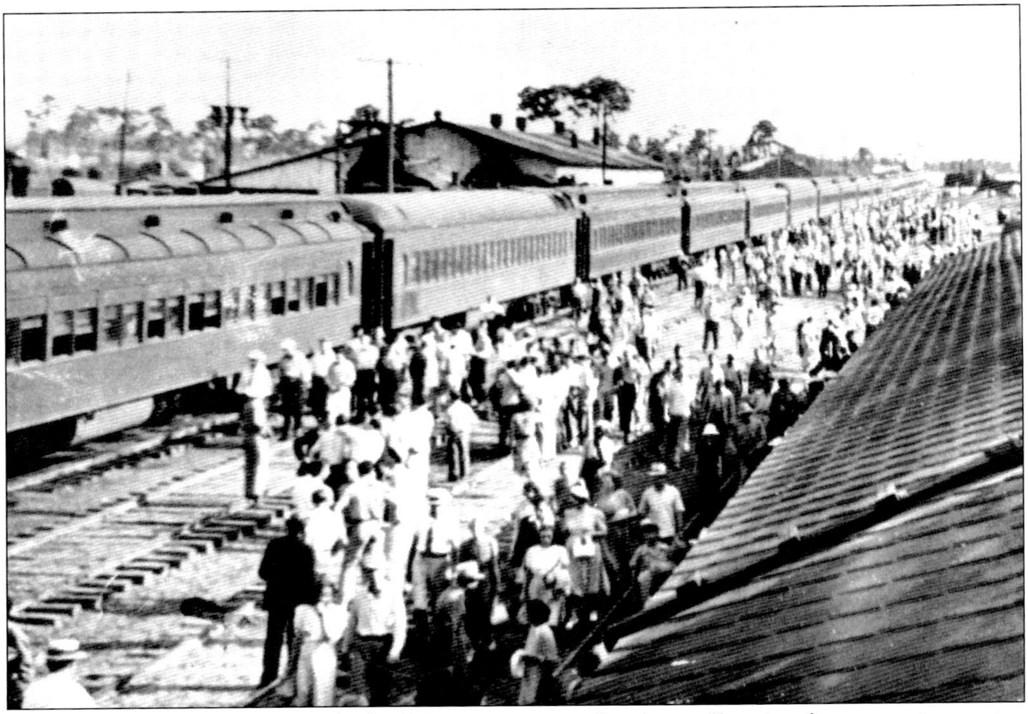

Daily passenger service through the Wiregrass required only small trains, but excursion trains to the beach were a different story. At the Bay Line depot in Panama City, Florida, scores of tourists board a northbound excursion at the end of their vacations. The Bay Line shops are in the background. (Courtesy of David Kirkland.)

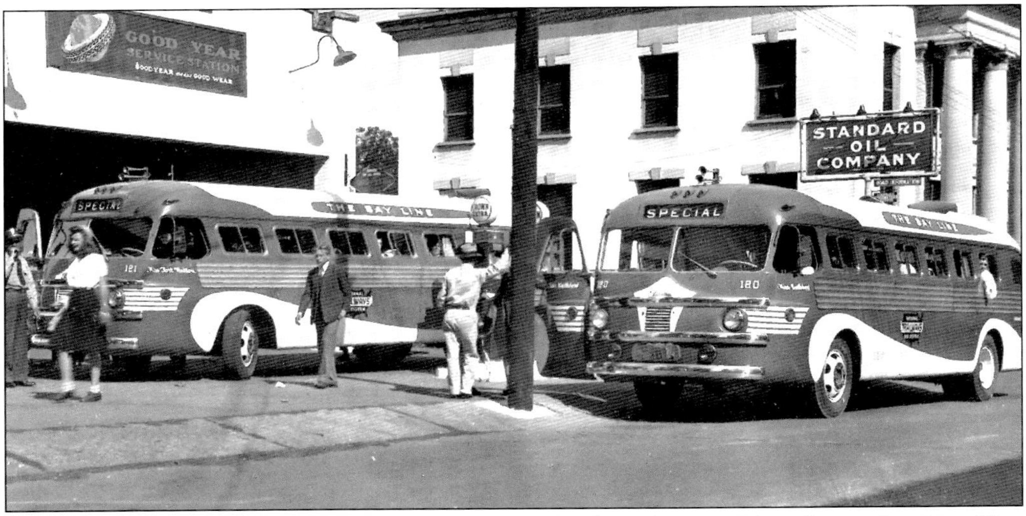

Railroads became full transportation services with the advent of bus lines. At City Tire Company in Dothan, the Dothan High School Band boards Bay Line busses to watch their Tigers football team tie the Sidney Lanier Poets at Montgomery's Crampton Bowl on October 24, 1941. (Courtesy of Quinton Bruner.)

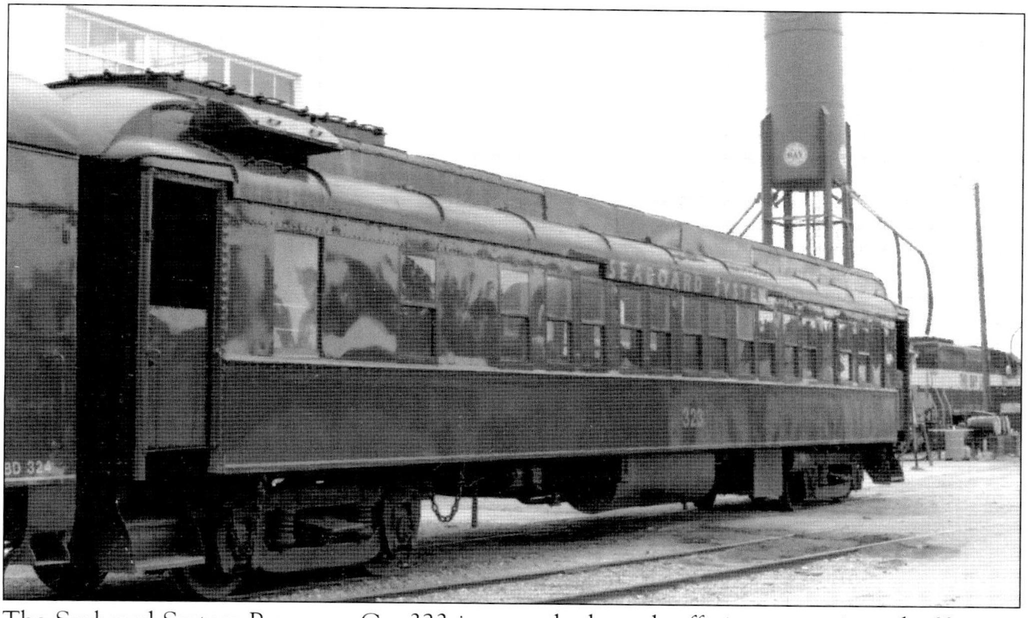

The Seaboard System Passenger Car 323 is a standard coach offering approximately 60 seats. Passengers could choose between it, Pullman sleepers, or observation-lounges on most east-west lines. This restored car is pictured at the Bay Line depot in Panama City, Florida, in the 1980s. (Courtesy of David Kirkland.)

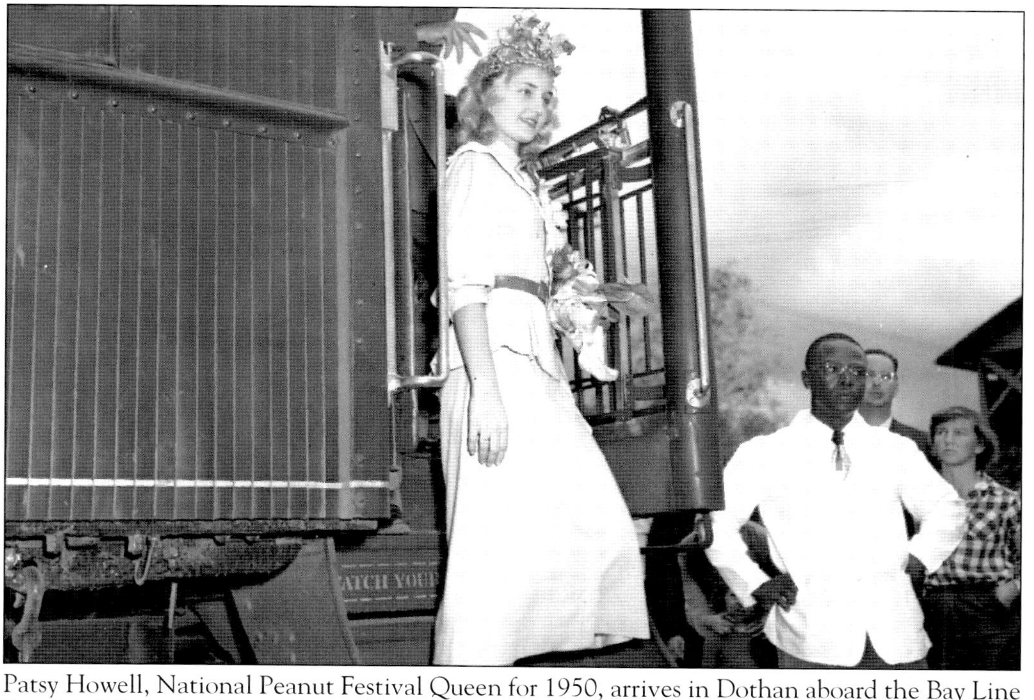

Patsy Howell, National Peanut Festival Queen for 1950, arrives in Dothan aboard the Bay Line Special Office Car No. 100, a self-propelled business railcar equipped with a galley, lounge, bedrooms, washrooms, and meeting room. A no-nonsense porter in white jacket looks on. (Courtesy of Quinton Bruner.)

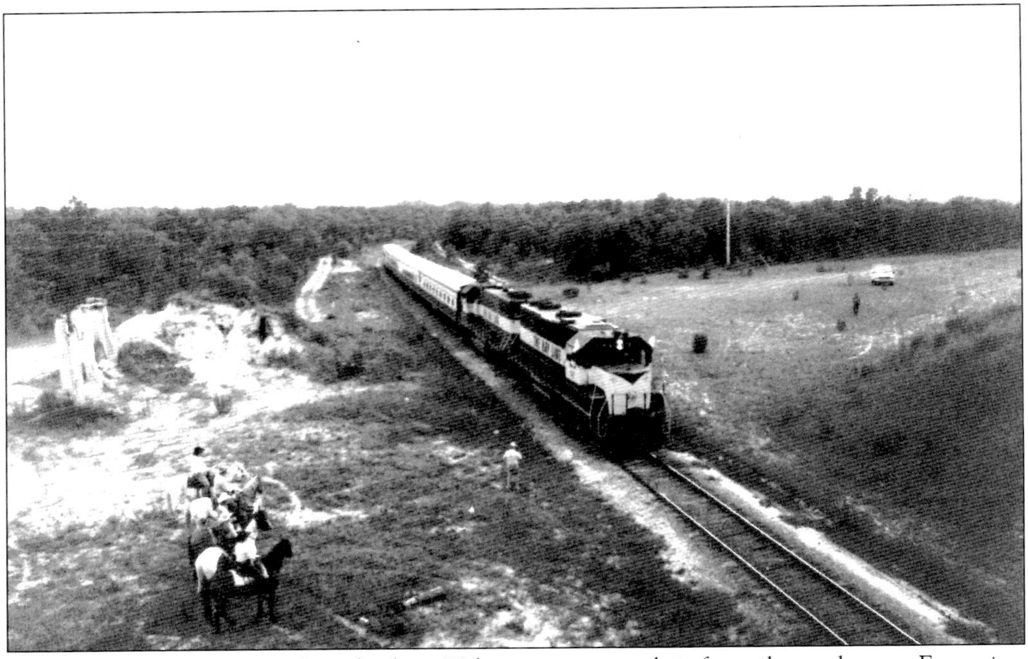

As passenger service waned in the late 20th century, nostalgia for rail travel grew. Excursion and charter lines served this emerging market. This 1989 photo shows a photographer taking a promotional picture for the *American Orient Express* as horse-mounted spectators watch the train pass on the Bay Line tracks in Florida. (Courtesy of David Kirkland.)

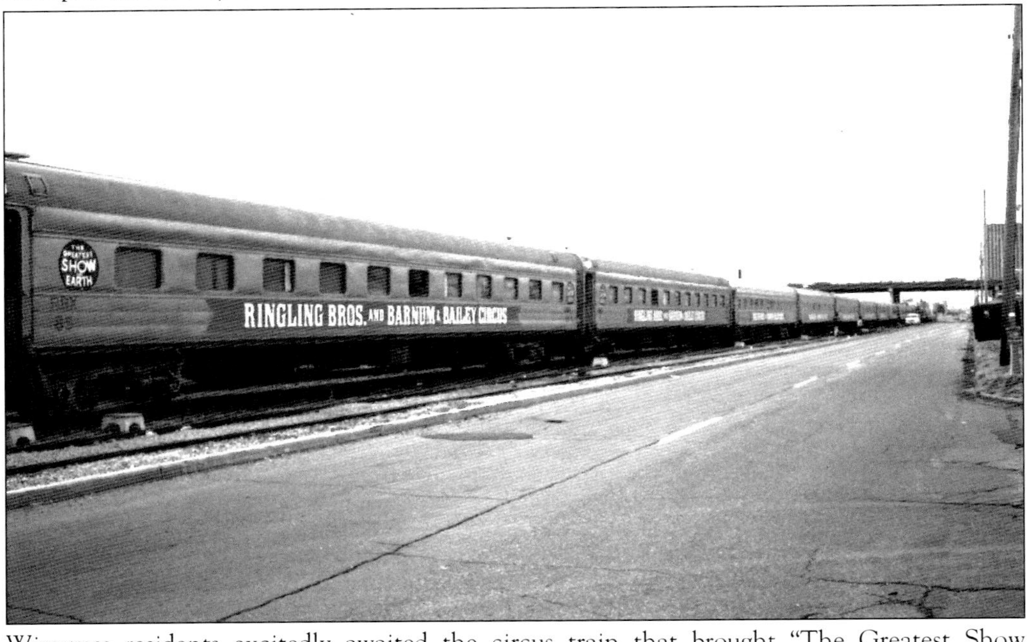

Wiregrass residents excitedly awaited the circus train that brought "The Greatest Show on Earth" and other acts through on their way to winter quarters in Florida. Trains such as this one stopped to allow the circus to put on shows in small towns along the route. (Courtesy of David Kirkland.)

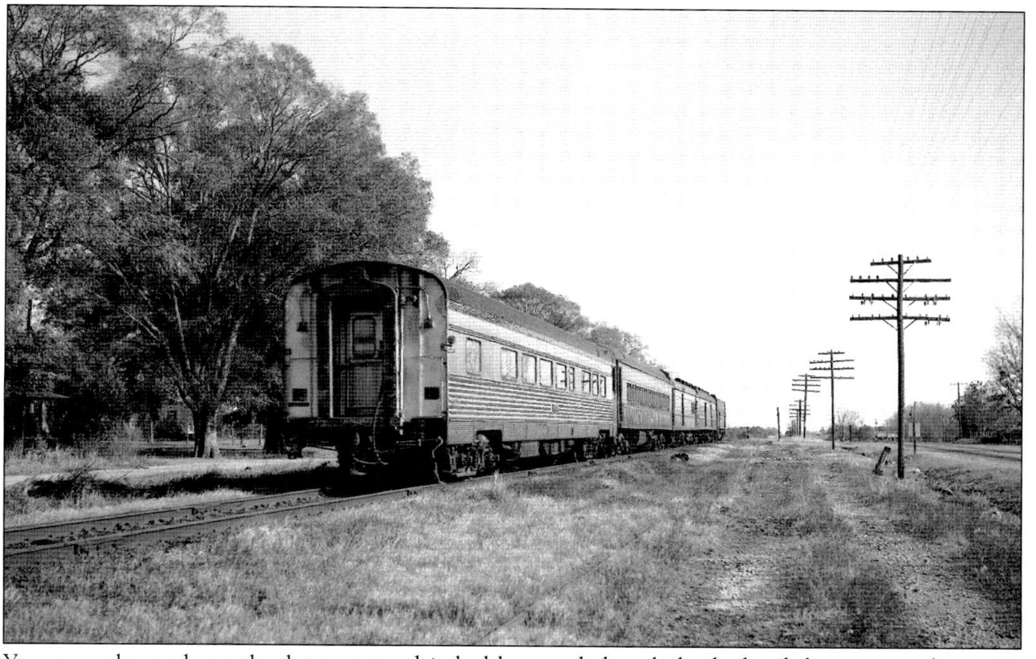

You can almost hear the lonesome whistle blow and the click-clack of the cars as the ACL No. 180 makes its way past Ashford, Alabama, toward Saffold, Iron City, Thomasville, and Waycross, Georgia. This picture is dated November 30, 1963. (Courtesy of the Tom Solomon Collection, DLF.)

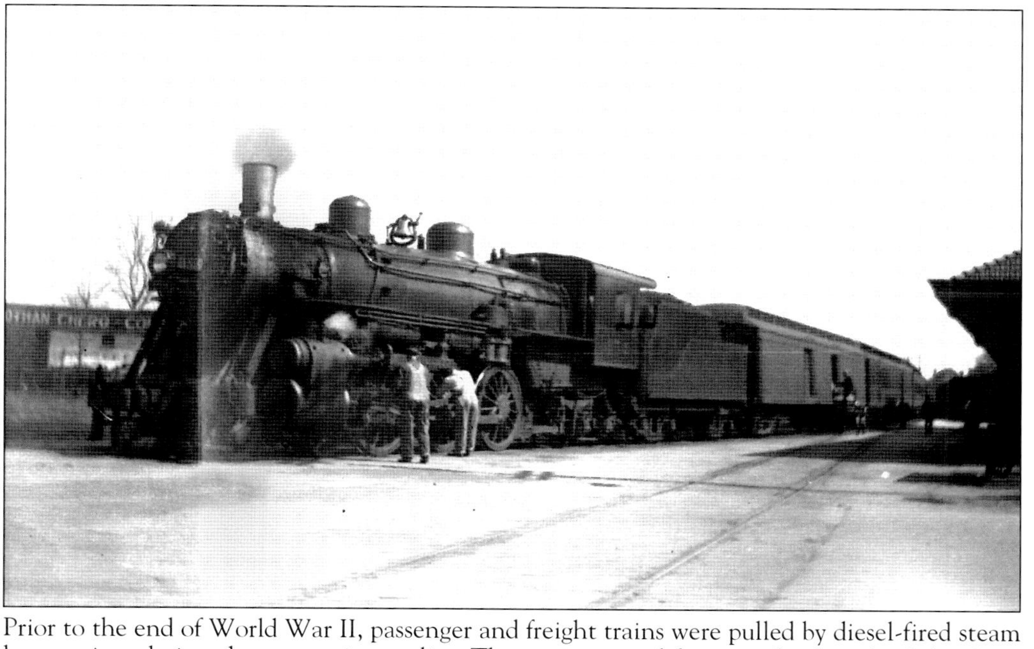

Prior to the end of World War II, passenger and freight trains were pulled by diesel-fired steam locomotives designed a generation earlier. The engineer and fireman check and oil the drive train on the ACL No. 454, a Light Pacific locomotive pulling Train No. 189 through Dothan in 1935. (Courtesy of the Tom Solomon Collection, DLF.)

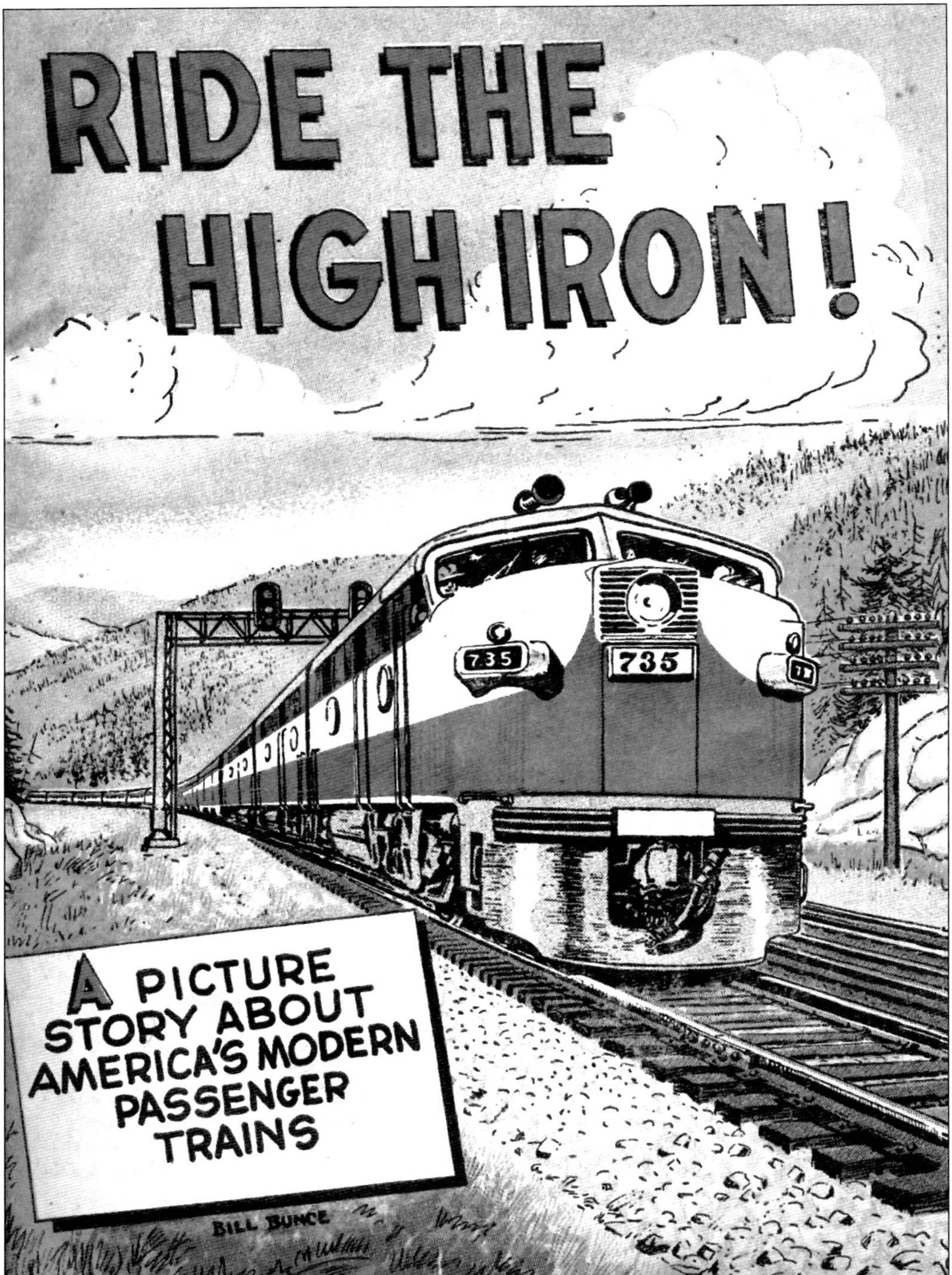

The 1950s witnessed a comic book craze, providing the American Association of Railroads a perfect medium to educate potential teen-aged riders about the drama and practical advantages of rail travel. Unfortunately for the railroads, automobiles captured that generation's imagination instead. (Courtesy of the DLF Dixie Depot Collection, AWHC.)

Three

CARRYING THE GOODS

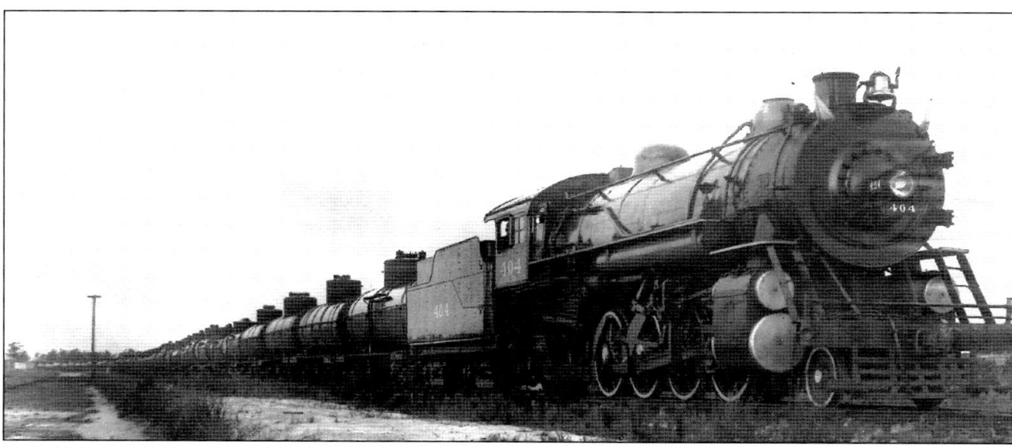

In addition to wood products, manufactured goods, agricultural crops, and fertilizer, a chemical industry has grown up at the edge of the Wiregrass. In this undated photograph, the Bay Line No. 404, a massive diesel-fired steam locomotive, pulls 100 tanker cars to the Panama City docks. (Courtesy of the Tom Solomon Collection, DLF.)

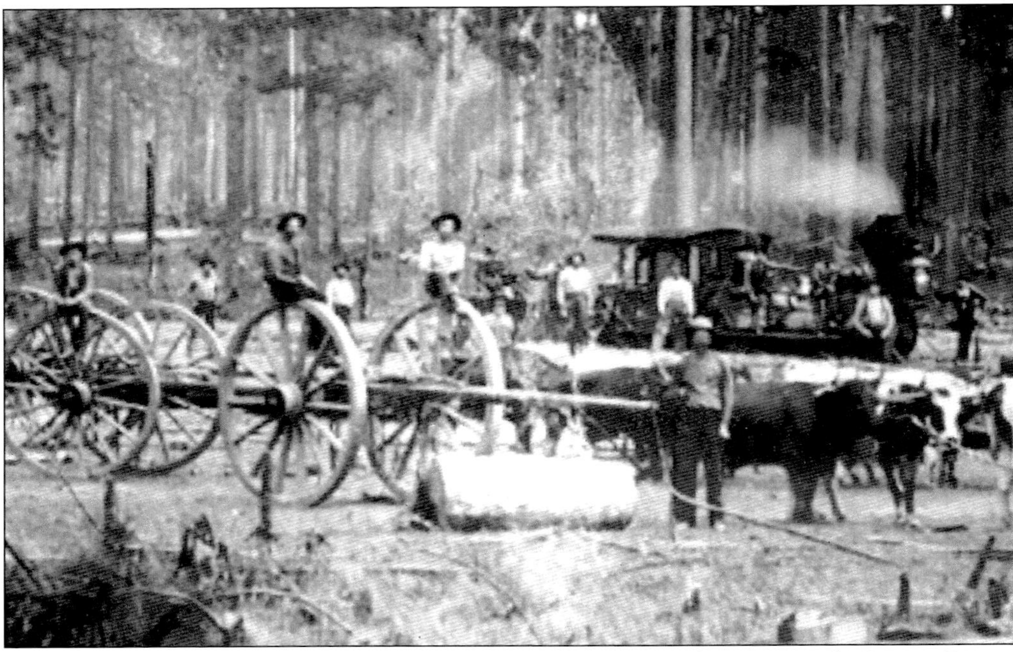

The forest products industry was significant in the Wiregrass in the post–Civil War era. Dozens of companies hauled logs for lumber and pulpwood. Before the advent of mechanical skidders and cranes, specially designed ox-driven wagons brought the wood to the narrow-gauge train for transfer to the mill. (Courtesy of David Kirkland.)

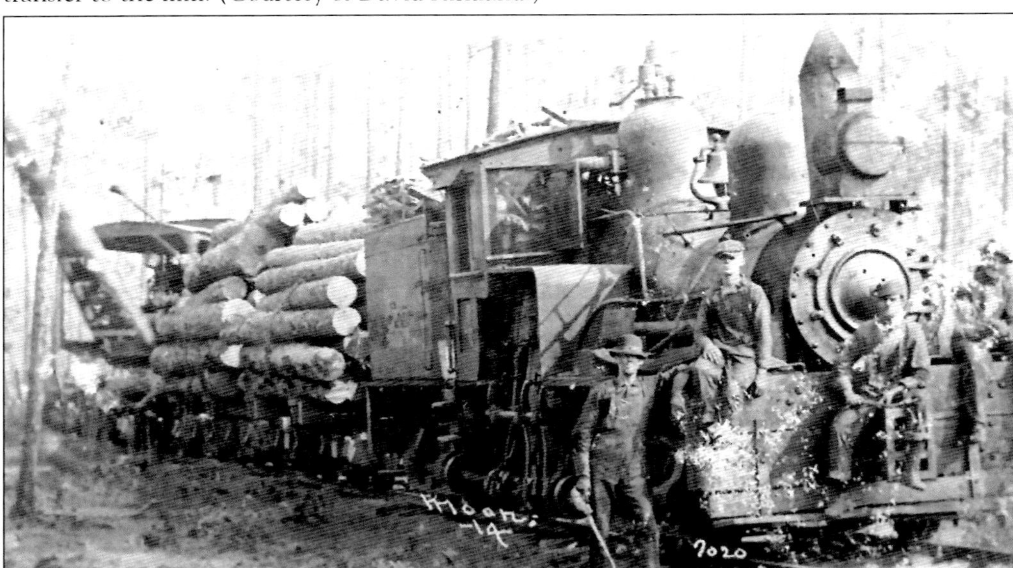

When lumber companies grew large enough to cut one million board feet per mile per year for 20 years, they could afford to haul logs by train rather than by oxen. In 1914, the crew pictured worked this narrow-gauge lumber railroad outside Panama City, Florida. Note the crane at the rear end of the train loading logs onto the cars. (Courtesy of the Bay County [Florida] Public Library Local History Room.)

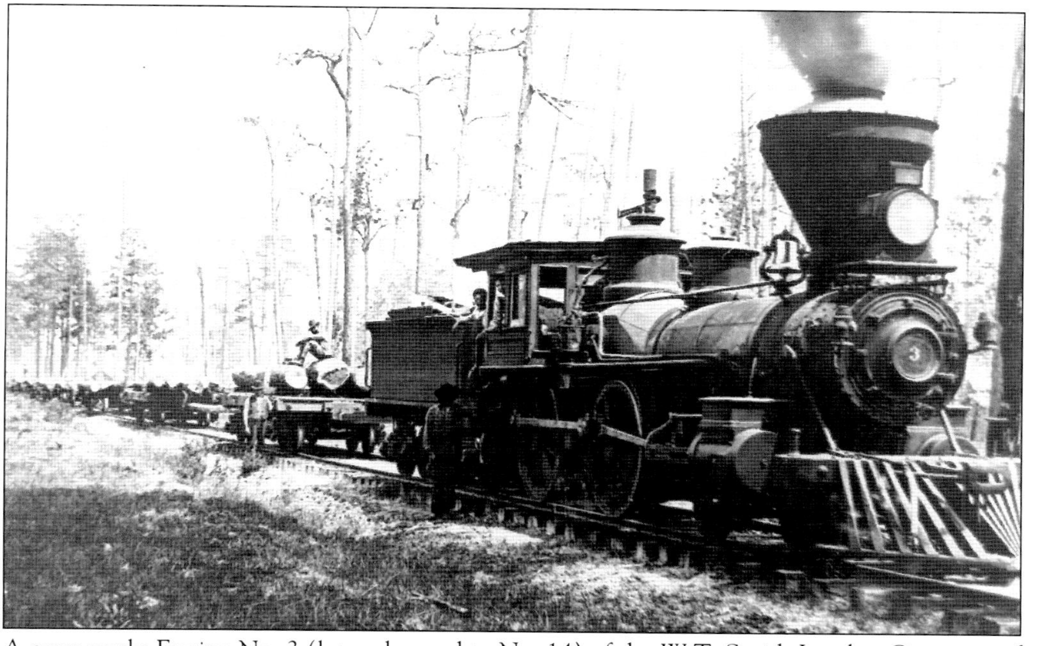

A crew works Engine No. 3 (later changed to No. 14) of the W.T. Smith Lumber Company of Chapman, Alabama. The cars are separated by extensions, called "rooster poles," to allow logs to hang over their ends. Also, they are lightly loaded because they had no brakes and because stopping quickly resulted in breaking the rooster poles or derailing the cars. (Courtesy of the Pioneer Museum of Alabama.)

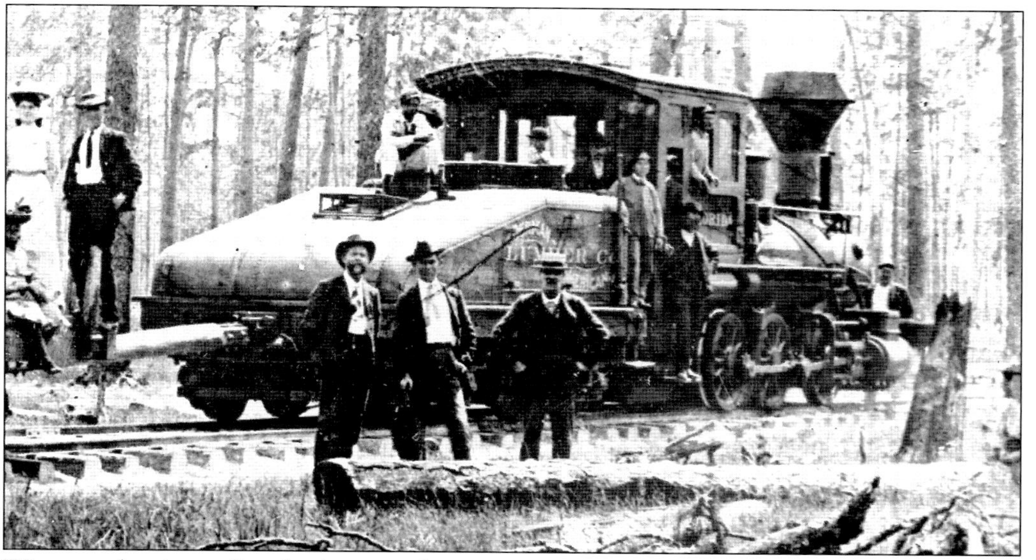

Wiregrass logging railroads also served as passenger transport in the backwoods. Like many of its competitors, the Sherman Lumber Company of Florida allowed its workers to catch the company train to leave the isolated logging camps and villages on Sundays, as well as during the week when the company ran excursions. Portable "peckerwood" sawmills, which were cheap and easily brought to the downed logs, replaced the railroads. (Courtesy of the Ashford Depot Restoration Foundation.)

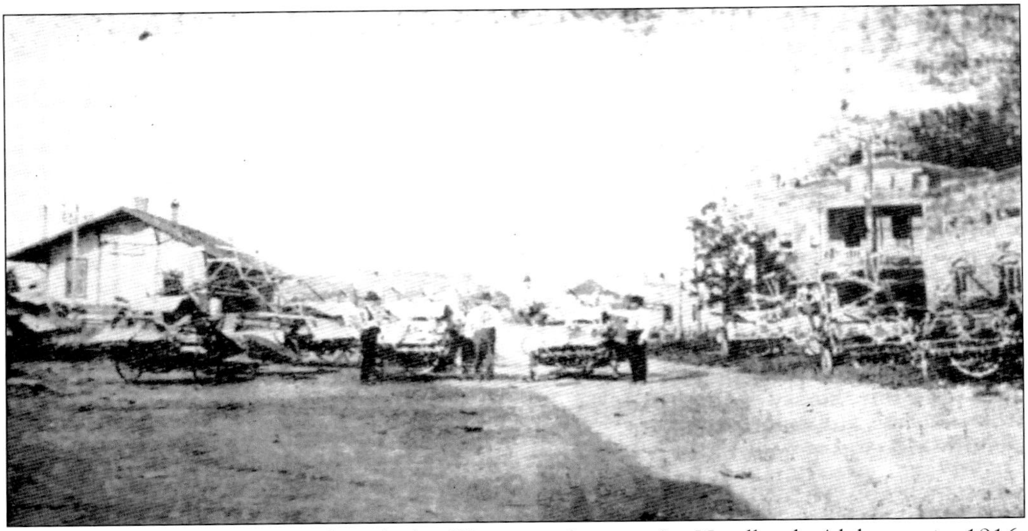

Railroads shipped agricultural tools for Wiregrass farmers. In Headland, Alabama, in 1916, workers display reapers on the ground and street between the depot (left) and the Alice Hotel (right.) These reapers were delivered to Hawkins Hardware to the right, outside of the picture. (Courtesy of the Henry County Historical Group.)

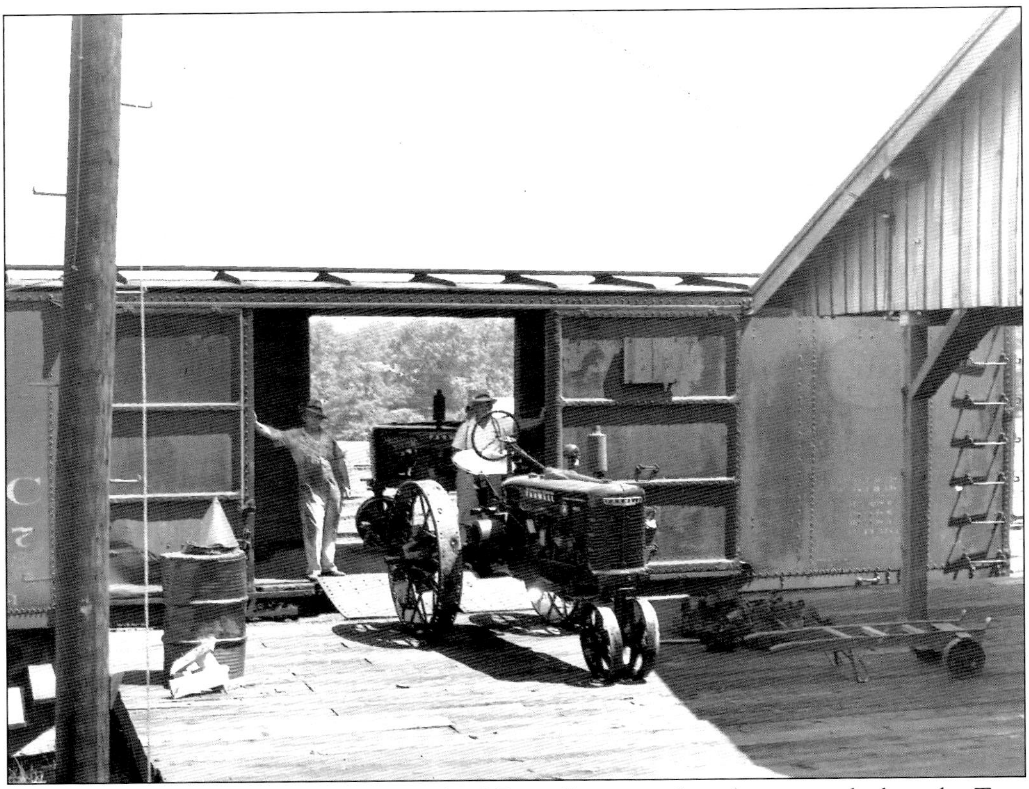

In this undated photo, freight agents unload Farmall tractors from boxcar to dock at the Troy (Alabama) freight depot of the Atlantic Coast Line. (Courtesy of the Troy Public Library.)

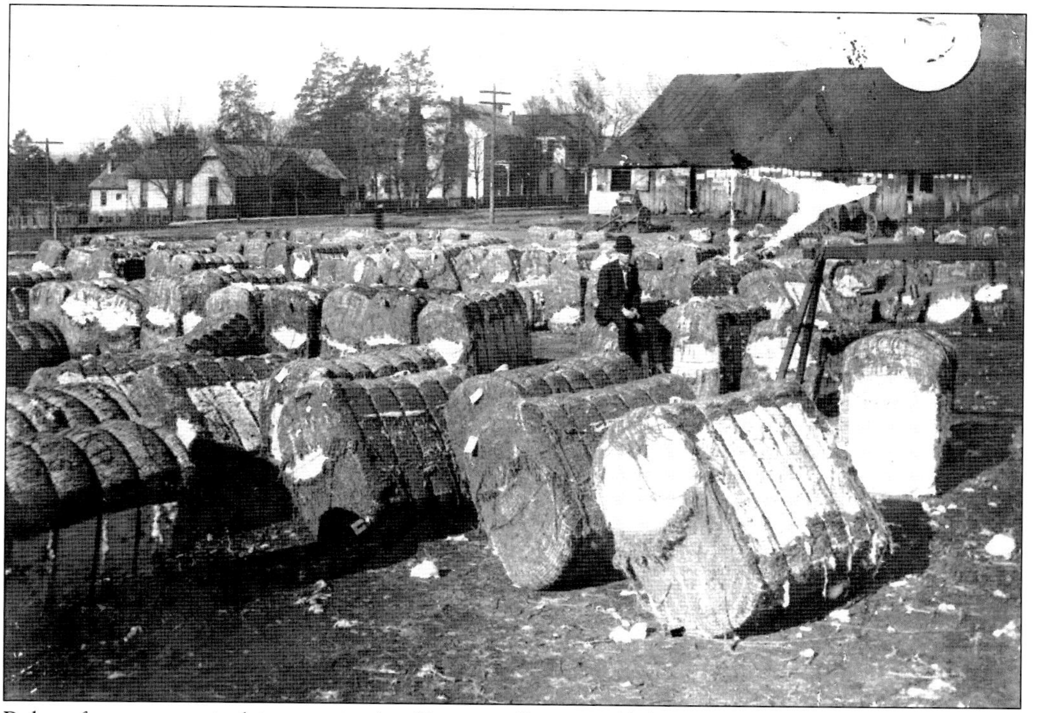

Bales of cotton await shipment in this Houston County, Alabama photograph. Note the cotton scales to the right of the well-dressed cotton broker. The cotton crop declined significantly with the invasion of the boll weevil after 1915. (Courtesy of the DLF.)

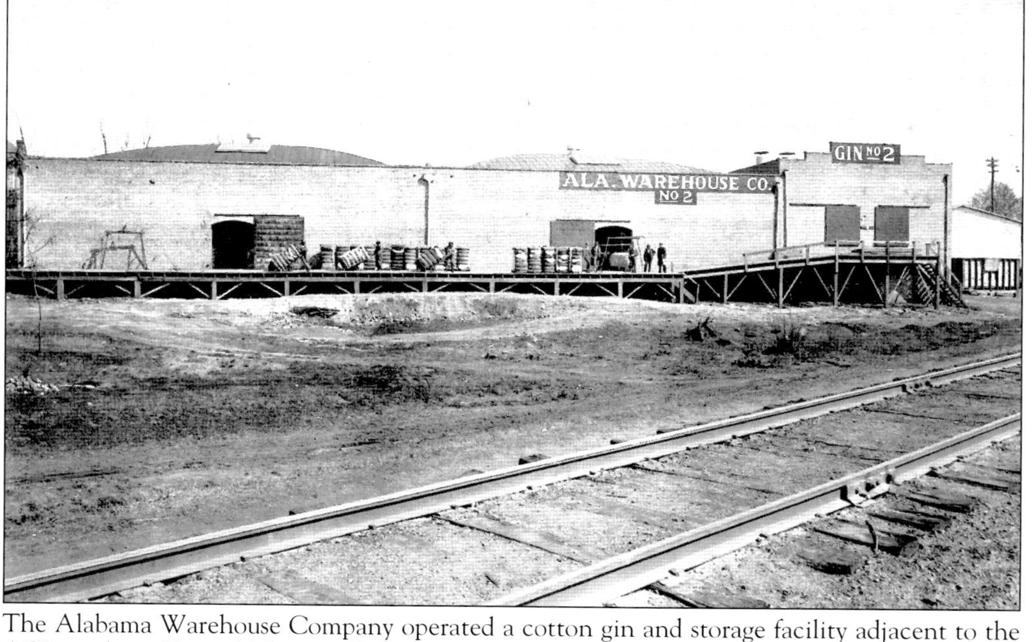

The Alabama Warehouse Company operated a cotton gin and storage facility adjacent to the ACL tracks in Troy, Alabama. Though no longer in operation, this faculty is still standing and is visible from Three Notch Road. (Courtesy of the Pioneer Museum of Alabama.)

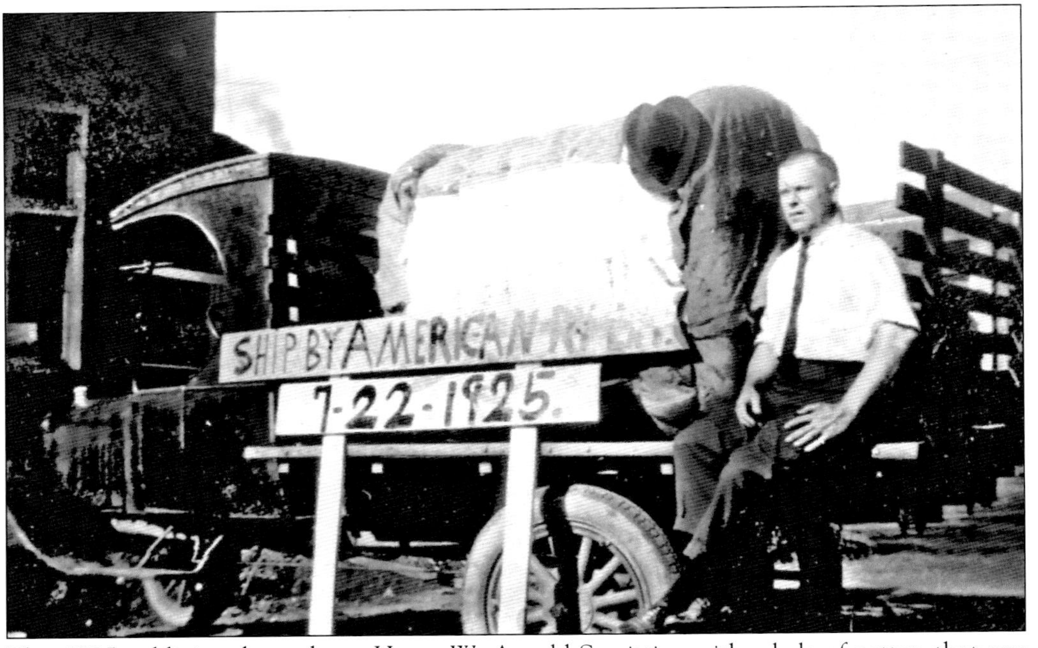

This 1925 publicity photo shows Henry W. Arnold Sr. sitting with a bale of cotton that was delivered by the American Railway Express. Arnold owned a small grocery in Dothan and was the city's first inspector of business licenses. (Courtesy of Theresa Adkison.)

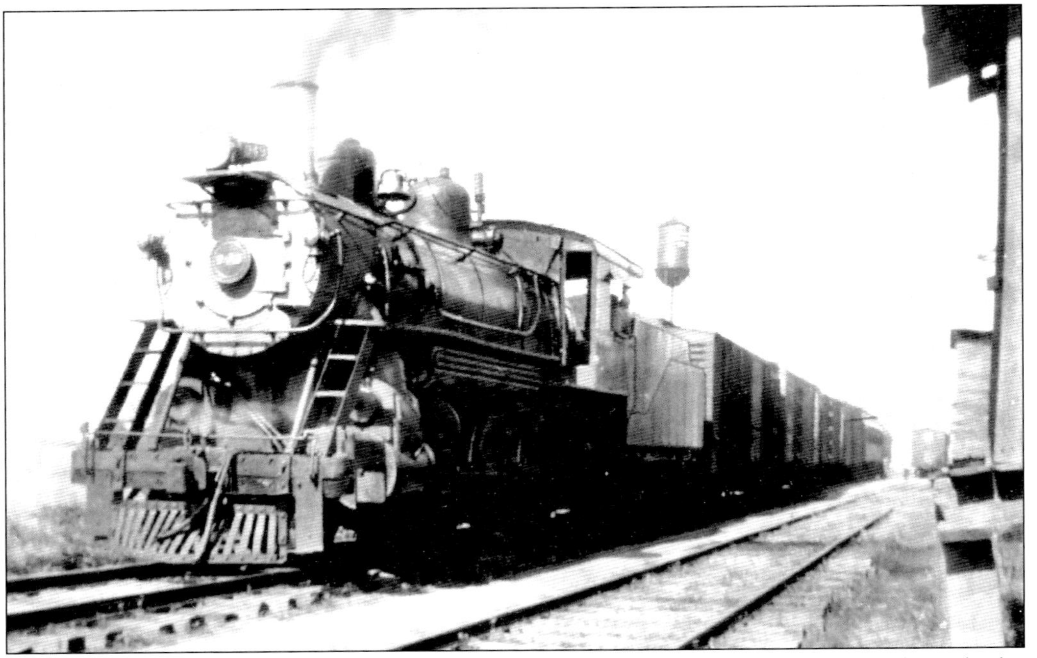

Atlantic Coast Line Engine No. 949 pulls a mixed freight and passenger train through the Headland, Alabama station in 1932. The water tower visible behind the train served the Dothan Oil Mill, producers of cottonseed and peanut oil. (Courtesy of the Abbeville [Alabama] Memorial Library.)

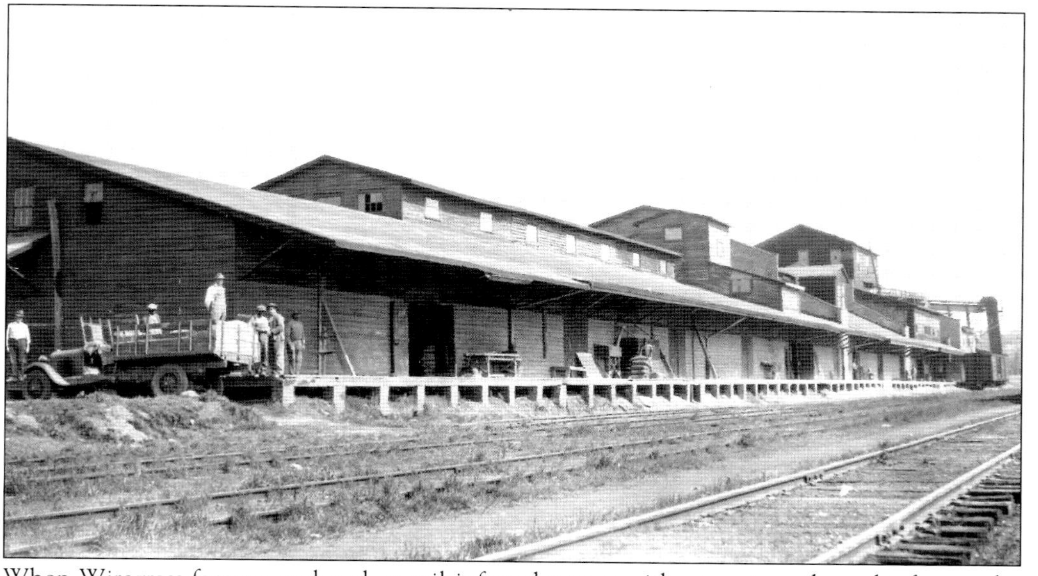

When Wiregrass farmers replaced weevil-infested cotton with peanuts as their chief crop, the Alabama Warehouse Company of Troy built a new peanut-shelling plant. Like the company's cotton gin, this plant relied on the railroads to move both raw and processed product. (Courtesy of the Pioneer Museum of Alabama.)

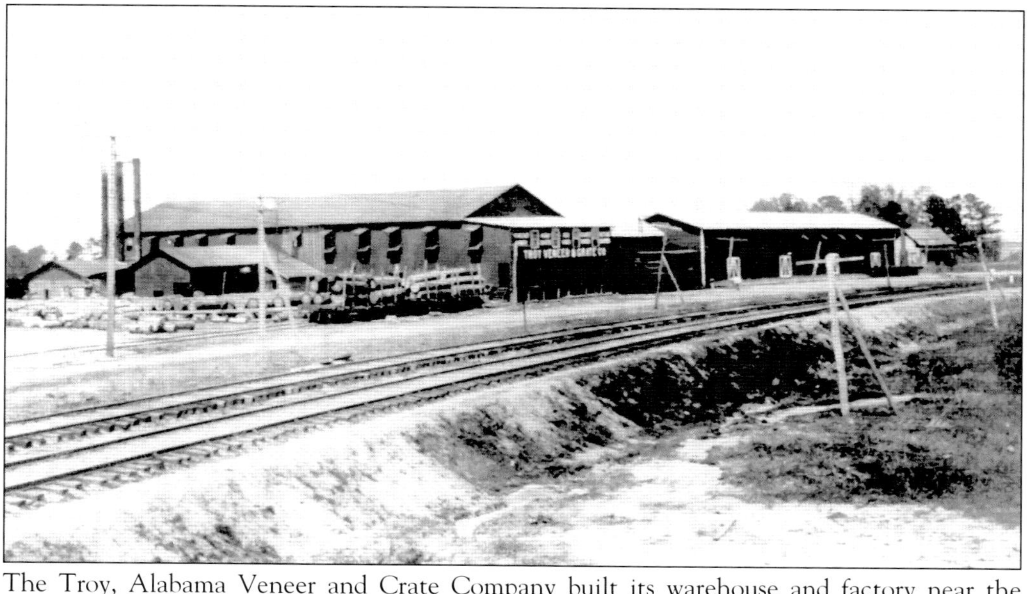

The Troy, Alabama Veneer and Crate Company built its warehouse and factory near the railroads that brought logs and took baskets and unassembled crates to markets around the world. Originally known as the Georgia Alabama Fruit Growers' Veneer Factory, it sat at the intersection of Butter and Egg Roads. (Courtesy of the Pioneer Museum of Alabama.)

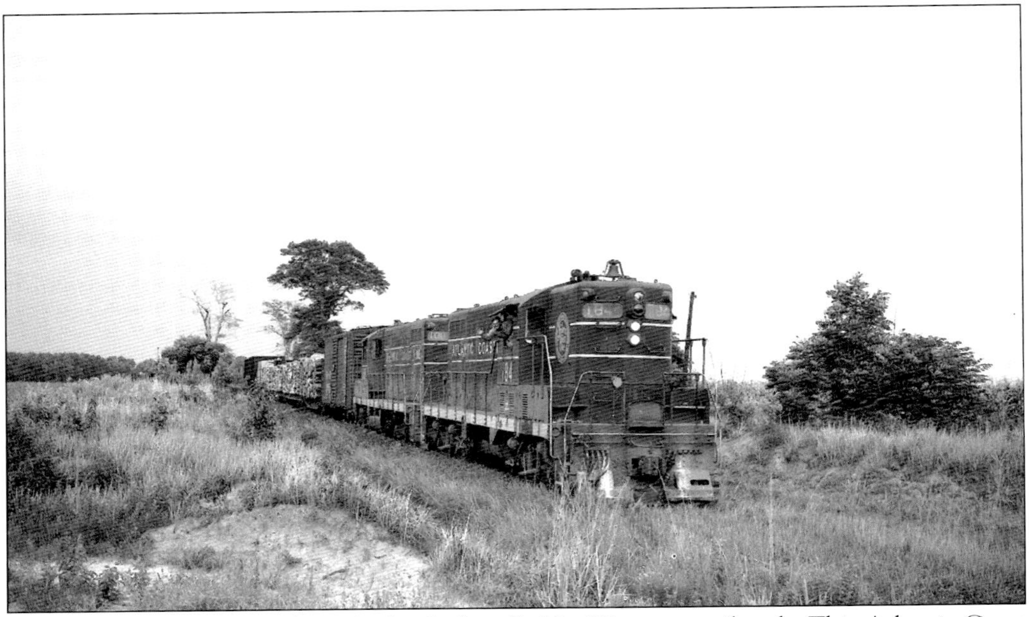

Wood products were not the only freight handled by Wiregrass railroads. This Atlantic Coast Line double-header hauls not only two cars of pulpwood but also a number of boxcars of weather-sensitive freight. Engineer Gerald Everett waves from the cab window on July 10, 1964. (Courtesy of the Tom Solomon Collection, DLF.)

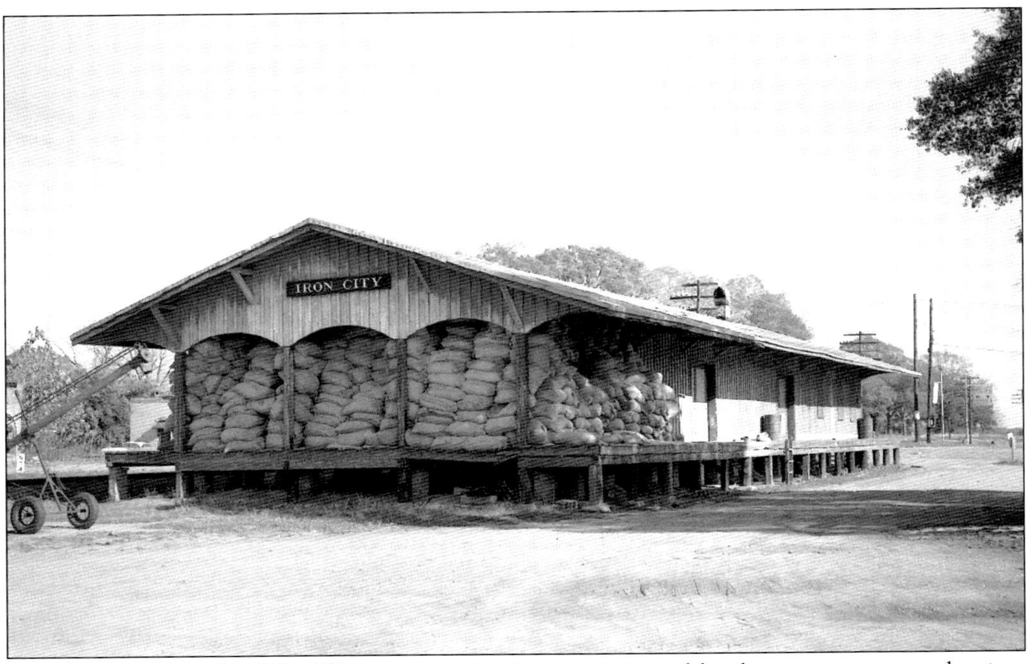

The poor, sandy soils of the Wiregrass require large amounts of fertilizer to remain productive. Hundreds of bags of soil nutrients await transfer from the Iron City, Georgia depot along the ACL track on on November 30, 1963. (Courtesy of the Tom Solomon Collection, DLF.)

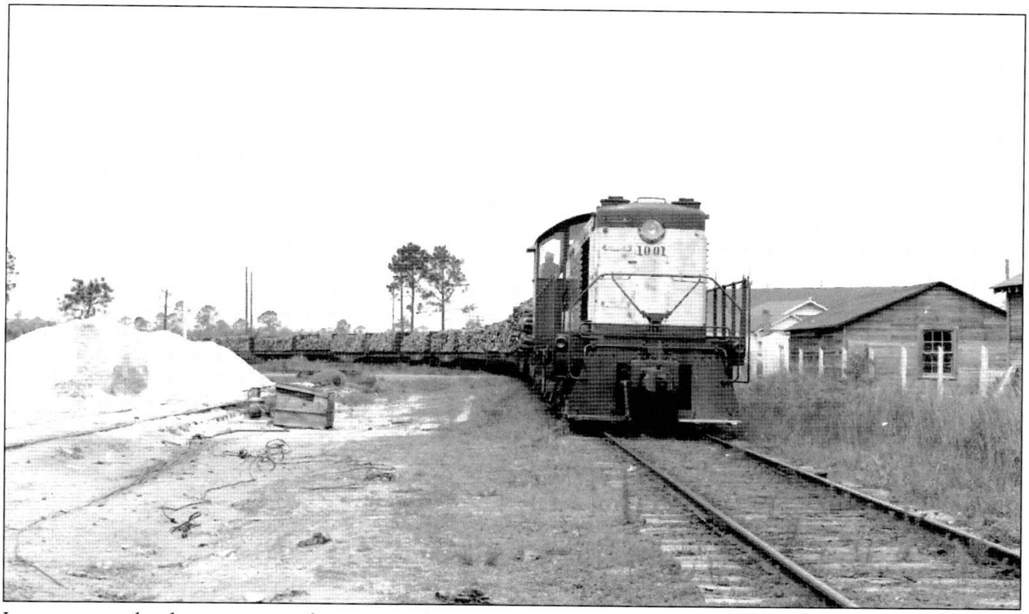

Loggers might have stopped using rail transport, but pulpwooders have taken it up with a vengeance. Here, the Bay Line No. 1101 pulls a full complement of flatcars filled with pine logs destined to become paper. (Courtesy of Quinton Bruner.)

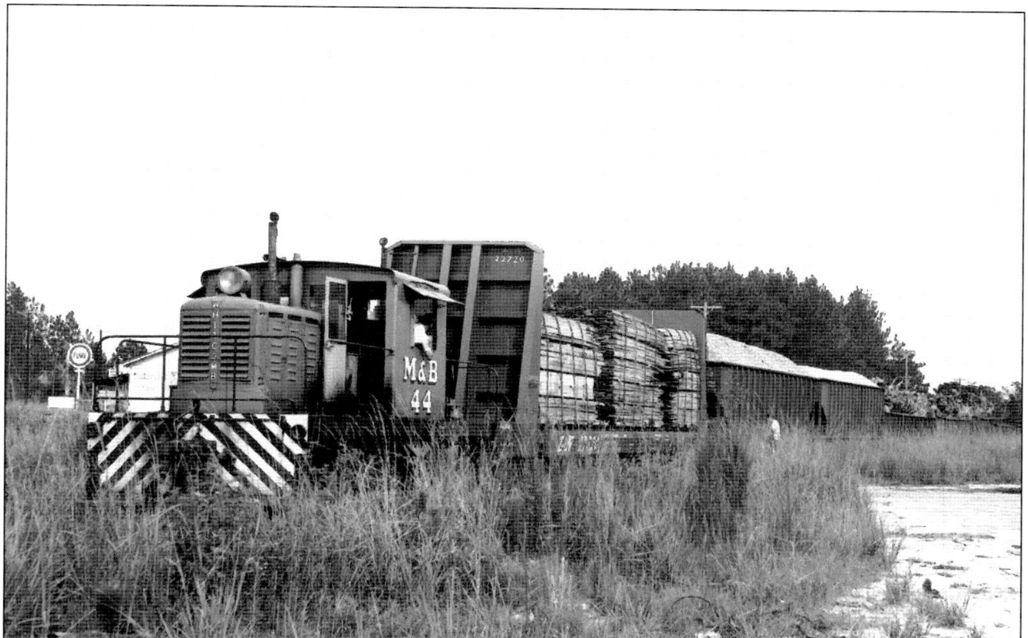

In August 1964, this Whitcomb 45-ton locomotive, the Marianna & Blountstown No. 44, towed a mixed freight train of finished plywood, woodchips, and pulpwood logs to their destinations in north Florida. (Courtesy of David Kirkland.)

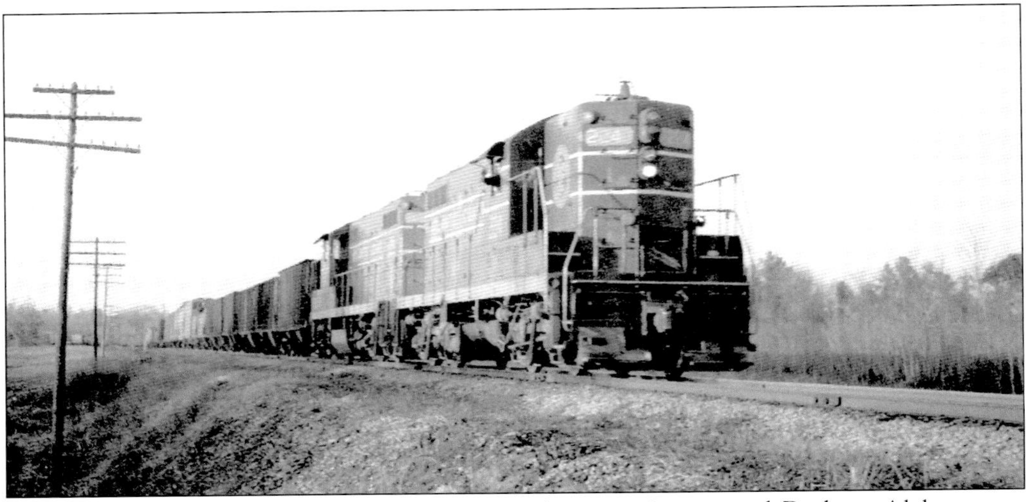

ACL No. 224 and No. 165 pull a local freight between Grimes and Dothan, Alabama, on February 10, 1965. Both engines were diesel locomotives built by General Motors in 1951. The 224 carried Electro-Motor Division (EMD) serial number 14968, while the 165 carried EMD serial number 13910. (Courtesy of the Tom Solomon Collection, DLF.)

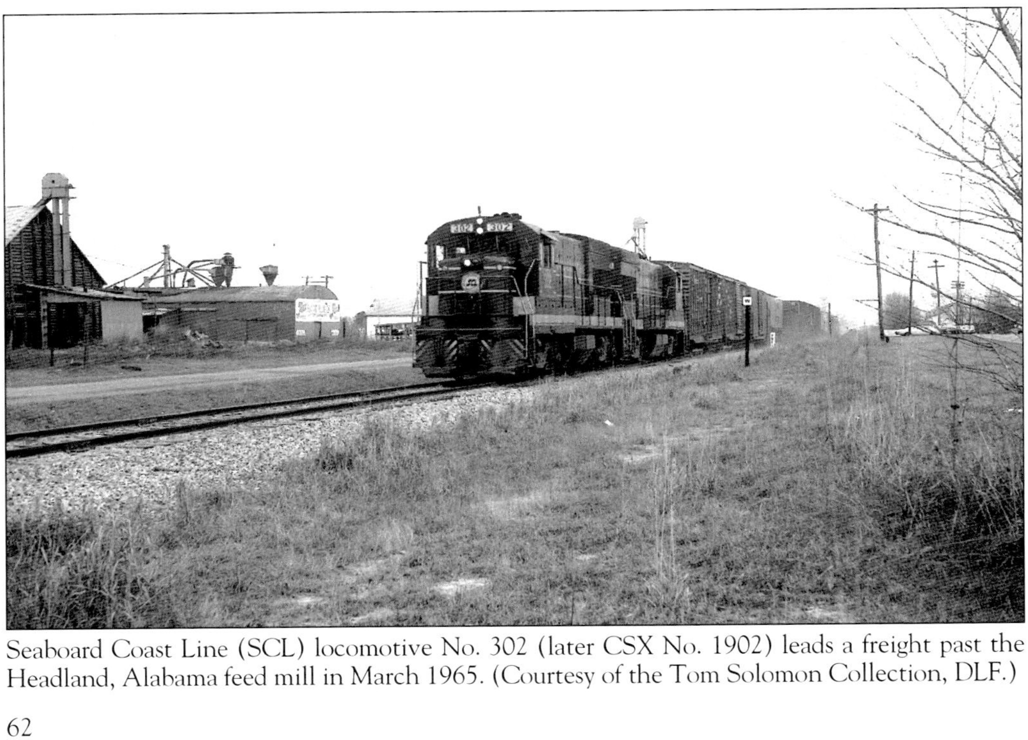

Seaboard Coast Line (SCL) locomotive No. 302 (later CSX No. 1902) leads a freight past the Headland, Alabama feed mill in March 1965. (Courtesy of the Tom Solomon Collection, DLF.)

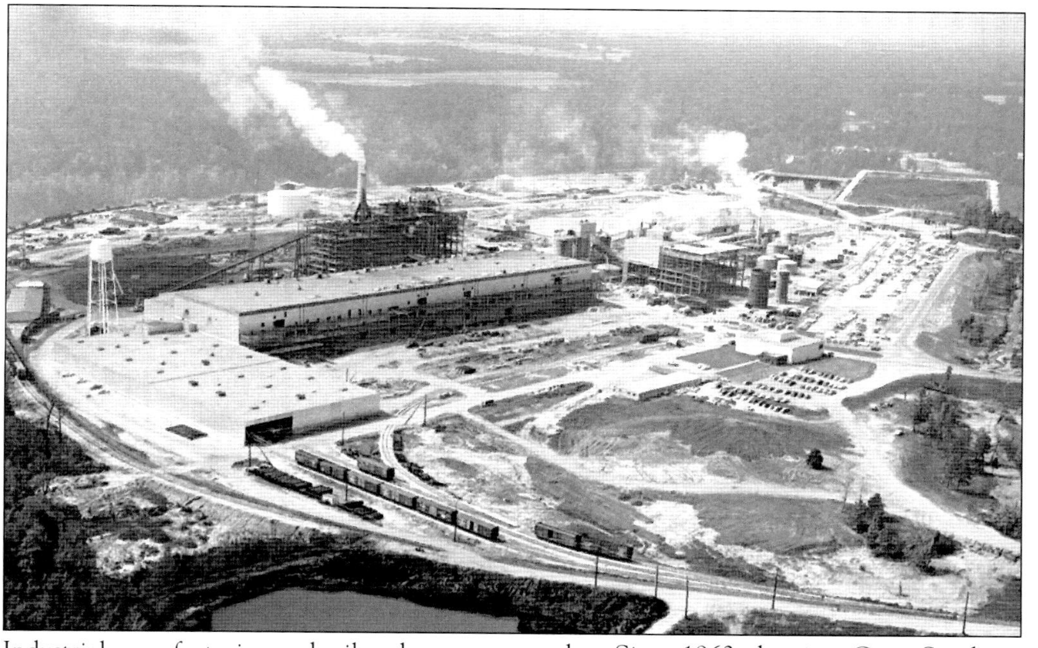

Industrial manufacturing and railroads grew up together. Since 1963, the giant Great Southern Paper mill in Early County, Georgia, has integrated rail service into its total shipping strategy. The Chattahoochee Industrial Railroad brings hoppers of wood chips to the plant and takes carloads of kraft paper from it. (Courtesy of Reid Smith.)

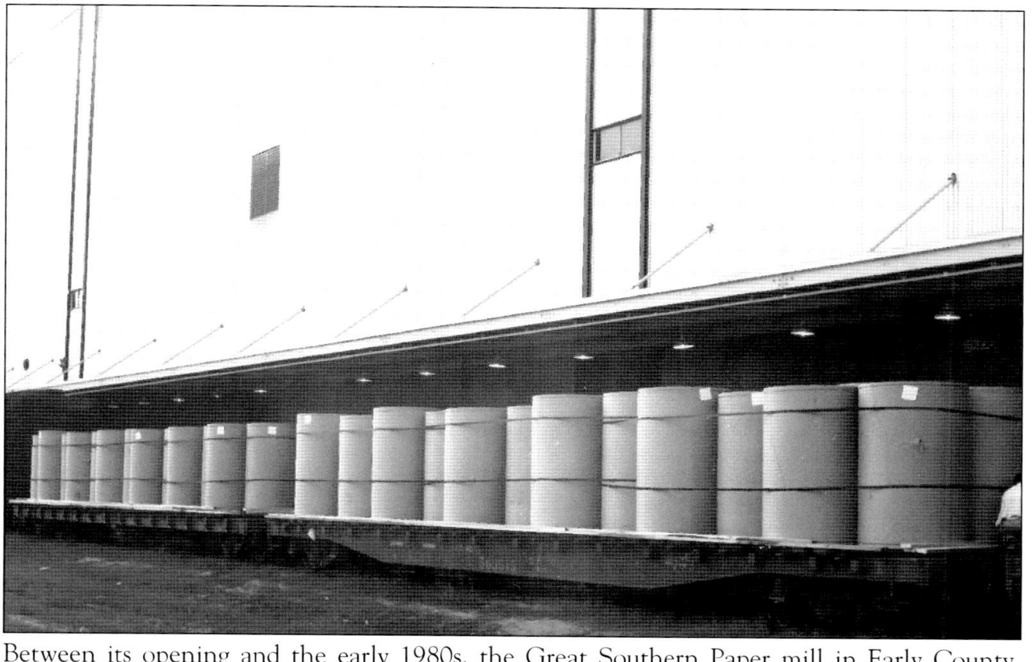

Between its opening and the early 1980s, the Great Southern Paper mill in Early County, Georgia, loaded its rolls of finished product onto flatcars. To save shipping costs and damage caused by these heavy but unstable rolls, the company changed to specially designed box cars. (Courtesy of the CIRR.)

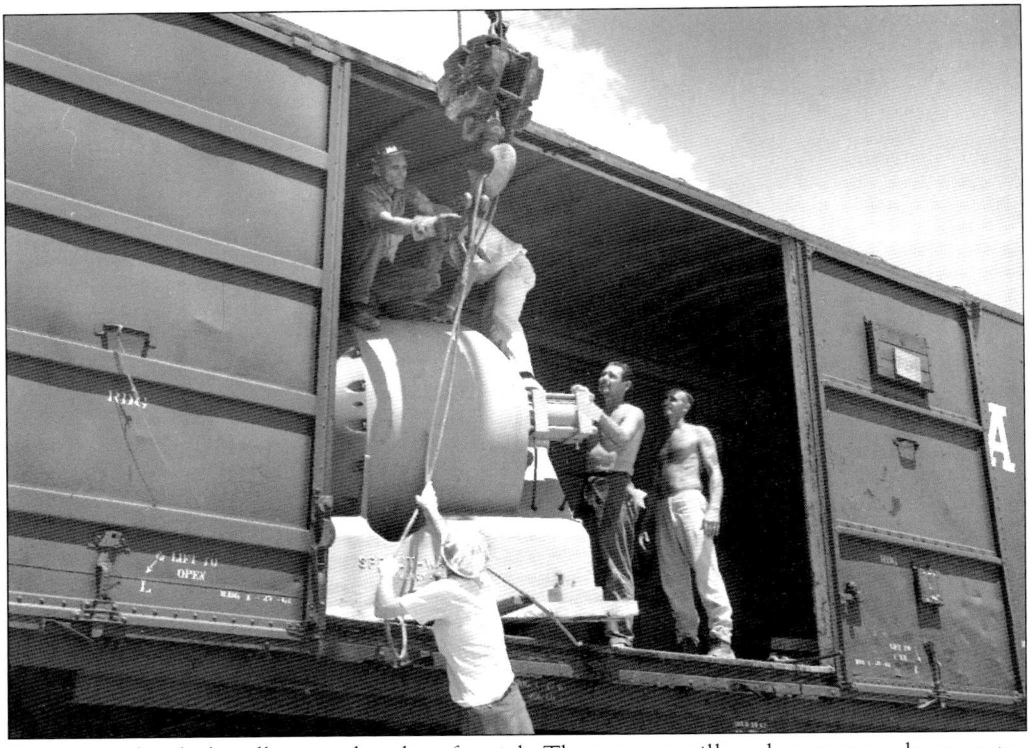

Sometimes freight handling can be a bit of a trick. These paper mill workers secure a large motor to a crane hoist for off-loading in Early County, Georgia, in the 1960s or 1970s. (Courtesy of the CIRR.)

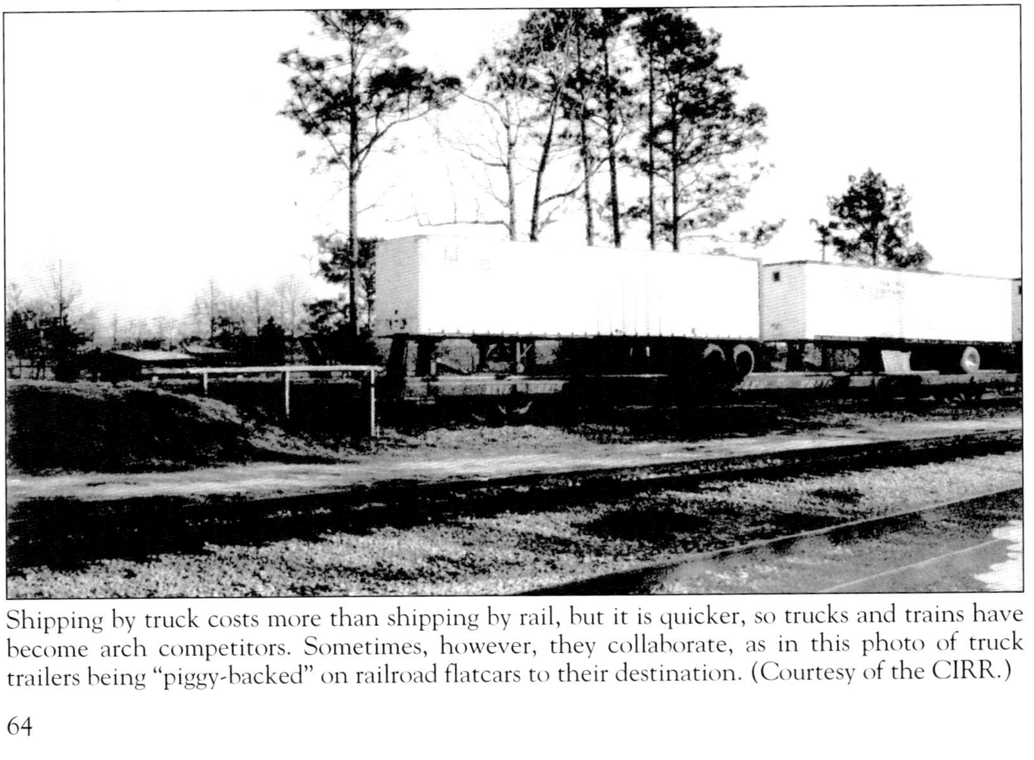

Shipping by truck costs more than shipping by rail, but it is quicker, so trucks and trains have become arch competitors. Sometimes, however, they collaborate, as in this photo of truck trailers being "piggy-backed" on railroad flatcars to their destination. (Courtesy of the CIRR.)

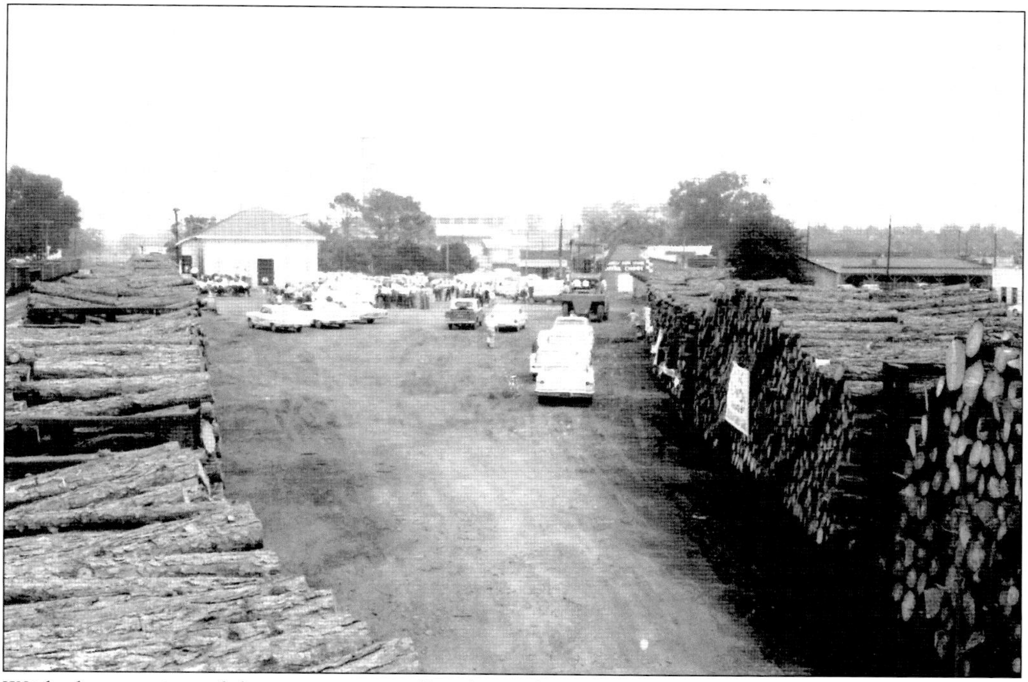

With the opening of the new paper mill only weeks away, the city of Blakeley, Georgia, hosted "Operation Silver Dollar" in late August 1963. For each cord of pulpwood delivered to the Chattahoochee Industrial Railroad depot, the railroad paid $15.50 in silver dollars. (Courtesy of the CIRR.)

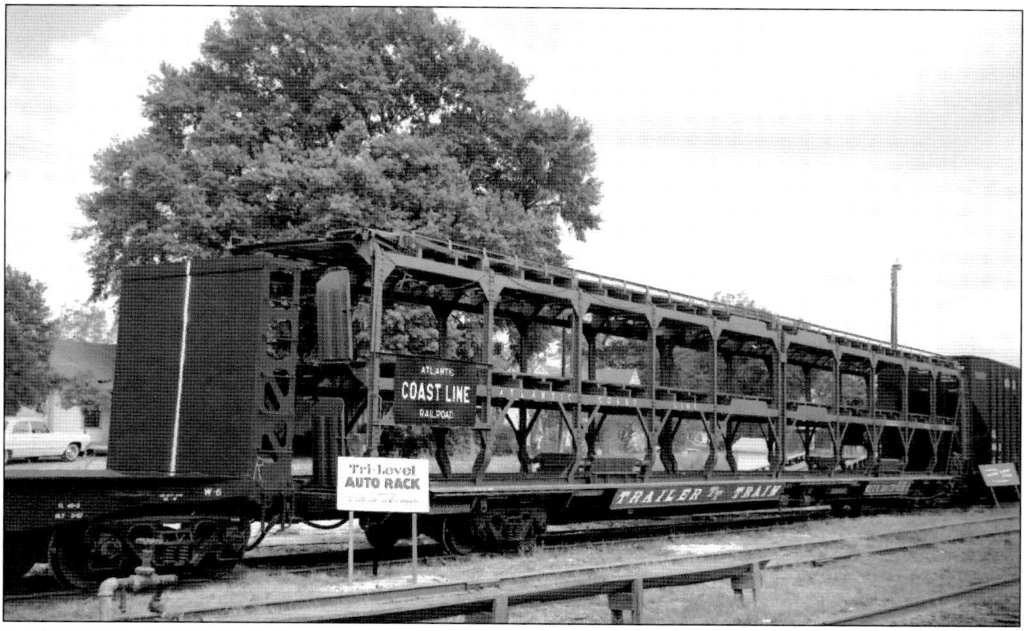

Rail is a cost-effective method of moving large quantities and many varieties of goods. This "auto rack" on display at the ACL yards in Dothan in 1964 is designed to transport 12 sedans or 18 compact cars on its three levels. (Courtesy of the Tom Solomon Collection, DLF.)

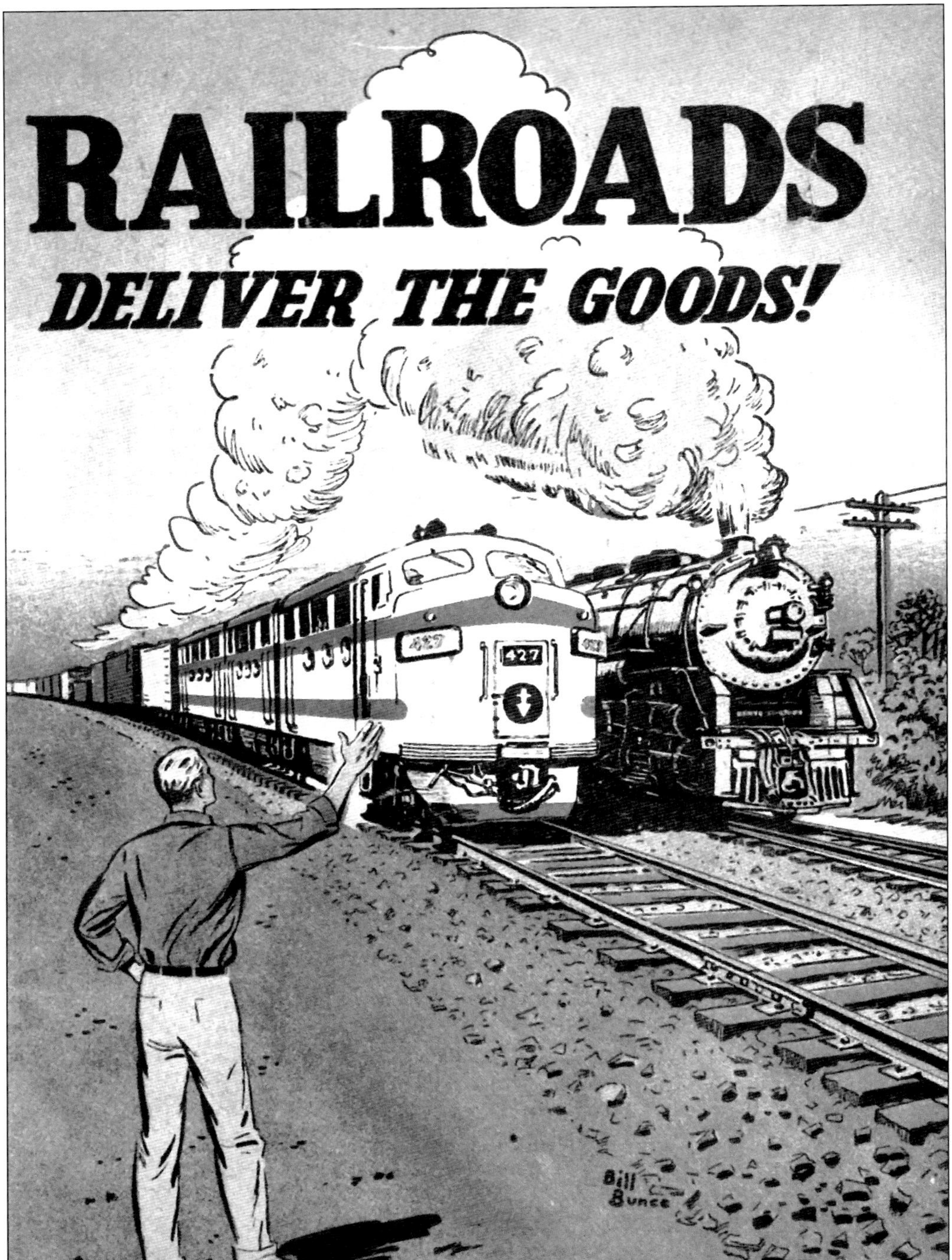

The Association of American Railroads represents railroads to lawmakers and the public. Its schools and college service produced a line of educational comic books about railroads during the 1950s, including this one about the history of freight trains. (Courtesy of the DLF Dixie Depot Collection, AWHC.)

Four

Rolling Stock and Equipment

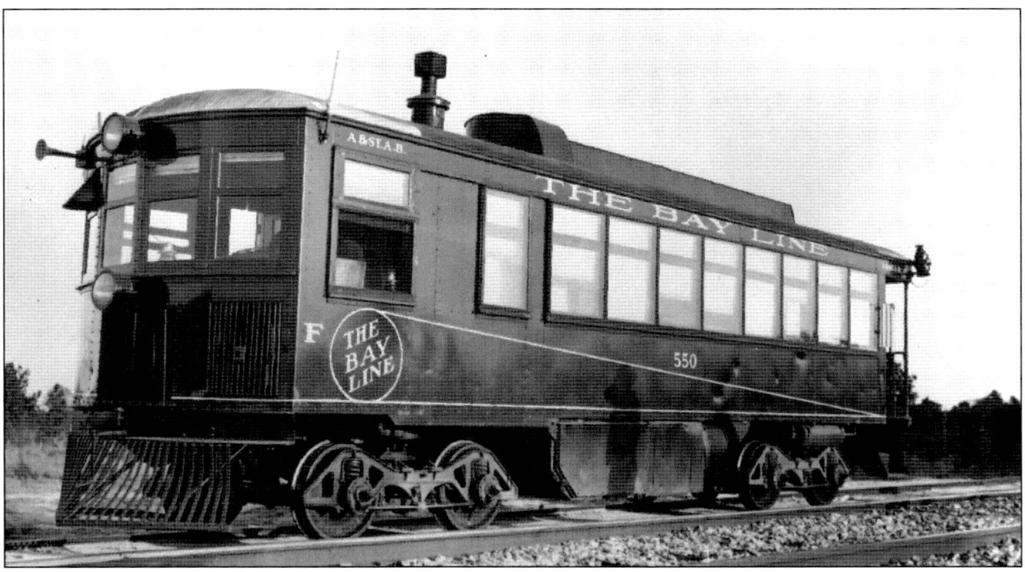

The Atlanta & St. Andrews Bay Railway—called the Bay Line—operated approximately 80 miles of track between Panama City, Florida, and Dothan, Alabama. It connected the port with the Central of Georgia, the L & N, the ACL, and now the CSX. Bay Line president J.A. Streyer used this gas-driven "executive car" as a moving office. (Courtesy of the Tom Solomon Collection, DLF.)

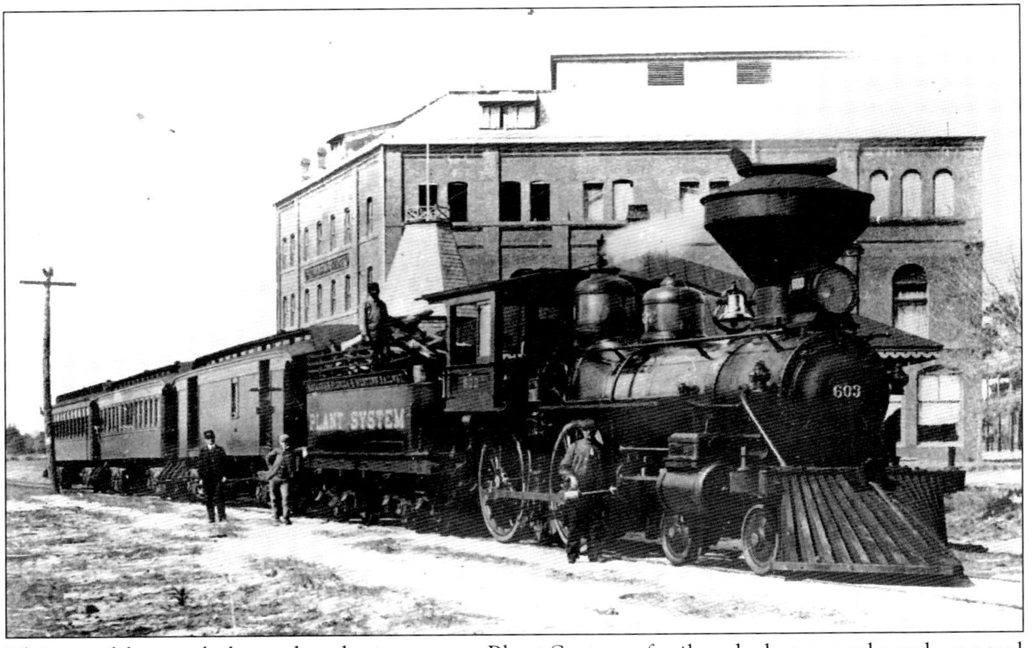

This wood-burner belonged to the important Plant System of railroads that served north-central Florida and southern Georgia. Henry Plant integrated rail and steamship travel with hotels in a post–Civil War empire that rivaled Henry Flagler's East Florida tourist empire. (Courtesy of the Tom Solomon Collection, DLF.)

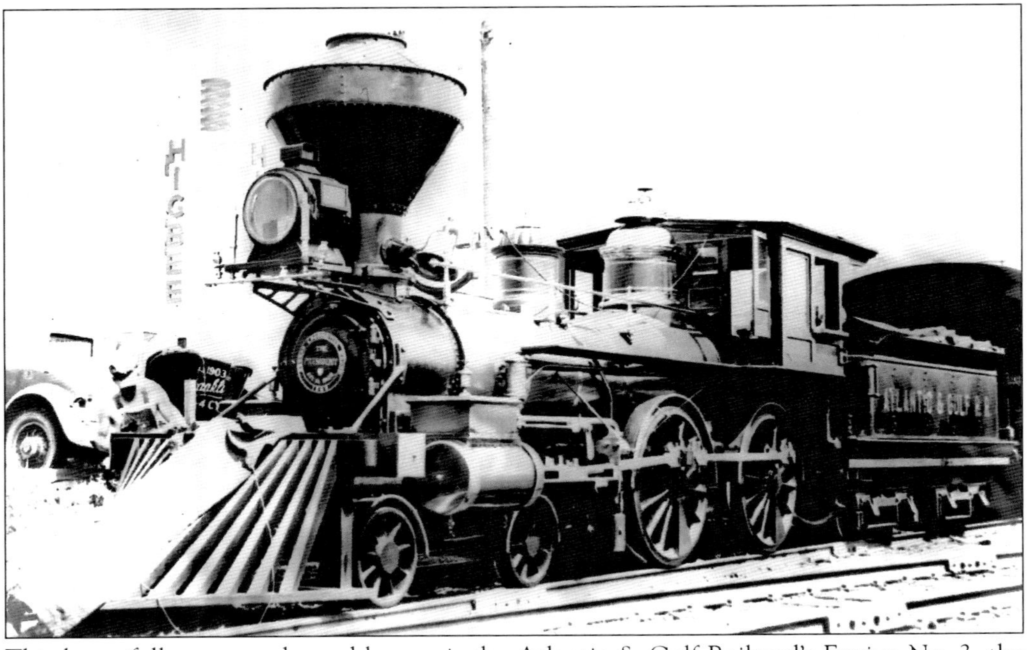

This beautifully preserved wood burner is the Atlantic & Gulf Railroad's Engine No. 3, the *Satilla*. Chartered in 1854, the A & G served the 237 miles between Bainbridge and Savannah, Georgia. Henry Plant purchased the road in 1879 and re-named it the Savannah, Florida & Western Railway. (Courtesy of the Tom Solomon Collection, DLF.)

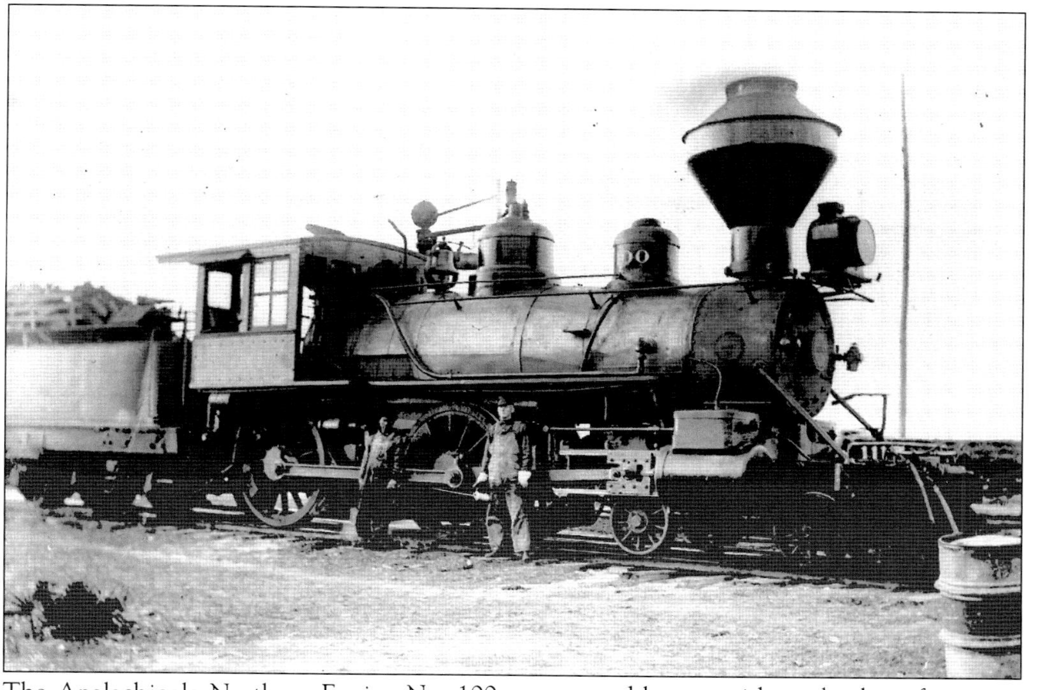

The Apalachicola Northern Engine No. 100 was a wood-burner with a wheel configuration of 4-4-0 (four pilot wheels in front, four drivers, and zero training wheels). This picture shows Fireman ? Waddell (left) and William H. Howell Sr. on their first run after Howell had been promoted to engineer. (Courtesy of the Tom Solomon Collection, DLF.)

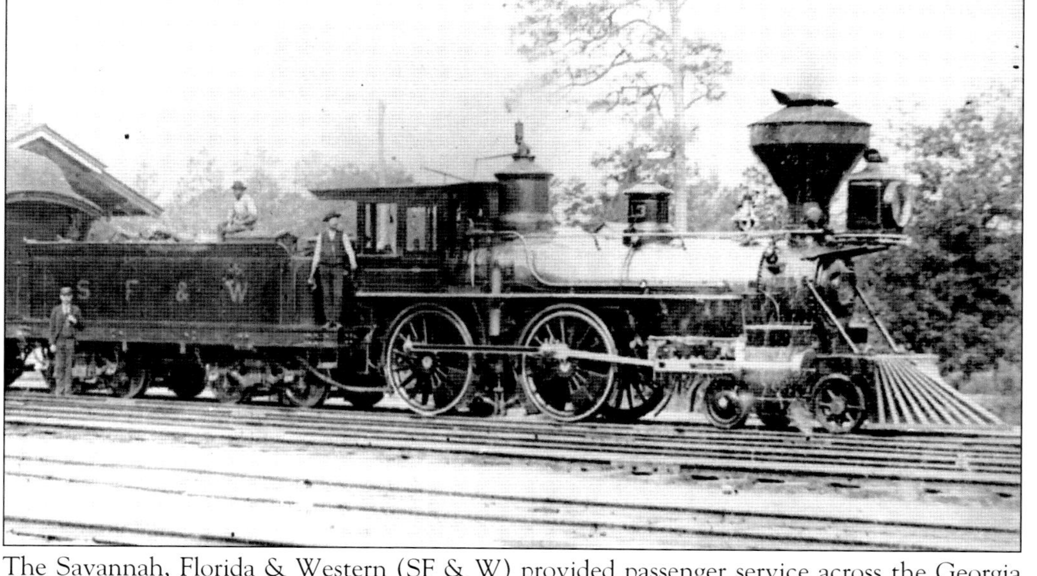

The Savannah, Florida & Western (SF & W) provided passenger service across the Georgia Wiregrass. This undated photo shows the crew posing with train. Note the fireman atop the wood pile in the tender. This is a typical, light-duty engine complete with cabbage stack for arresting sparks and a 4-4-0 wheel configuration. (Courtesy of the Tom Solomon Collection, DLF.)

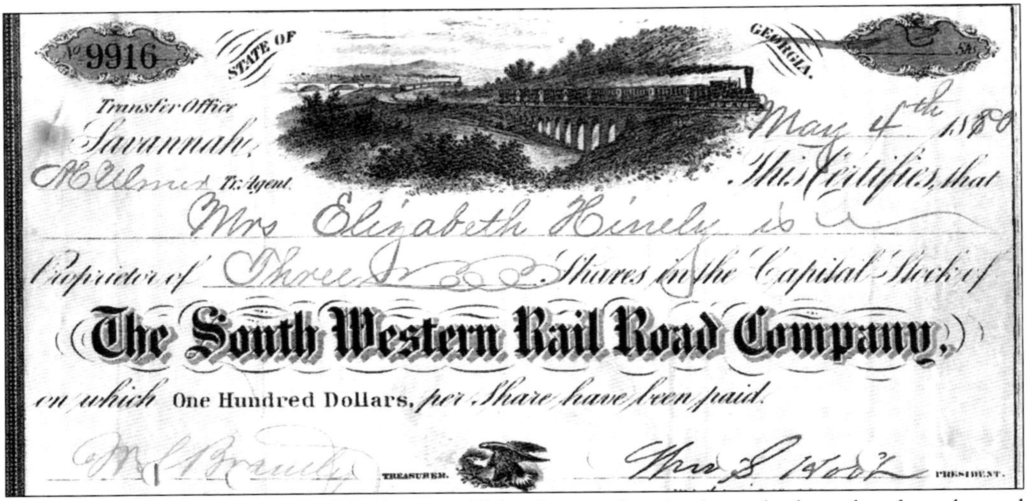
No 9916

STATE OF GEORGIA.

Transfer Office Savannah, May 4th 1880

Tr. Agent. This Certifies that

Mrs Elizabeth Hinely is a Proprietor of Three Shares in the Capital Stock of

The South Western Rail Road Company,

on which One Hundred Dollars, per Share have been paid.

TREASURER. PRESIDENT.

Railroads were so expensive that they could be financed only through the sale of stocks and bonds. Thus, the corporation replaced the single proprietor and the partnership as the most important business organization in the United States. In 1890, Mrs. Elizabeth Hinley bought three shares of South Western Rail Road Company stock for $300. In 2003, she would have paid $5,860. (Courtesy of the Clay County [Georgia] Public Library.)

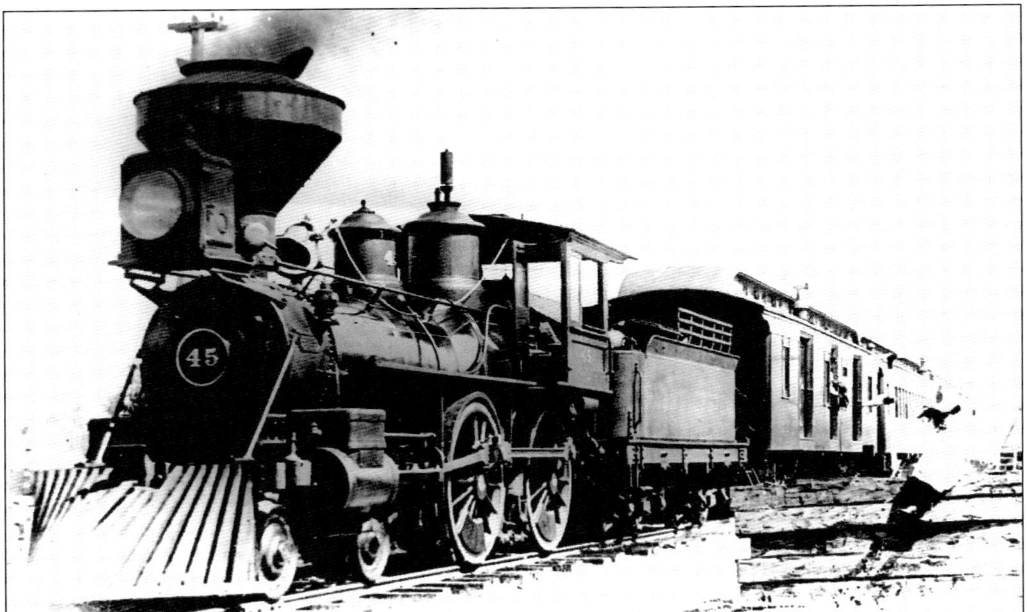

Wood was and is a prime necessity for railroads. The Plant System Engine No. 45, a 4-4-0, burned wood to make its steam, and the young lady seated to the right is atop a stack of wooden crossties cut from the local forests. (Courtesy of the Tom Solomon Collection, DLF.)

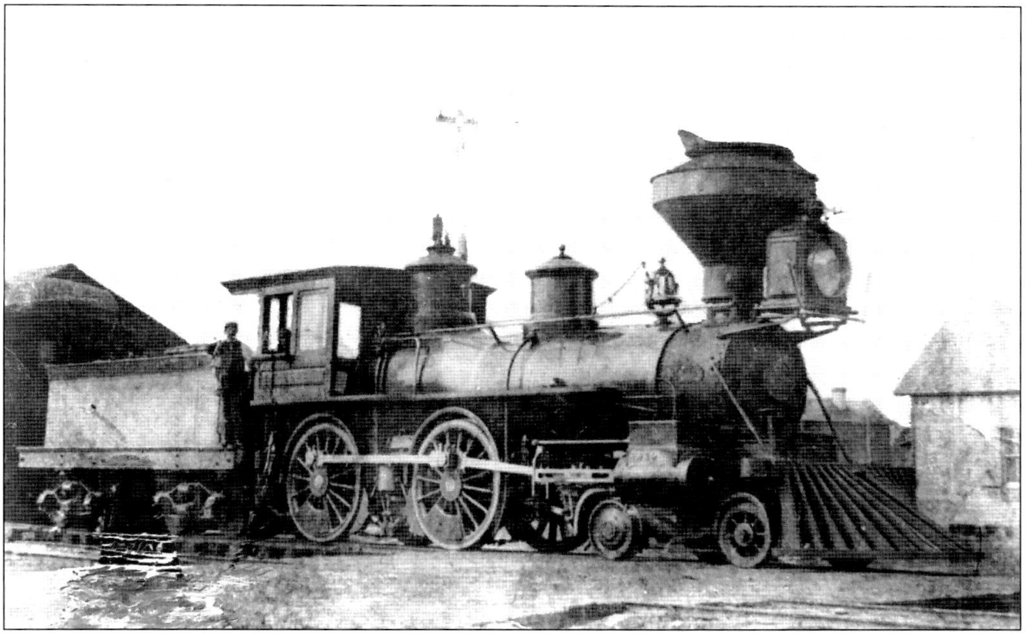

Engines in the wood-burning era were small because most pulled short trains. The Plant System No. 47, with its cabbage-stack spark arrestor and 4-4-0 wheel configuration, ran across the low hills and plains of the Wiregrass hauling only a few cars of passengers or freight. (Courtesy of the Tom Solomon Collection, DLF.)

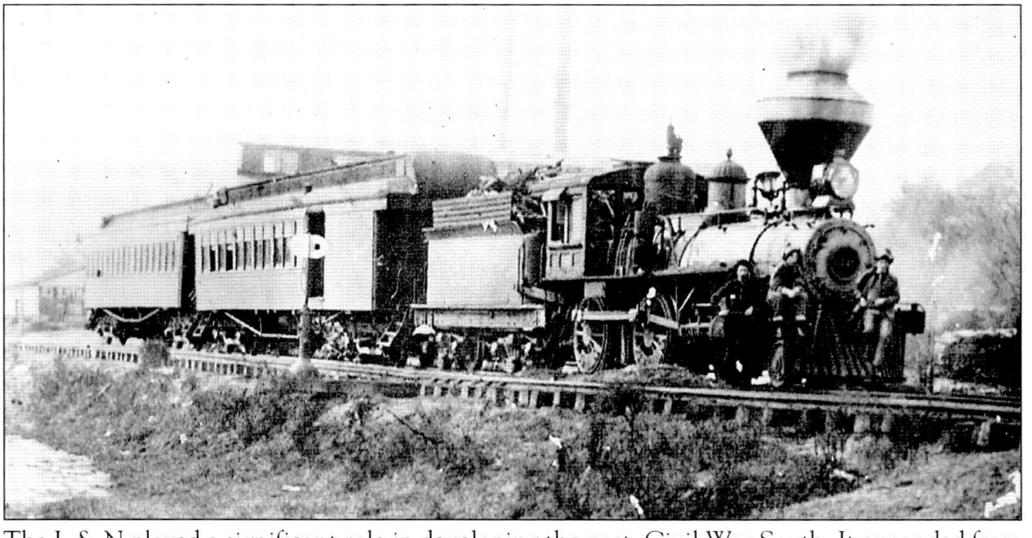

The L & N played a significant role in developing the post–Civil War South. It expanded from its original route from Louisville to Mobile and by the 20th century controlled passenger service across the Florida Panhandle. This small train was powered by a typical 4-4-0 wood-burner. (Courtesy of the Tom Solomon Collection, DLF.)

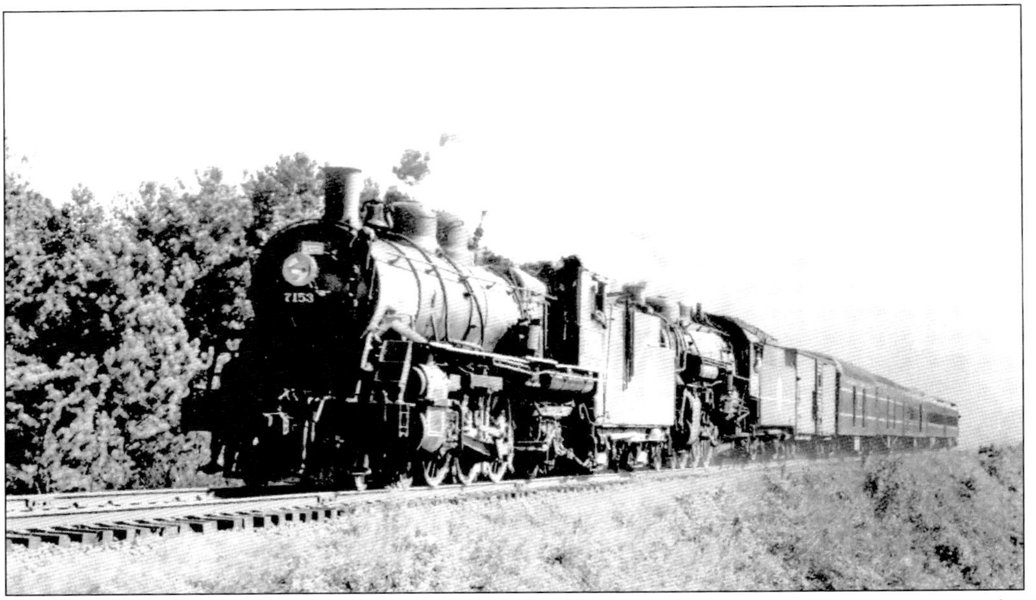

This is an unusual sight in the Wiregrass—a "double-headed" passenger train. In 1946, the Atlantic Coast Line acquired the Atlanta, Birmingham & Coast Railroad, including 13 second-hand Pacific-type locomotives. The No. 7153, built by the Lima Locomotive Works in 1914, came from the Great Northern Railroad. (Courtesy of the Tom Solomon Collection, DLF.)

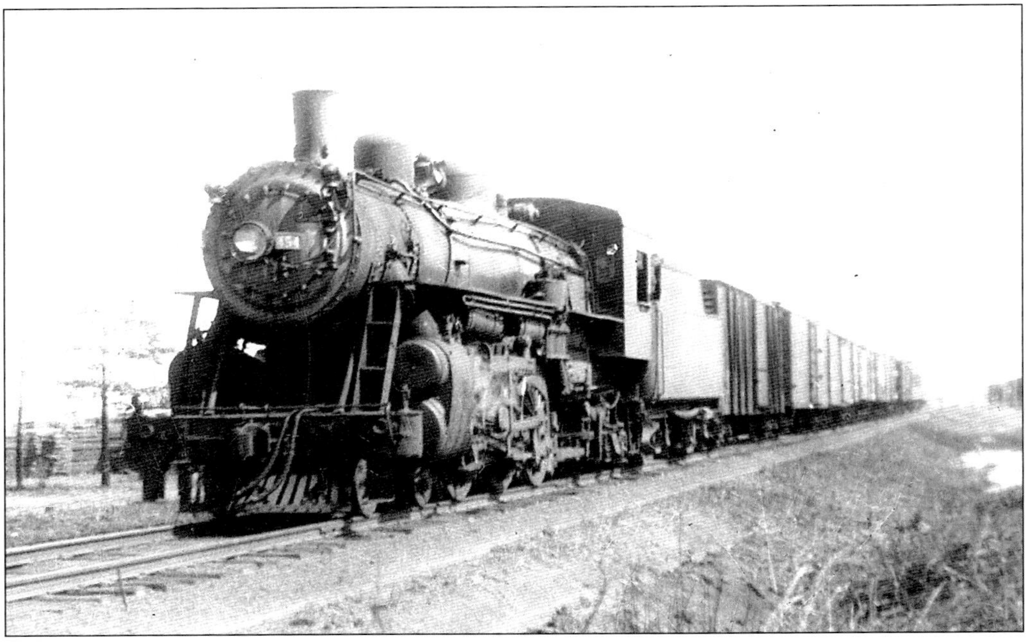

In 1914, the Atlantic Coast Line purchased 45 dual-purpose (passenger and freight) locomotives from the Baldwin Locomotive Works, including this one, the No. 454. Here, it pulls a mixed train from Headland to Grimes, Alabama, in June 1934. (Courtesy of the Tom Solomon Collection, DLF.)

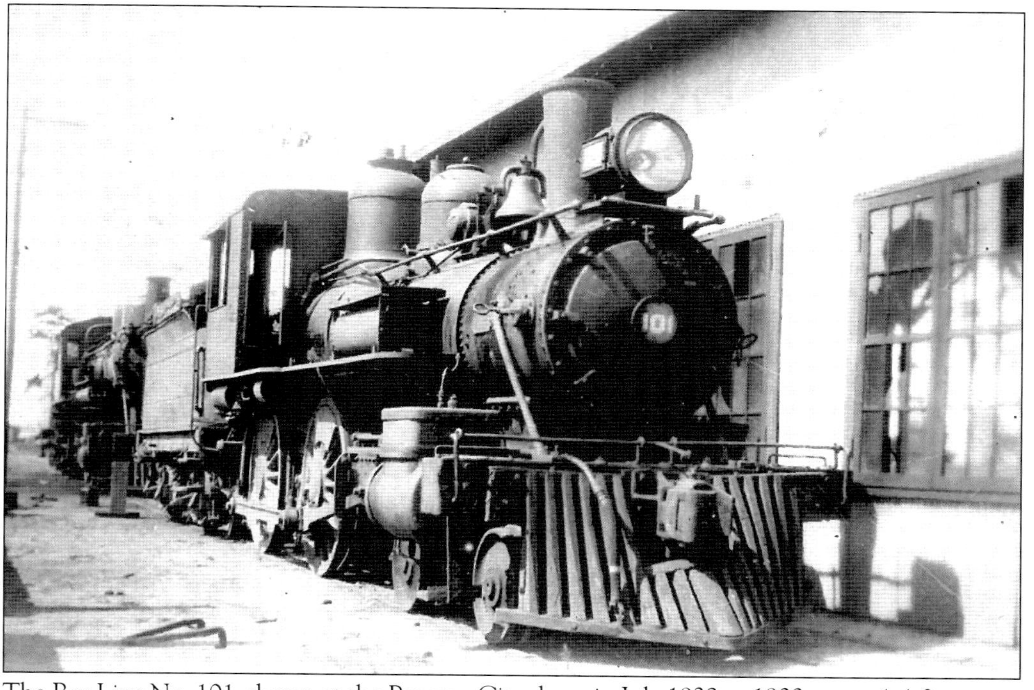

The Bay Line No. 101, shown at the Panama City shops in July 1932 or 1933, was a 4-4-0 steamer built in 1888 by the Rogers Locomotive Works of Patterson, New Jersey. It saw service with the Savannah, Florida & Western, the ACL, and the Georgia Car & Locomotive Co. (GC & L) before the Bay Line acquired it in 1906. (Courtesy of the Tom Solomon Collection, DLF.)

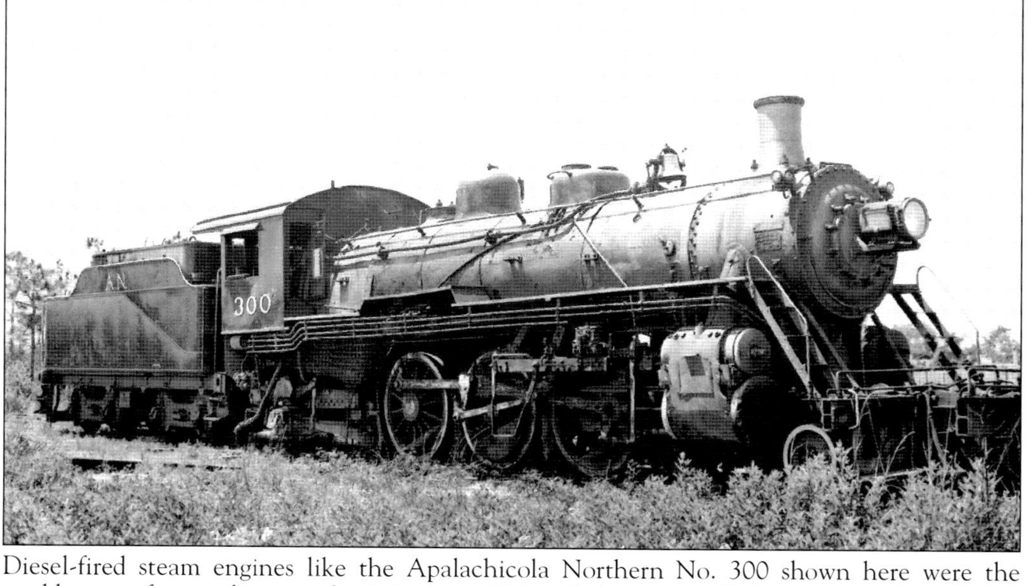

Diesel-fired steam engines like the Apalachicola Northern No. 300 shown here were the workhorses of many lines in the Wiregrass. This 4-6-4 engine pulled passenger trains to the L & N line in River Junction, Florida, until 1951, and then concentrated on hauling pulpwood, chips, paper, coal, and ice until replaced by diesel-electrics in 1954. (Courtesy of the Tom Solomon Collection, DLF.)

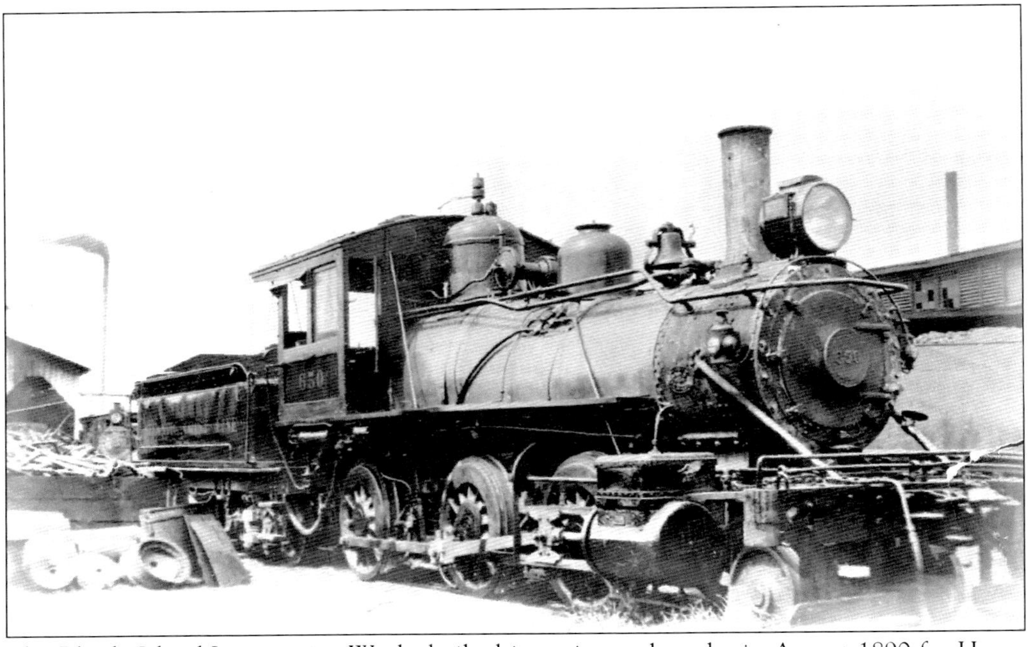

The Rhode Island Locomotive Works built this engine and tender in August 1890 for Henry Plant's Savannah, Florida & Western Railway. This 1917 photo shows the 2-6-0 locomotive as ACL No. 650, its designation until being scrapped on December 2, 1929. (Courtesy of the Tom Solomon Collection, DLF.)

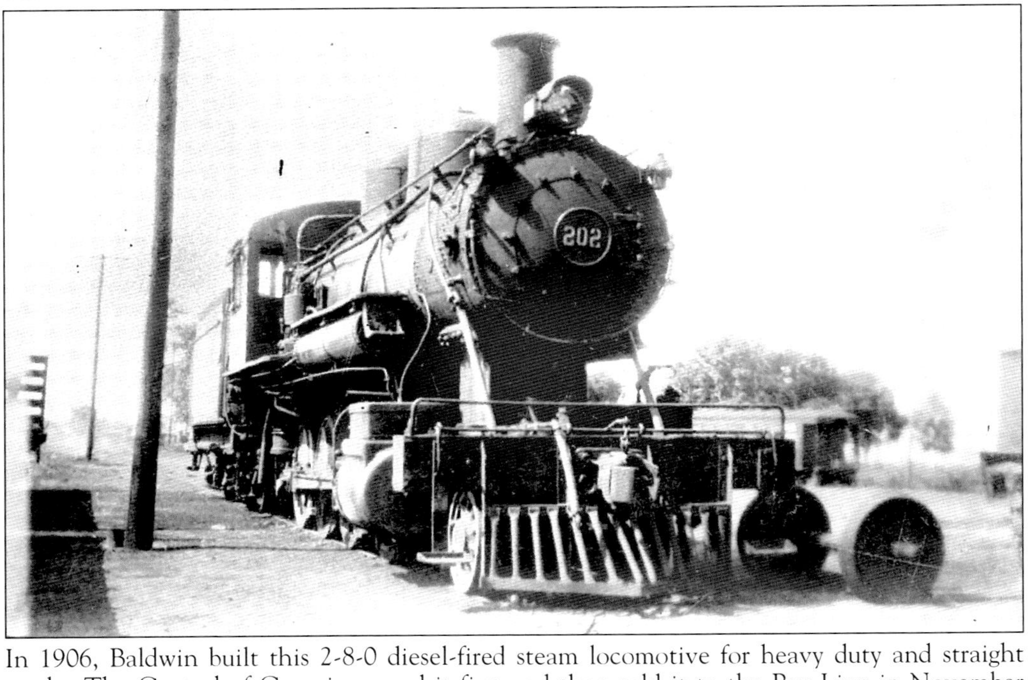

In 1906, Baldwin built this 2-8-0 diesel-fired steam locomotive for heavy duty and straight tracks. The Central of Georgia owned it first and then sold it to the Bay Line in November 1930. It served as Bay Line No. 202 until it was sold in 1945. (Courtesy of the Tom Solomon Collection, DLF.)

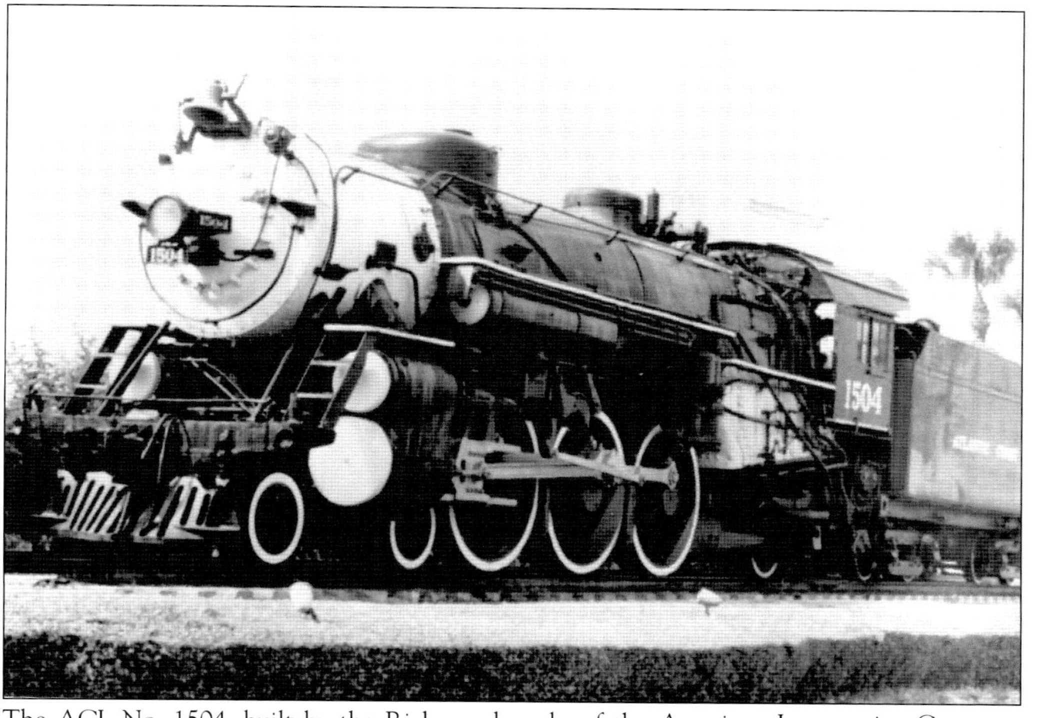

The ACL No. 1504, built by the Richmond works of the American Locomotive Company (ALCO) in 1919, was one of 81 in the "Light Pacific" design (4-6-2A). It pulled the 12-car *Southwind* and the *Florida Arrow* through the Wiregrass at 70 miles per hour for 30 years, and it then pulled freights in Tampa until 1952. (Courtesy of the Tom Solomon Collection, DLF.)

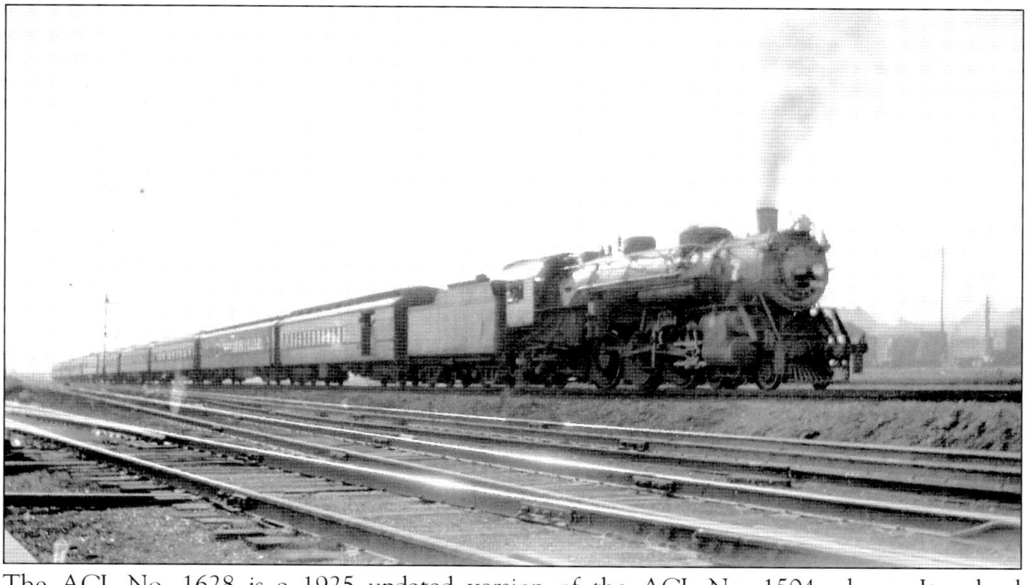

The ACL No. 1628 is a 1925 updated version of the ACL No. 1504, above. Its wheel configuration is the same—4-6-2—but its drive wheels are slightly smaller. It is shown pulling the *Florida Arrow* south of Montgomery in the winter of 1936–1937. ACL retired this engine after 1950. (Courtesy of the Tom Solomon Collection, DLF.)

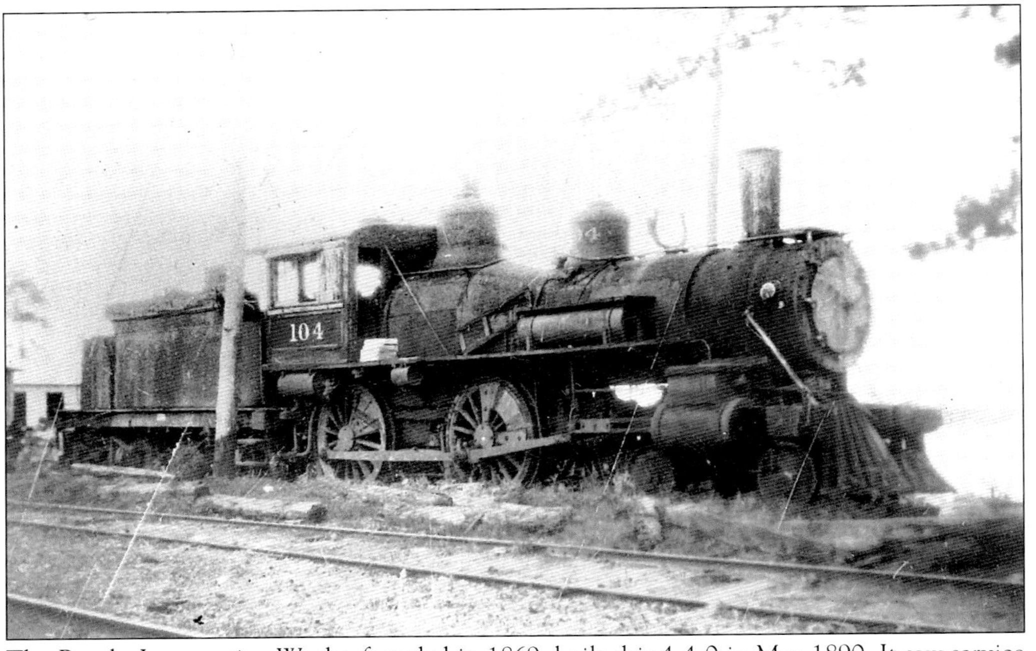

The Brooks Locomotive Works, founded in 1869, built this 4-4-0 in May 1890. It saw service in the extreme upper Midwest until the Bay Line acquired it in 1911. Renamed No. 104, this 31-ton locomotive worked until it was retired in 1931. (Courtesy of the Tom Solomon Collection, DLF.)

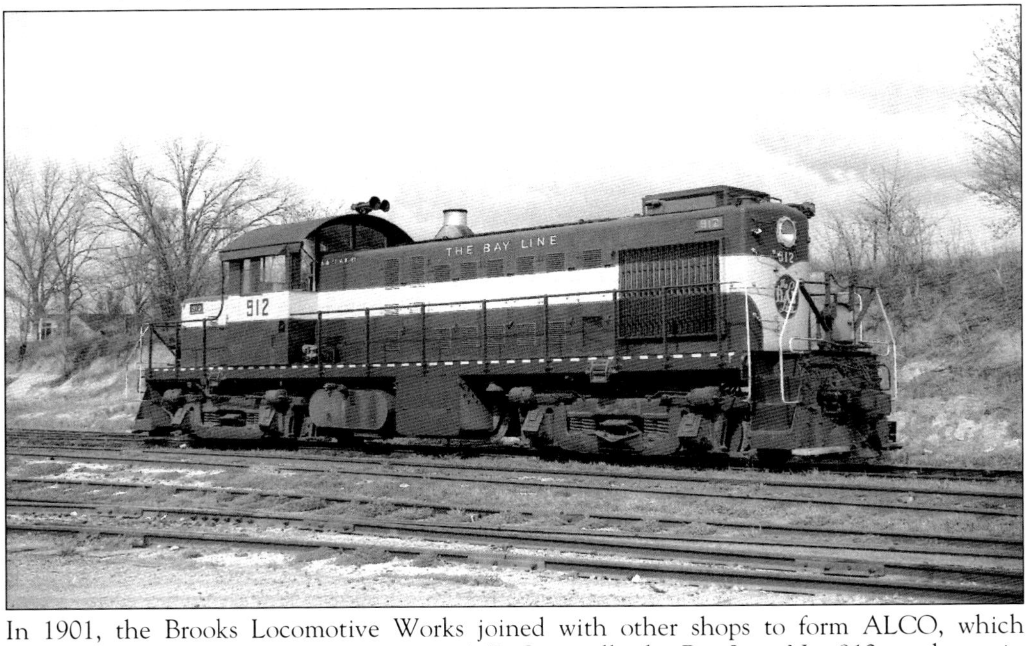

In 1901, the Brooks Locomotive Works joined with other shops to form ALCO, which built this RS-1 diesel-electric engine in 1947. Originally the Bay Line No. 912, as shown in this February 1964 photograph, it was sold to the Louisiana-Midland in 1977 and was parted out at the Chattahoochee Industrial Railroad in 1984. (Courtesy of the Tom Solomon Collection, DLF.)

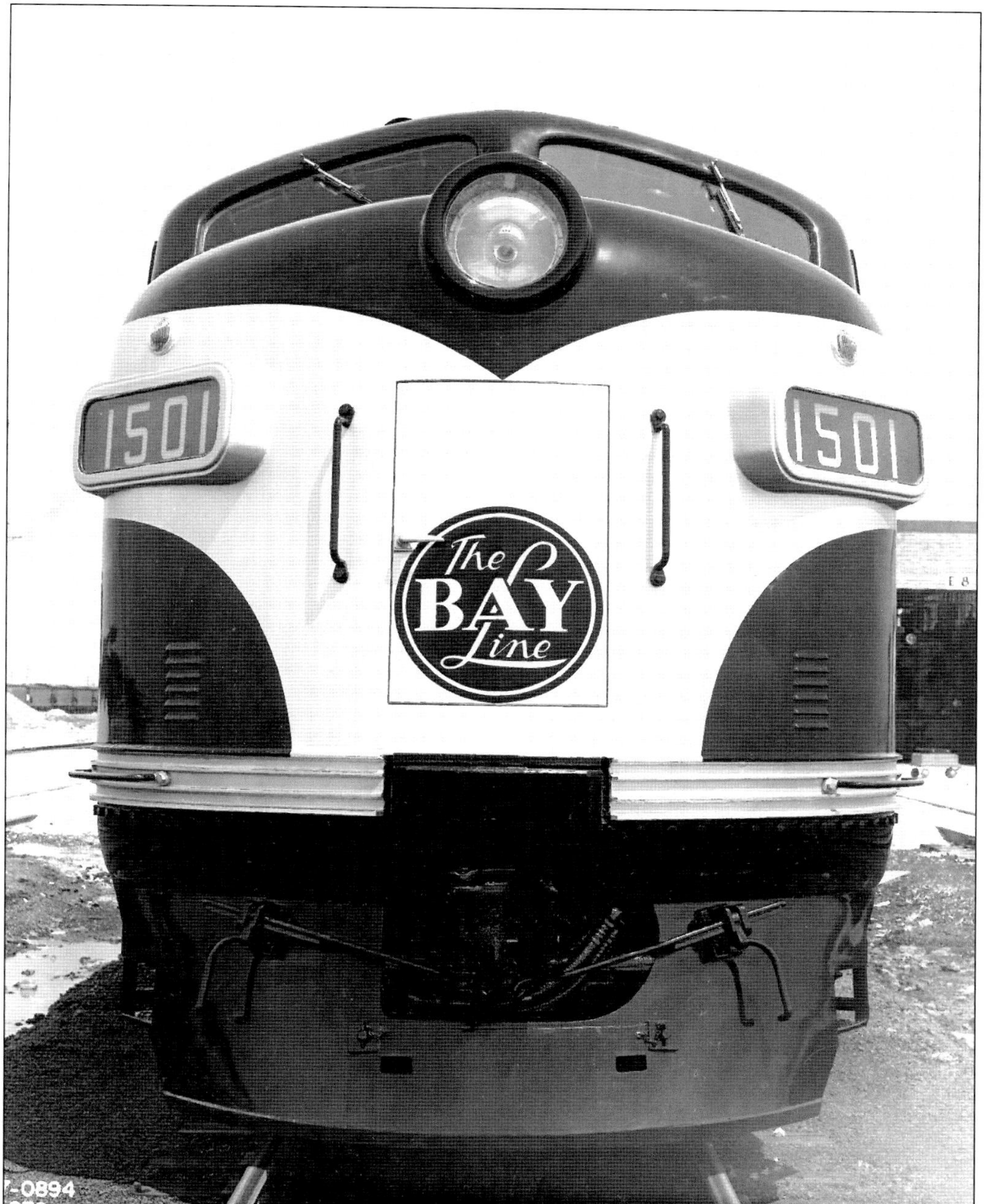

In 1947, the Bay Line upgraded its locomotive fleet with General Motor's EMD F-3s, the most recognizable of all American locomotives. In this publicity photo, Bay Line Engine No. 1501 rolls off the assembly line sporting the green and white logo of its parent company and the single-headlight, favored in the Eastern United States. (Courtesy of Quinton Bruner.)

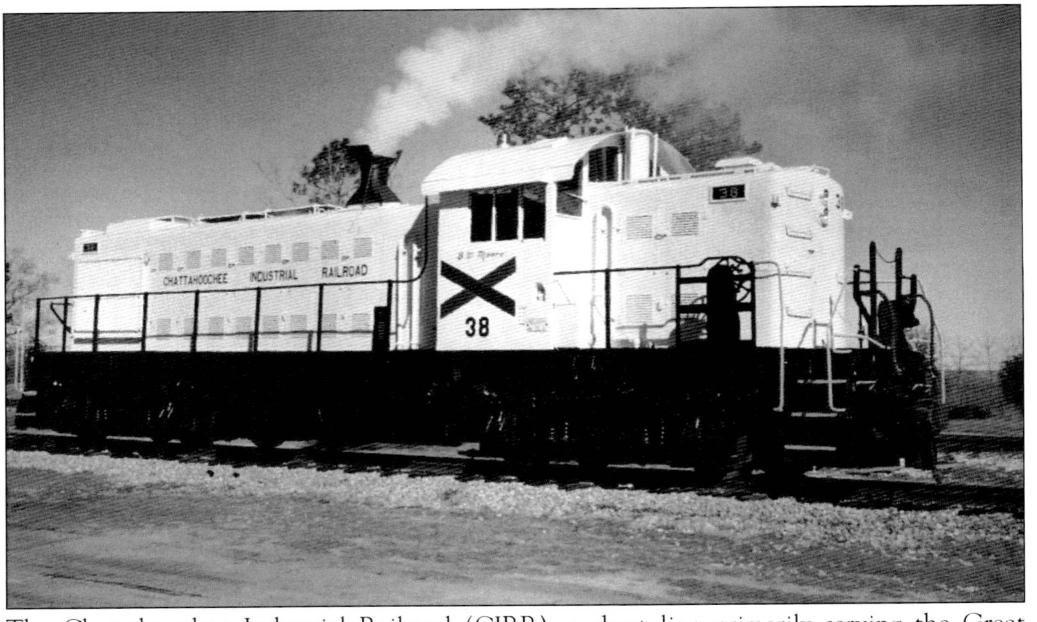

The Chattahoochee Industrial Railroad (CIRR), a short line primarily serving the Great Southern Paper mill in Early County, Georgia, christened its ALCO RS-1 Engine No. 38 the *B.W. Moore* in honor of the line's first construction engineer. (Courtesy of Reid Smith.)

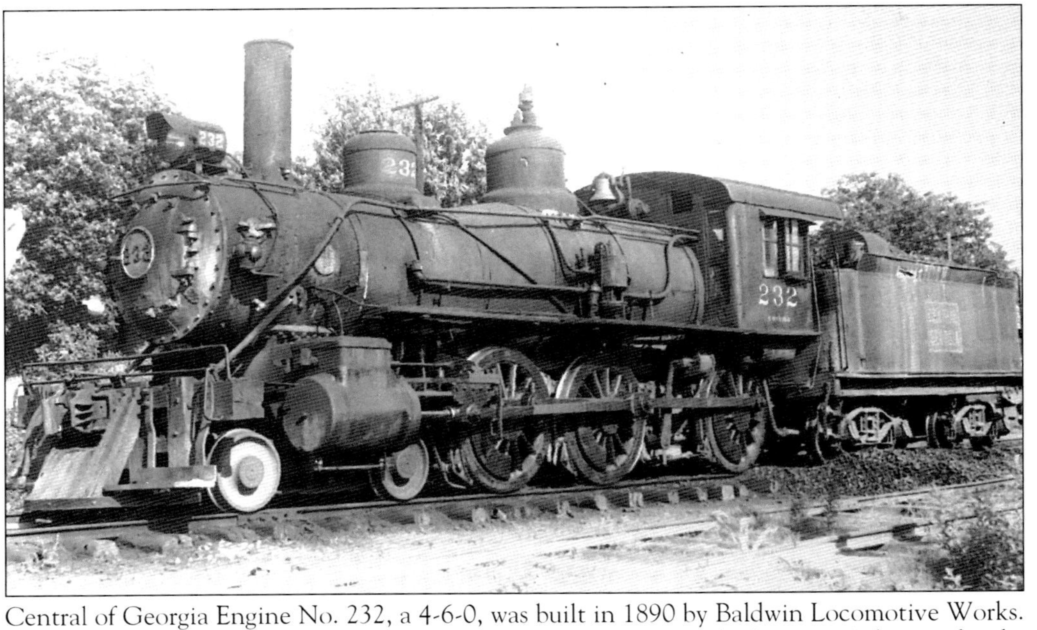

Central of Georgia Engine No. 232, a 4-6-0, was built in 1890 by Baldwin Locomotive Works. A small freight engine, it only weighed 114,800 pounds. Central of Georgia's largest freight engines weighed in at over 400,000 pounds. (Courtesy of the Tom Solomon Collection, DLF.)

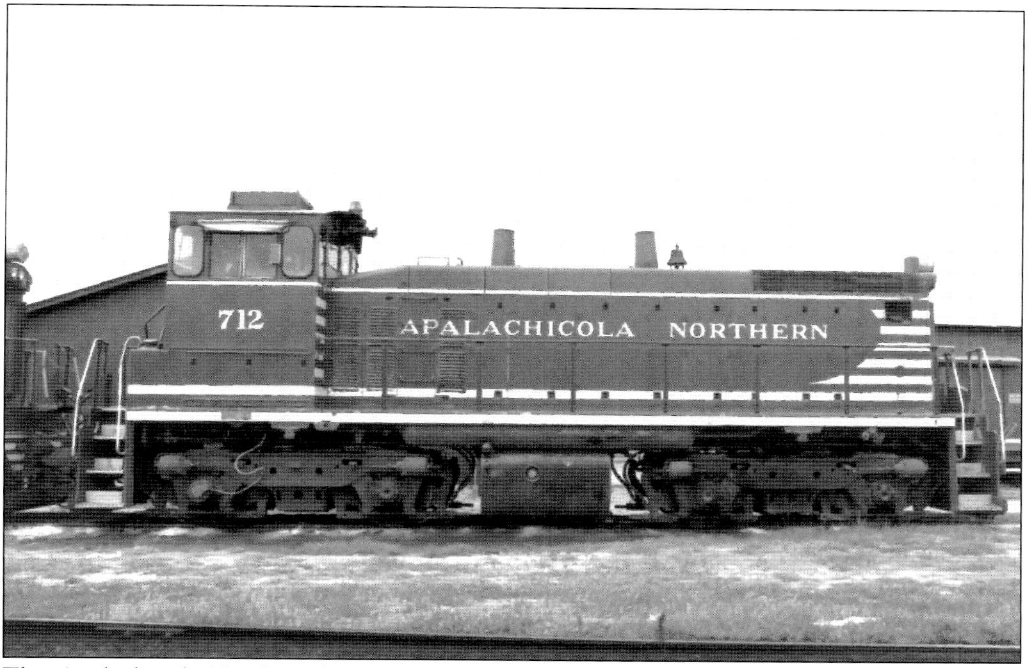

The Apalachicola Northern began operating an "oyster special" in 1907, carrying the justly famous mollusks packed in ice from the Gulf Coast to Atlanta. The AN transported timber and turpentine during their heyday and then changed to pulpwood, coal, and chemicals. (Courtesy of David Kirkland.)

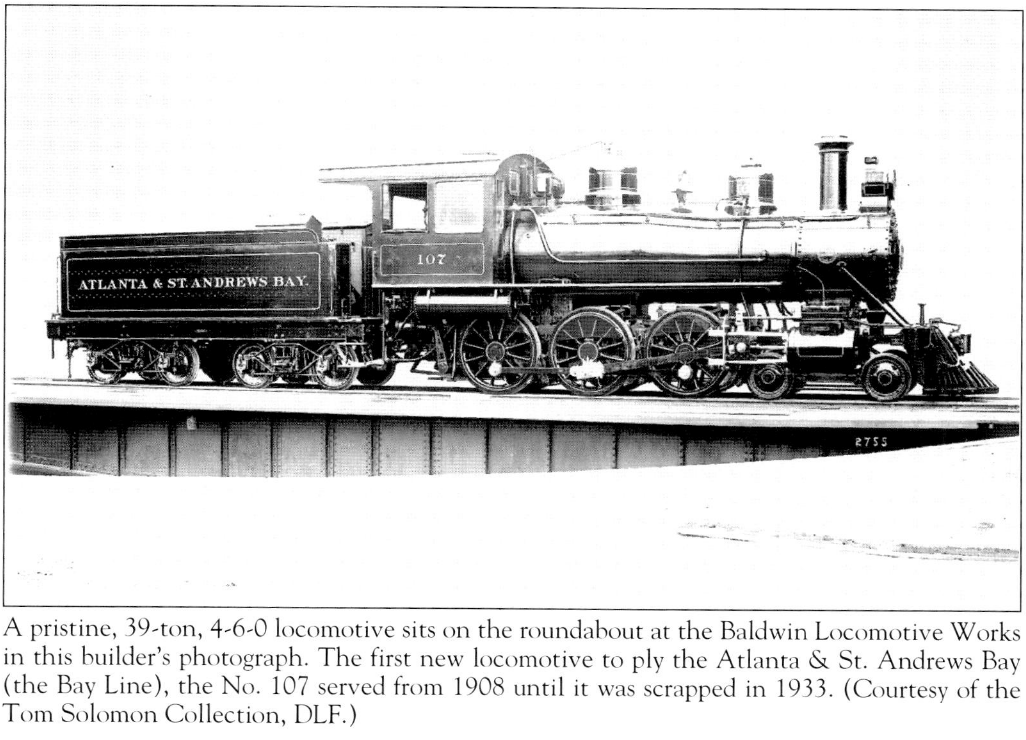

A pristine, 39-ton, 4-6-0 locomotive sits on the roundabout at the Baldwin Locomotive Works in this builder's photograph. The first new locomotive to ply the Atlanta & St. Andrews Bay (the Bay Line), the No. 107 served from 1908 until it was scrapped in 1933. (Courtesy of the Tom Solomon Collection, DLF.)

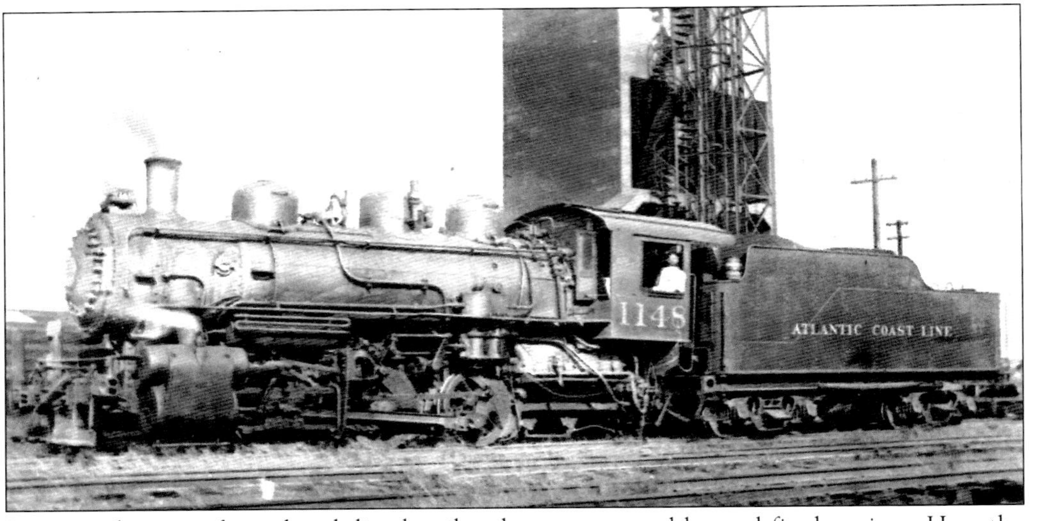

Between the eras of wood and diesel, railroads were powered by coal-fired engines. Here the ACL No. 1148, a switch engine, refills its tender at the coal chute in the Dothan, Alabama yard. (Courtesy of the Tom Solomon Collection, DLF.)

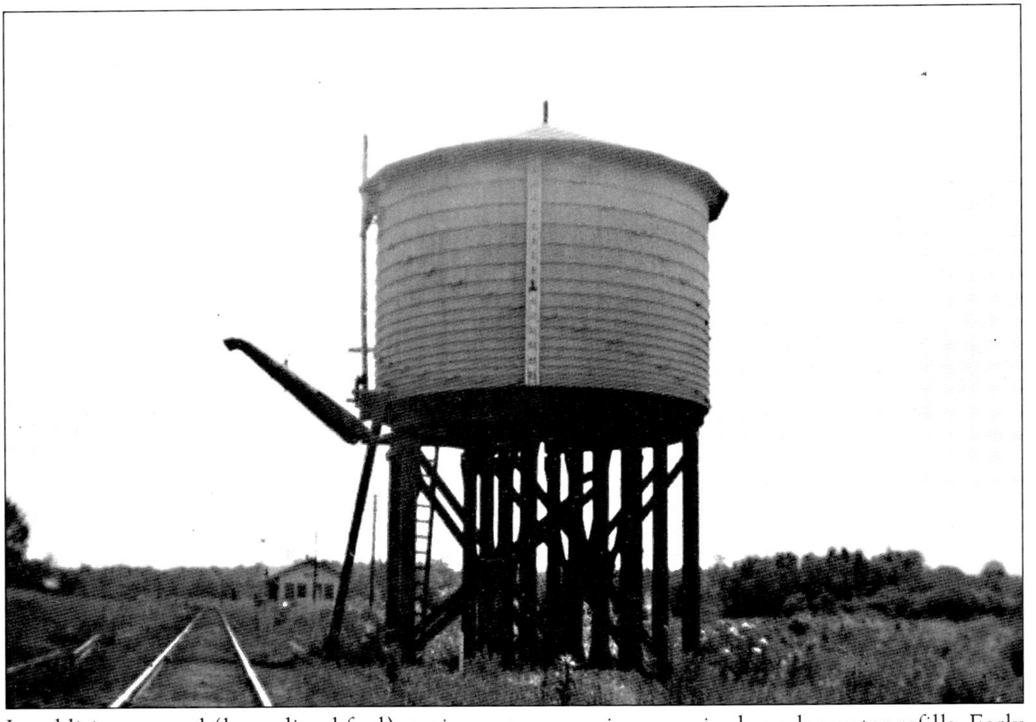

In addition to coal (later diesel fuel) stations, steam engines required regular water refills. Early on, railroads established tiny stations with water tanks every five to seven miles. This photo looks west toward the Alaga, Alabama station. The water tank and pull-down spout appear in the foreground. (Photo Courtesy of the Tom Solomon Collection, DLF.)

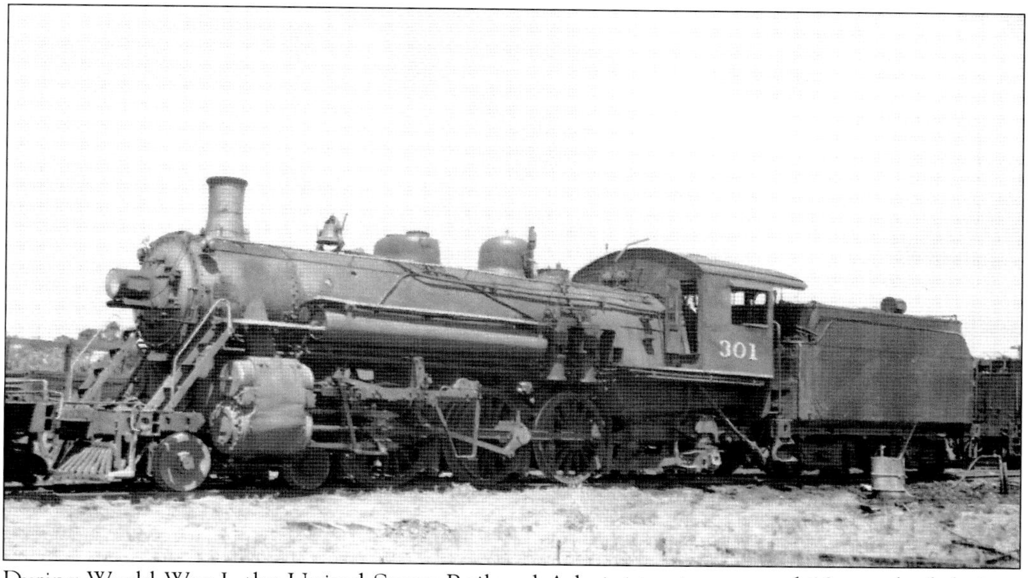

During World War I, the United States Railroad Administration created 12 standard designs for locomotives. One was the 4-6-2 "Light Pacific" design of the Apalachicola Northern No. 301. Diesel-fired steam locomotives worked the AN until 1954, when modern diesel-electrics replaced them. (Courtesy of the Tom Solomon Collection, DLF.)

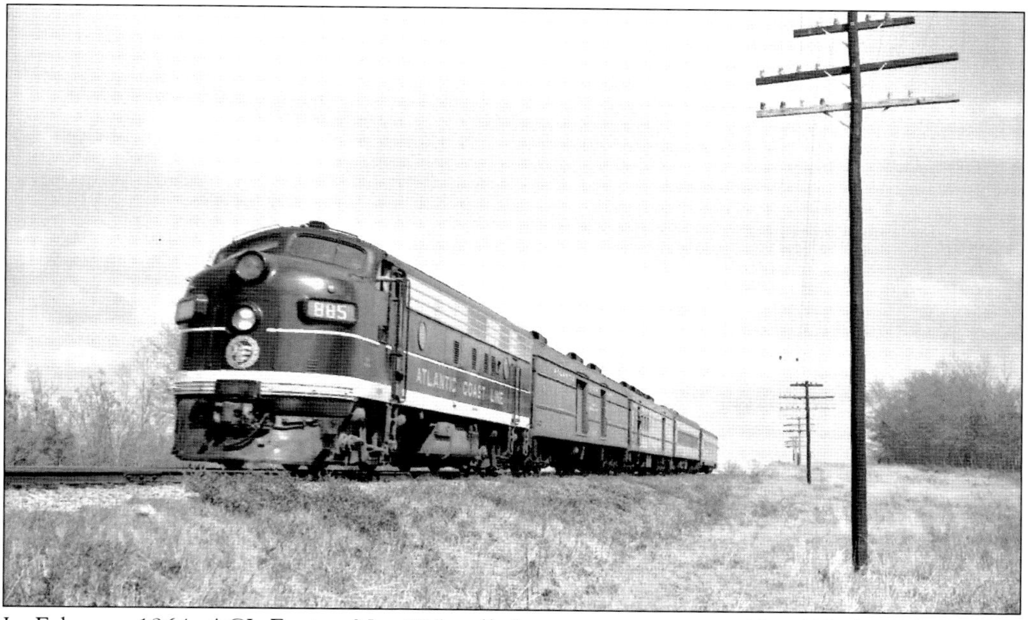

In February 1964, ACL Engine No. 885 pulled passengers on train No. 189 through Pansey, Alabama. The ACL ran the line between 1902, when it absorbed the entire Plant System, and 1967, when it merged with the Seaboard Air Line Railroad to become the Seaboard Coast Line. (Courtesy of the Tom Solomon Collection, DLF.)

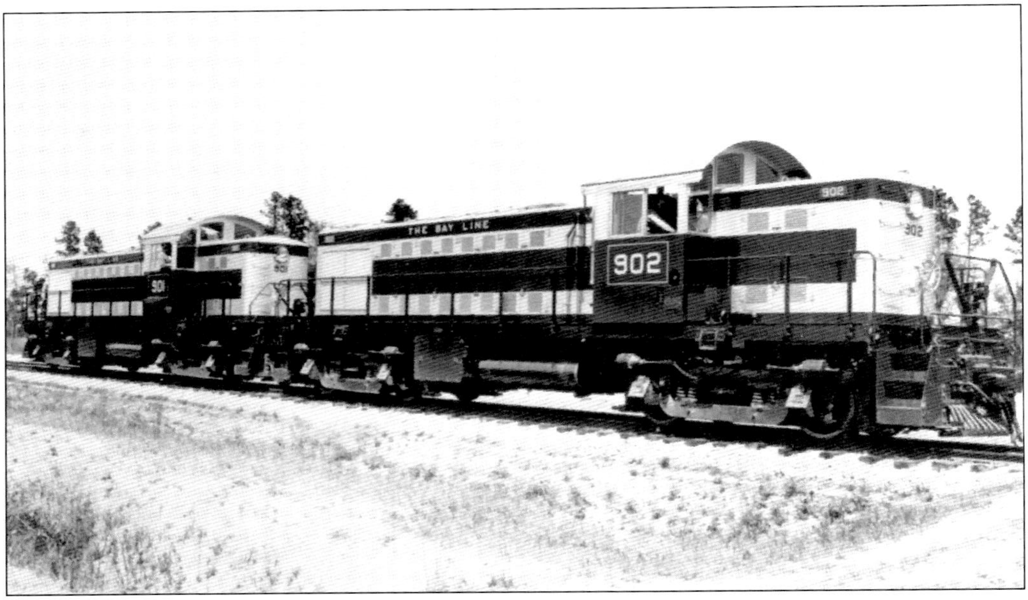

The Bay Line was the first railroad to convert from steam to diesel-electric locomotion. Prior to World War II, the line bought 3 of the first 13 diesel-electric engines ever produced in the United States (made by General Electric). The No. 901 and No. 902 were ALCO RS-1s. During World War II, the government requisitioned all Bay Line diesel-electrics, forcing it to revert to steam engines for the duration. (Courtesy of Quinton Bruner.)

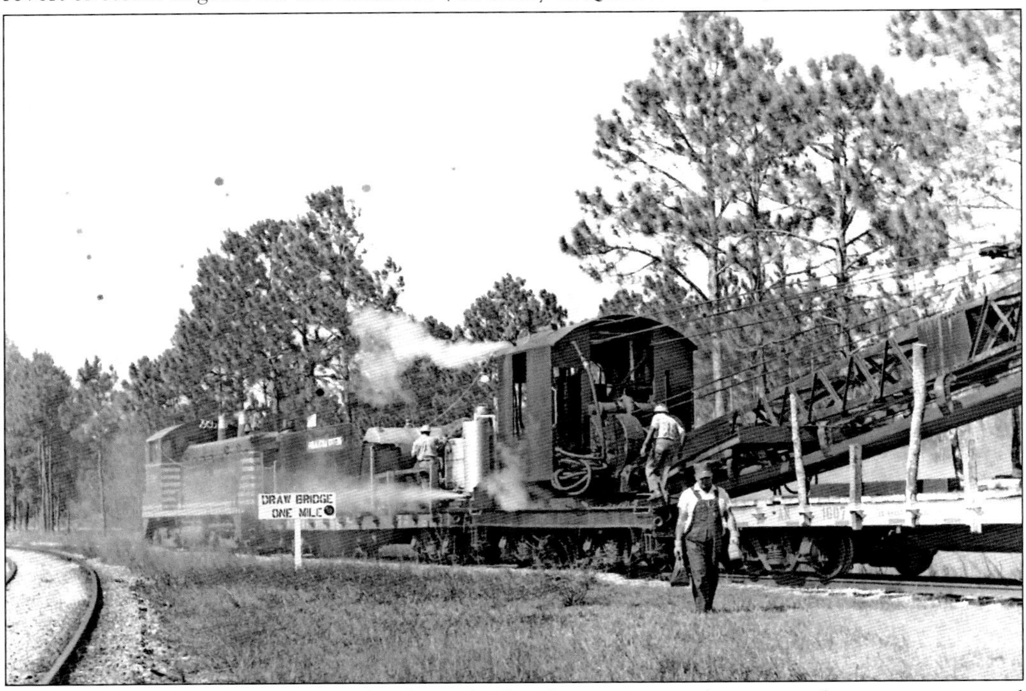

The Apalachicola Northern tracks through Florida encountered so many bogs, swamps, and streams that the pile driver, shown here, was among its most important pieces of equipment. (Courtesy of David Kirkland.)

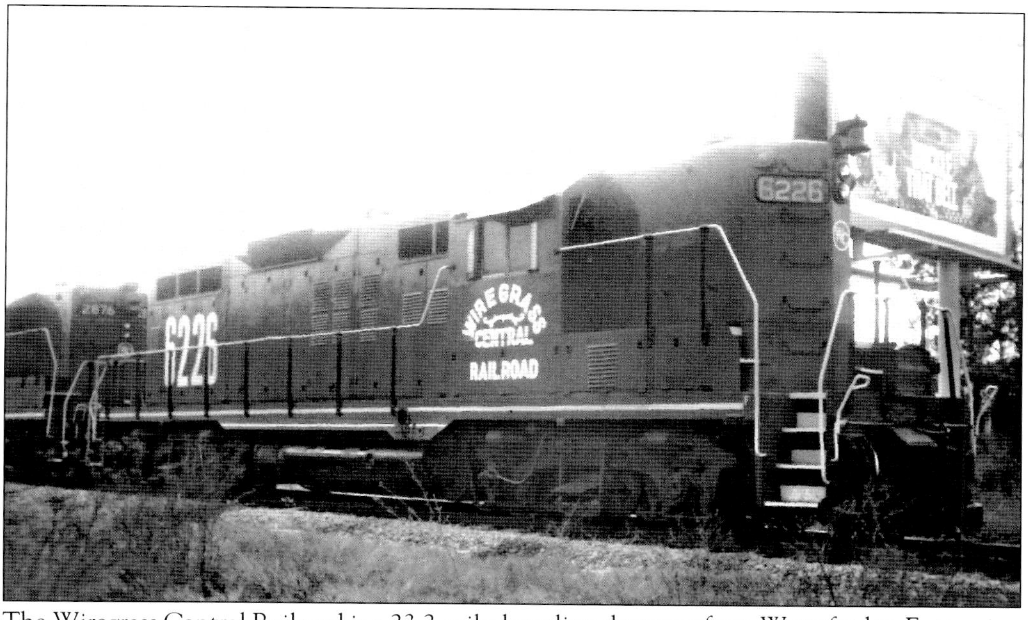

The Wiregrass Central Railroad is a 23.2-mile-long line that runs from Waterford to Enterprise, Alabama. It is one of three short lines comprising the Gulf & Ohio group and was purchased from Seaboard in 1987. The Wiregrass Central carries grain and peanuts. (Courtesy of David Kirkland.)

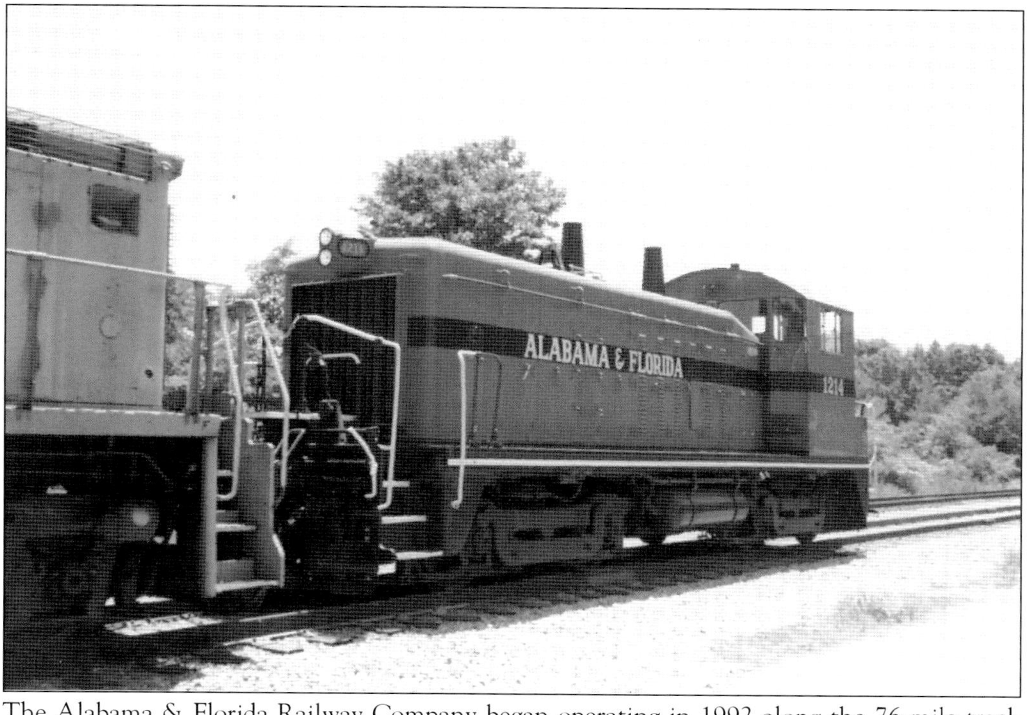

The Alabama & Florida Railway Company began operating in 1992 along the 76-mile track from Georgiana to Geneva, Alabama. Engine No. 1214 is decked out in its bright orange paint scheme accented with a black stripe and yellow letters. (Courtesy of David Kirkland.)

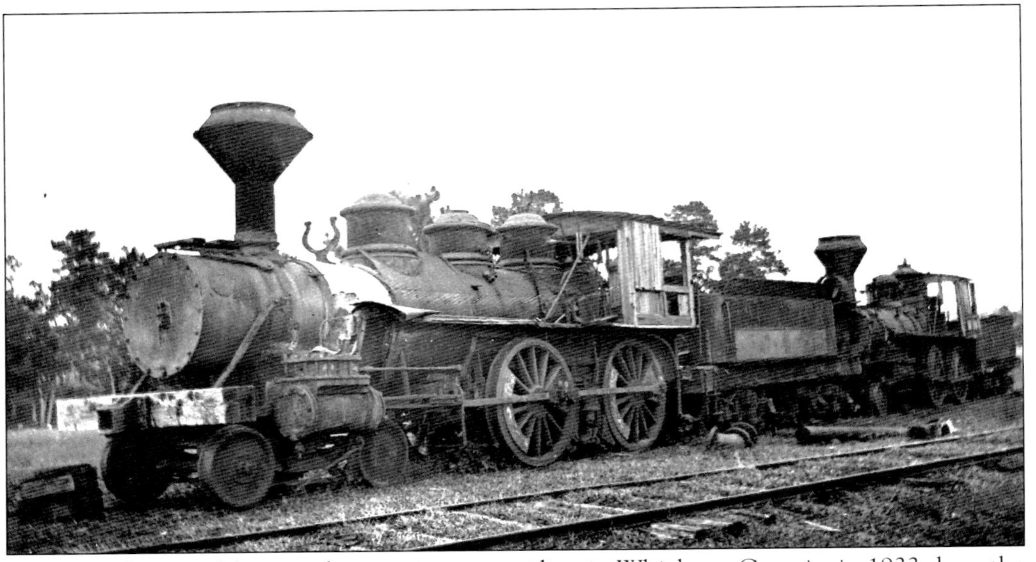

These derelict wood-burning locomotives on a siding in Whigham, Georgia, in 1933 show the rigors of freight and lumber hauling. Note the wooden bumper and cab siding slats that indicate "field updates." (Courtesy of the Tom Solomon Collection, DLF.)

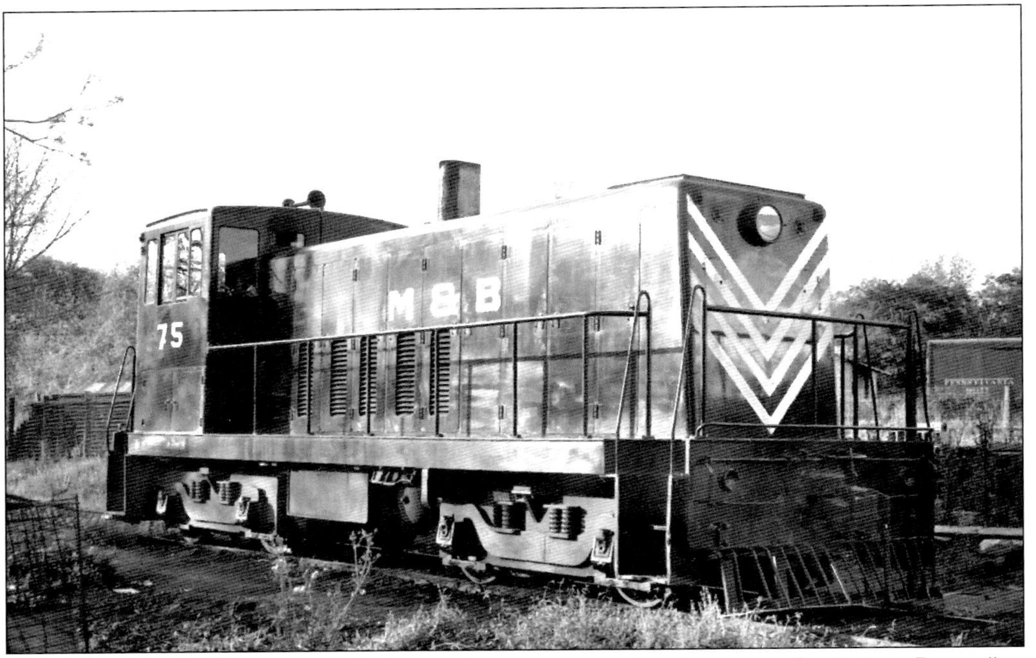

The Marianna & Blountstown Railroad—known among local users as the "Many Bumps"—ran the shortest line in Florida between 1909 and 1972. Throughout its life it carried wood and agricultural products, and before 1929, it provided passenger service as well. (Courtesy of David Kirkland.)

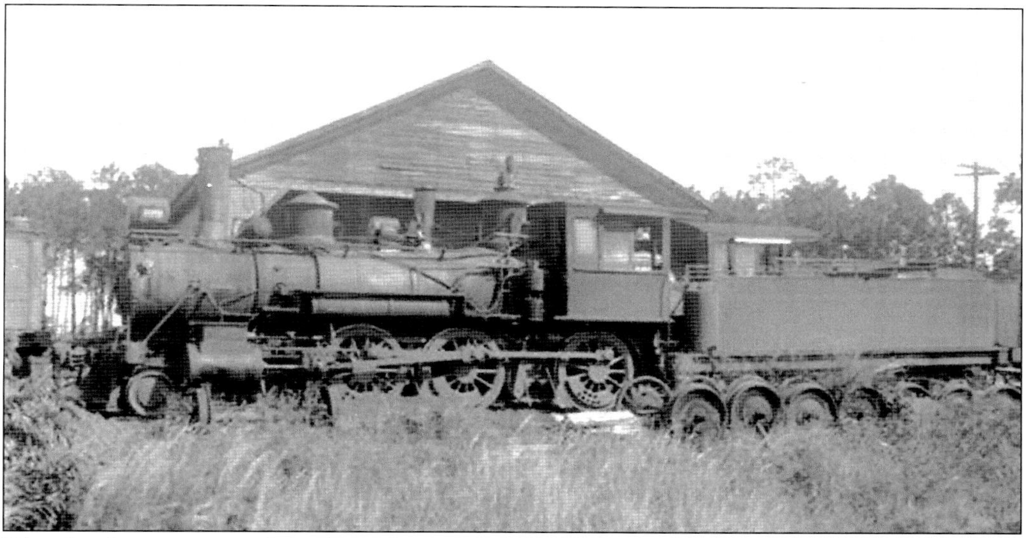

This derelict engine and tender, a 4-6-0, served the Birmingham, Columbus & St. Andrews Railroad in the 1920s. Later, the BC & StA became the Alabama & Western Florida Line. (Courtesy of David Kirkland.)

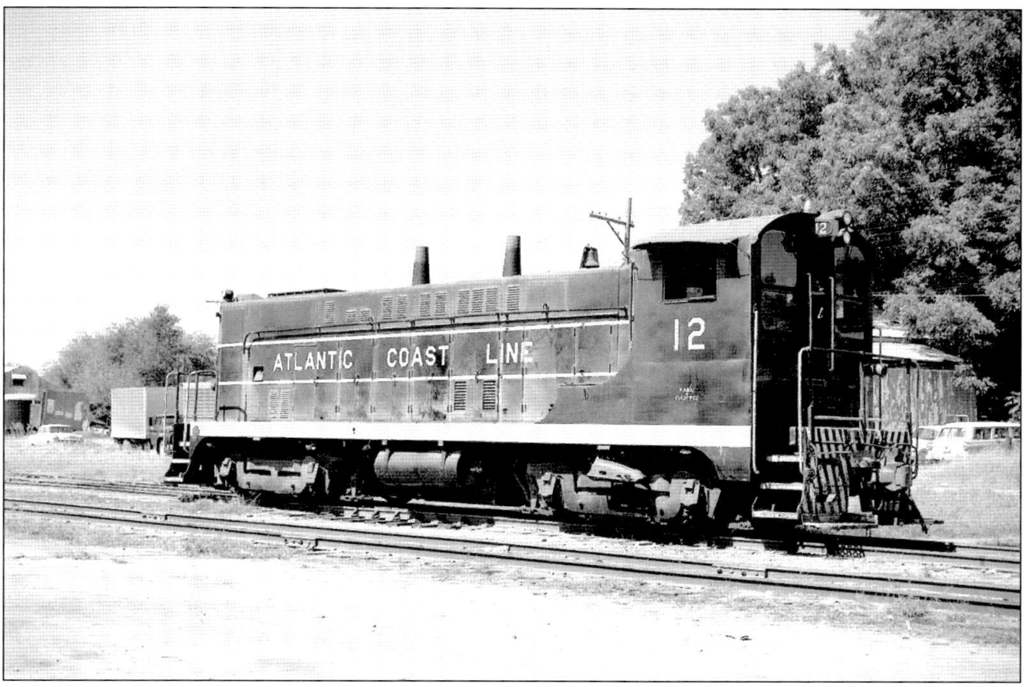

All railroads needed switch engines to transfer cars from one train to another. This is ACL's Switcher No. 12 in the Dothan, Alabama rail yard on September 2, 1964. (Courtesy of the Tom Solomon Collection, DLF.)

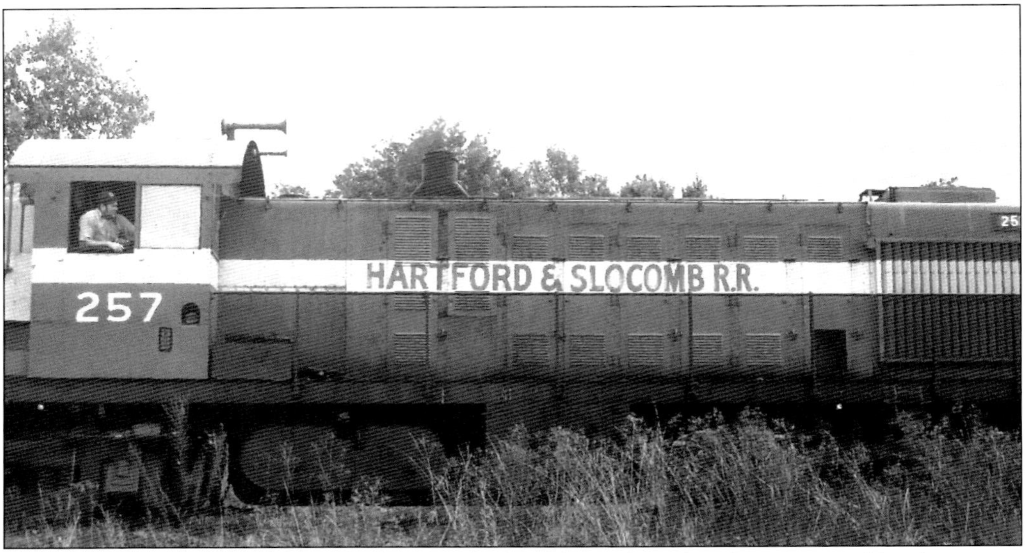

Engine No. 257 (ALCO RS-1) of the Hartford & Slocomb Railroad was painted bright orange with a black stripe and yellow numbers. The H & S operated along a 22-mile track west from Dothan to Hartford, Alabama, beginning in the 1970s. (Courtesy of Fred Fisher.)

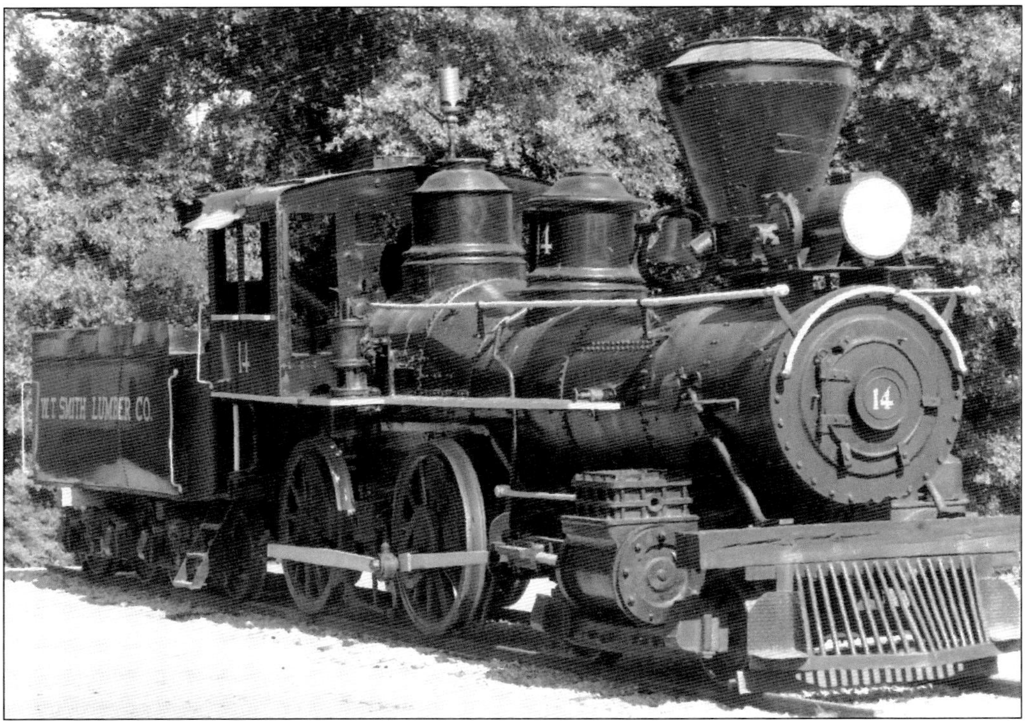

This 4-4-0 began life in 1881 at the Baldwin Locomotive Works. Its original owner, the Central of Georgia, christened it the *Madison*. The W.T. Smith Lumber Company acquired Engine No. 14 in 1912 and logged with it until 1927, after which the McGowin family of Chapman, Alabama, used it to log their private land. It was donated for display in 1992 to the Pioneer Museum of Alabama in Troy. (Courtesy of the Pioneer Museum of Alabama.)

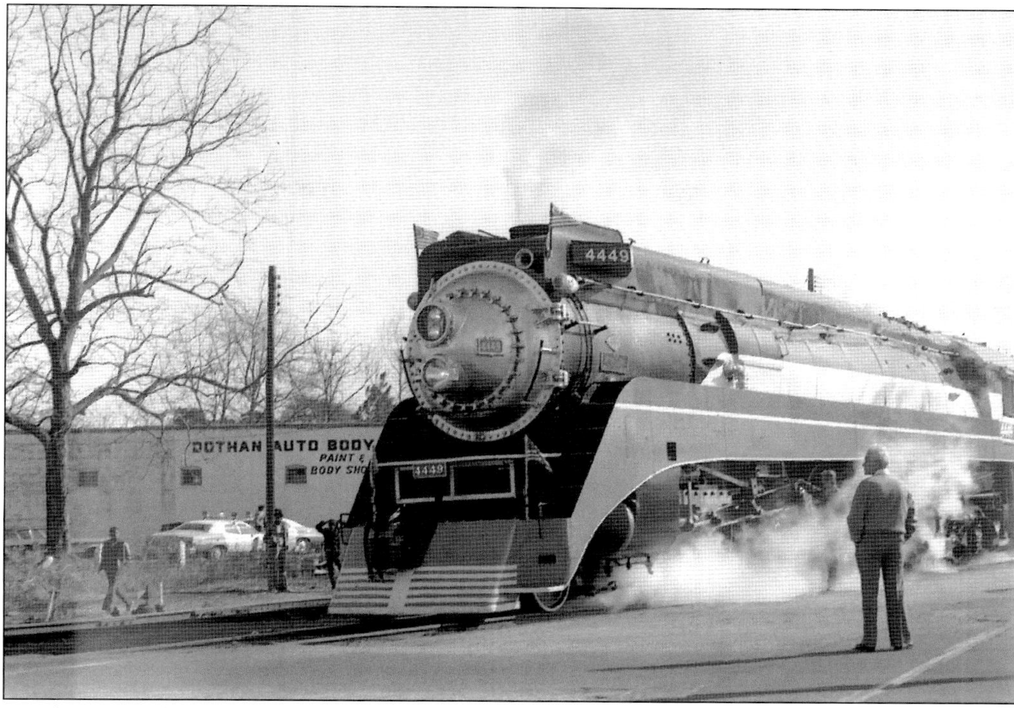

Southern Pacific Engine No. 4449 is a 4-8-4, GS-4 class, built by Lima in 1941. It ran West Coast routes until 1955 and was donated to the City of Portland, Oregon, in 1958. Ross Rowland, a New York commodities broker and rail enthusiast, brought the No. 4449 out of retirement to pull his *American Freedom Train* for the 1976 United States Bicentennial. (Courtesy of the Tom Solomon Collection, DLF.)

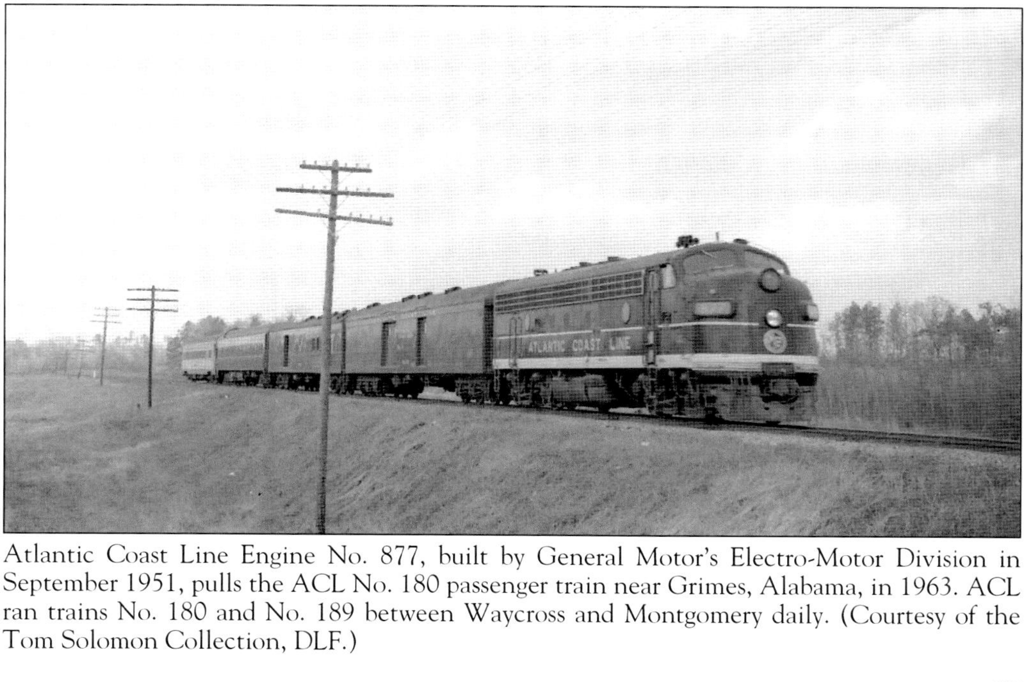

Atlantic Coast Line Engine No. 877, built by General Motor's Electro-Motor Division in September 1951, pulls the ACL No. 180 passenger train near Grimes, Alabama, in 1963. ACL ran trains No. 180 and No. 189 between Waycross and Montgomery daily. (Courtesy of the Tom Solomon Collection, DLF.)

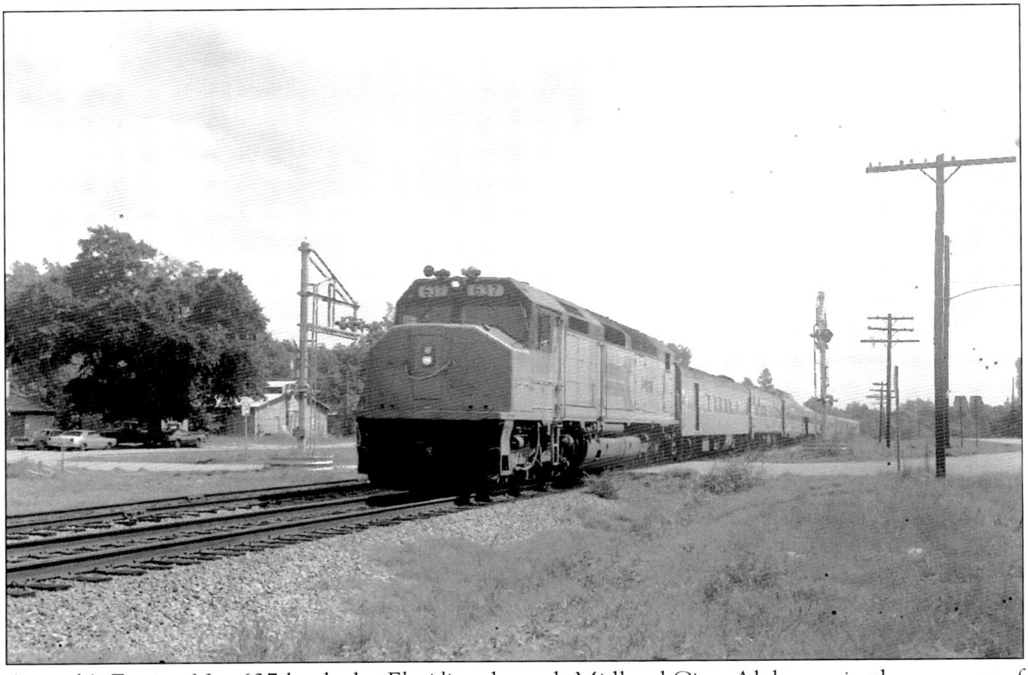

Amtrak's Engine No. 637 leads the *Floridian* through Midland City, Alabama, in the summer of 1979, just weeks before it discontinued service on September 30. Amtrak bought a fleet of these 3,000-horsepower EMD model SDP-40-F locomotives in 1973, but it sold them in the 1980s because of yawing problems. (Courtesy of the Tom Solomon Collection, DLF.)

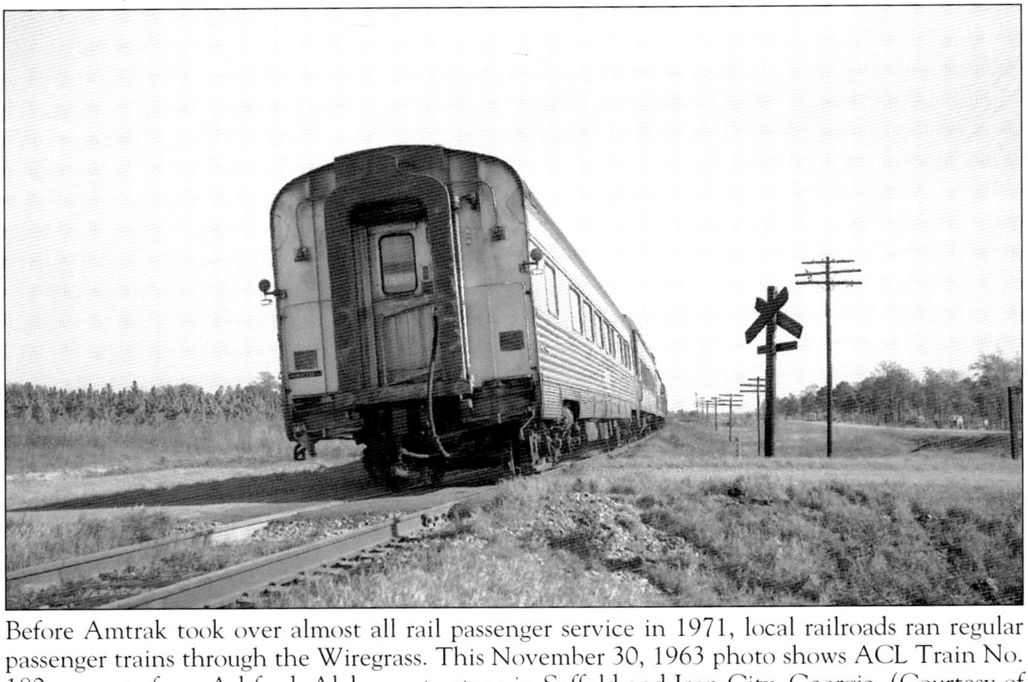

Before Amtrak took over almost all rail passenger service in 1971, local railroads ran regular passenger trains through the Wiregrass. This November 30, 1963 photo shows ACL Train No. 180 en route from Ashford, Alabama, to stops in Saffold and Iron City, Georgia. (Courtesy of the Tom Solomon Collection, DLF.)

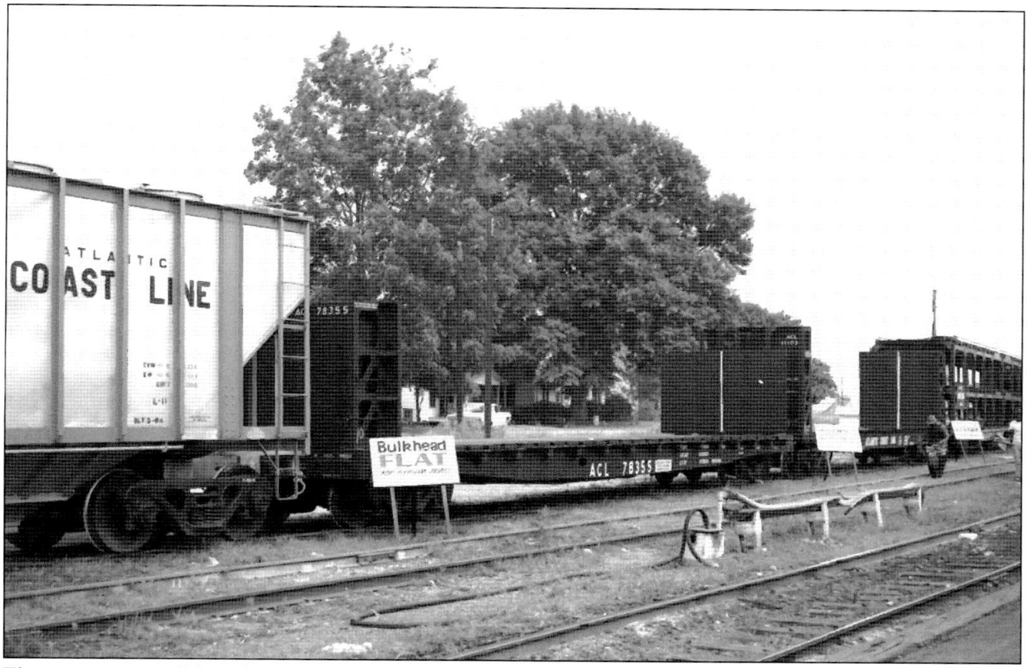

Flat cars carry all kinds of products that are not thrown off balance by swaying, enabling easy loading and off loading. Engineers designed this ACL bulkhead flatcar to haul up to 50 tons of gypsum board on pallets. Similar cars carry lumber, machinery, and pulpwood. This photo was taken in Dothan in 1964. (Courtesy of the Tom Solomon Collection, DLF.)

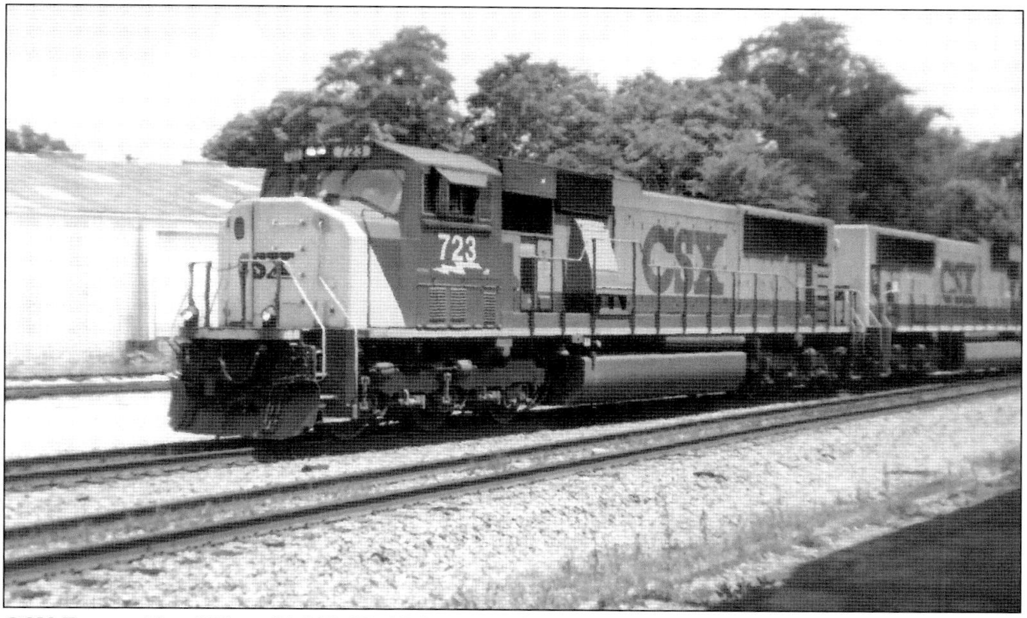

CSX Engine No. 723, a GM EMD SD70MAC diesel-electric that was introduced into service in 1992, trundles along the Bay Line tracks in this 2002 photograph. The Chessie System and the Seaboard Coast Line (created from a merger of the SAL and ACL in 1967) merged in 1980 to form CSX. (Courtesy of David Kirkland.)

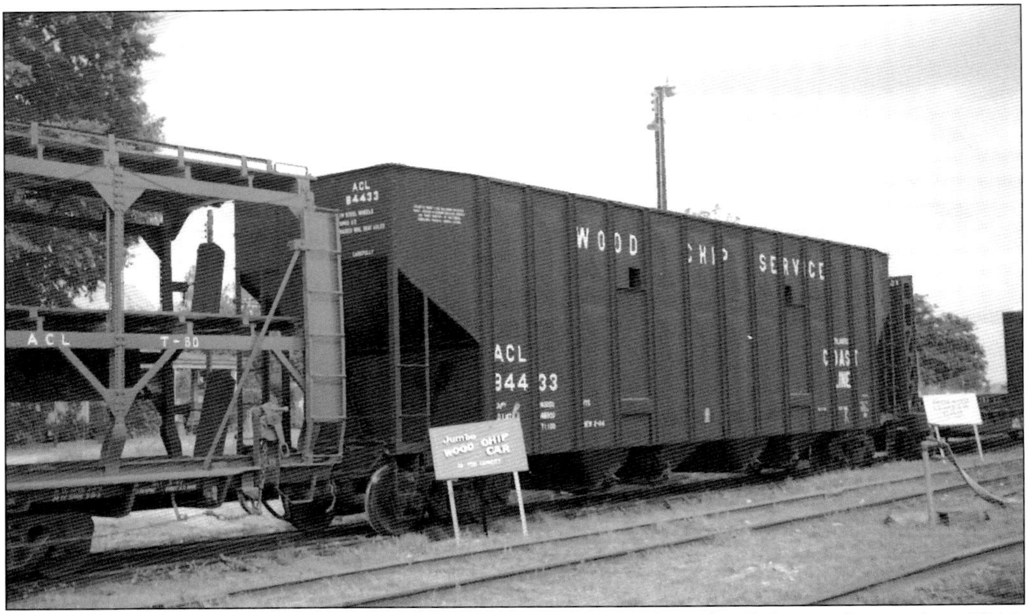

The Atlantic Coast Line displays new cars in a Dothan rail yard exhibit in September 1964. National rail use standards require shipping wood chips only in dedicated cars. This ACL jumbo wood ship car can hold 140,000 pounds of chips. Paper mills use "clean" chips to make paper and "fuel" chips from stumps to fire steam-powered generators. (Courtesy of the Tom Solomon Collection, DLF.)

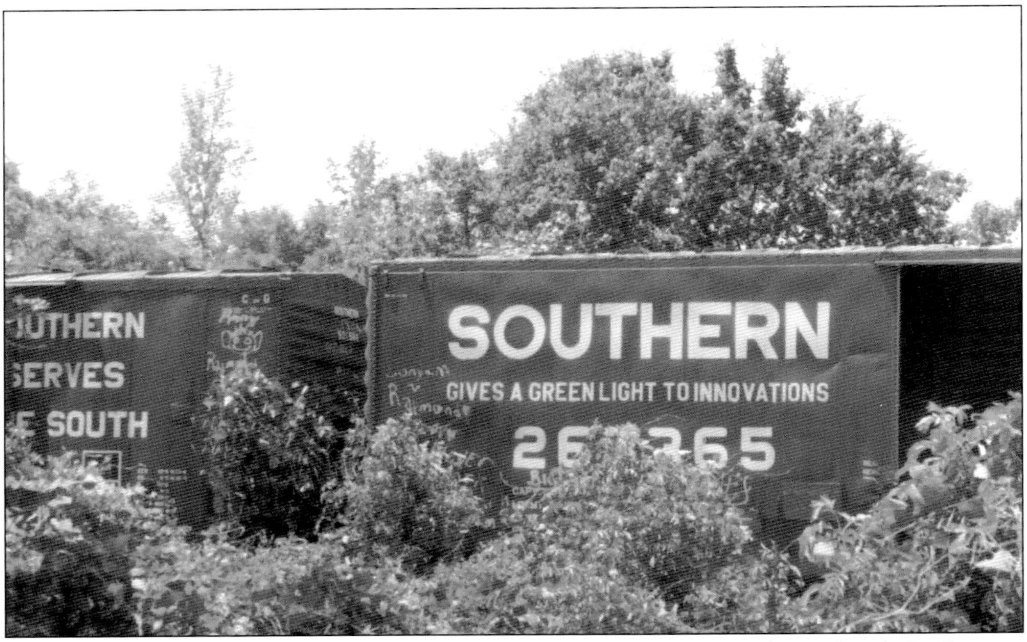

"Bit" Folger of Fort Gaines, Georgia, was intrigued when she saw "miles and miles" of empty boxcars overrun with kudzu on a siding in Barbour County, Alabama. They are waiting to be upgraded or repaired at the shops in Dothan or Birmingham. (Courtesy of the Clay County [Georgia] Public Library.)

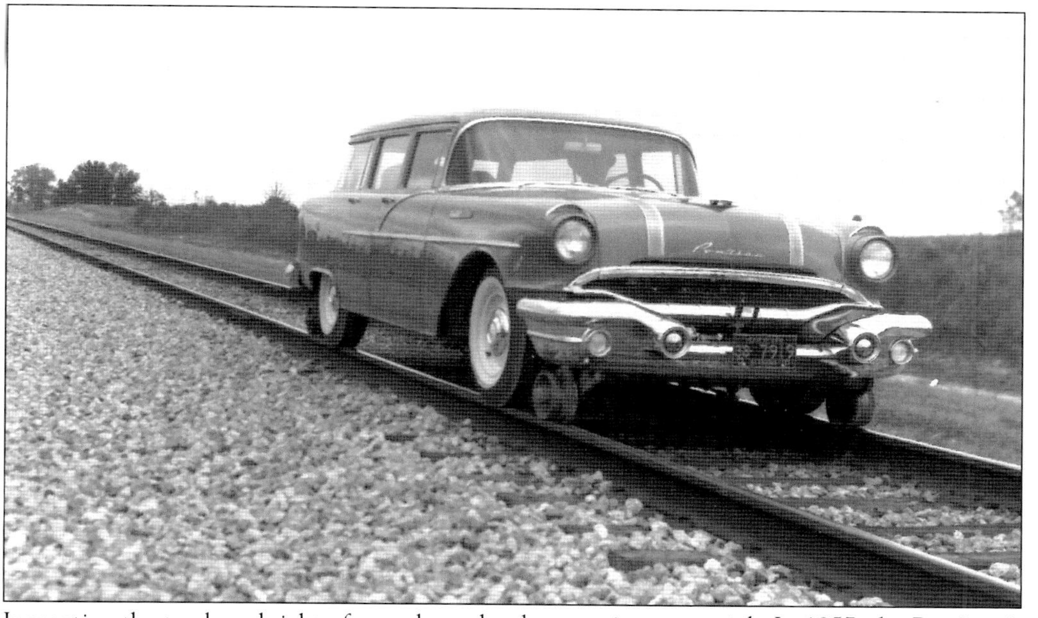

Inspecting the track and right of way always has been an important job. In 1957, the Bay Line's chief engineer and road master used this specially equipped Pontiac station wagon to check the rails for damage and wear. A custom hydraulic system lowered the flanged wheels to keep the car on the tracks and raised them to allow the car to drive on the roadway. (Courtesy of Quinton Bruner.)

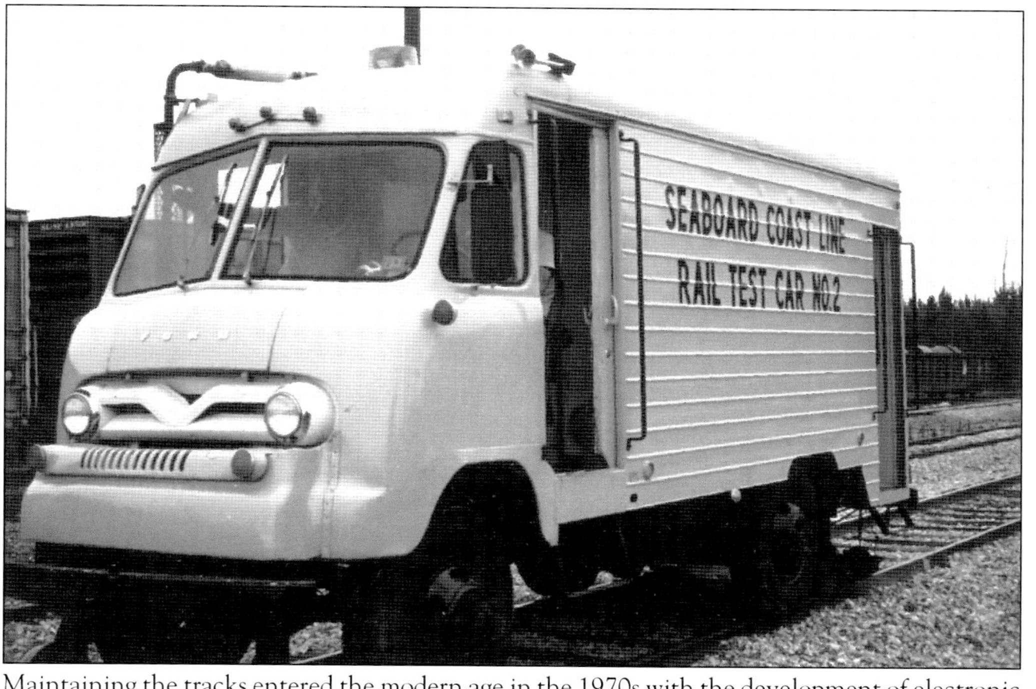

Maintaining the tracks entered the modern age in the 1970s with the development of electronic testing to "detect hidden defects and flaws in rails." This rail test car created miles of yard-wide print-outs resembling giant electrocardiogram tapes. (Courtesy of the CIRR.)

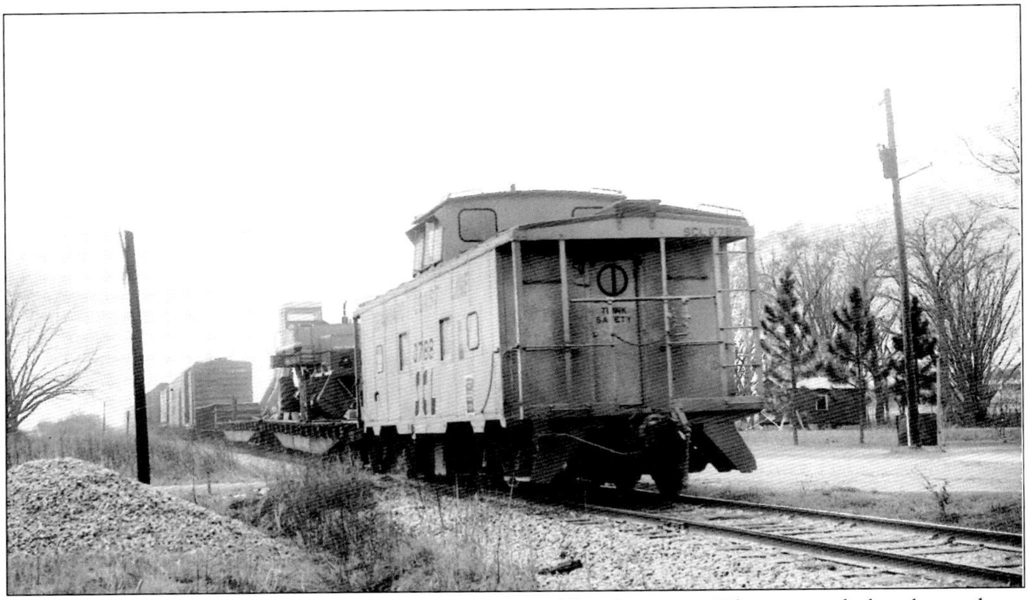

Traditionally, cabooses have brought up the rears of freight trains. They provided a place where the freight conductor and rear brakeman could do office work and be available for switching duty. In 1965, this SCL caboose on the Abbeville, Alabama branch line included a cupola where the crew could watch the entire length of the train. (Courtesy of the Tom Solomon Collection, DLF.)

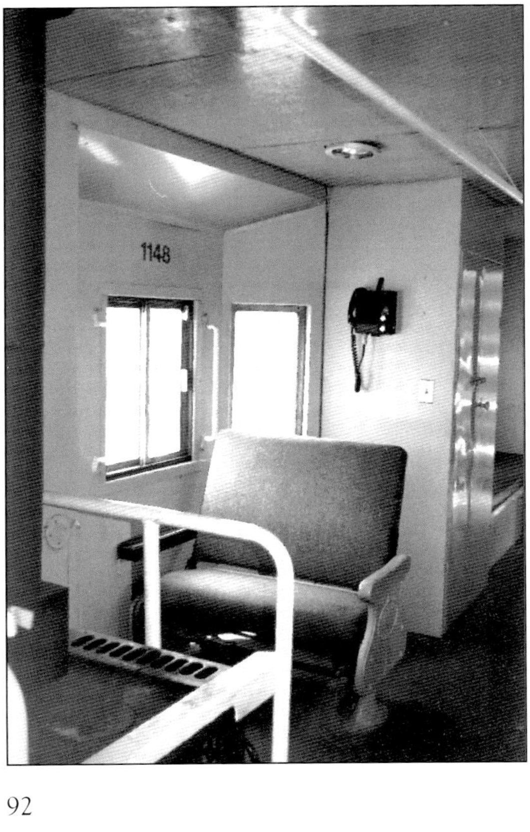

The interior of this caboose, located at the West Florida Railroad Museum in Milton, shows comfortable seats, modern steel lockers, and a radio intercom through which the rear crew can communicate with the engineer. On this caboose, bays are the observation ports. (Courtesy of David Kirkland.)

Five

Working on the Railroad

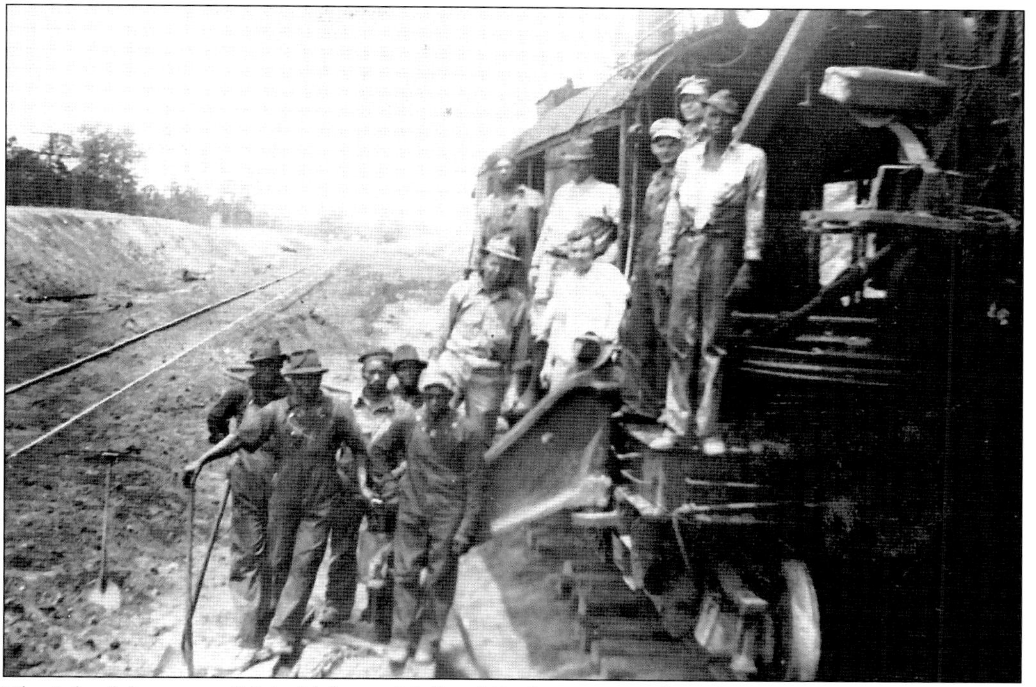

The job of the crew of this Alabama Midland Railway steam shovel was to cut grade, ditch, and generally move earth to make room for the tracks. The only person identified is fireman C.V. Oliver, standing on the deck with his left hand on his hip. He became an engineer. (Courtesy of the Tom Solomon Collection, DLF.)

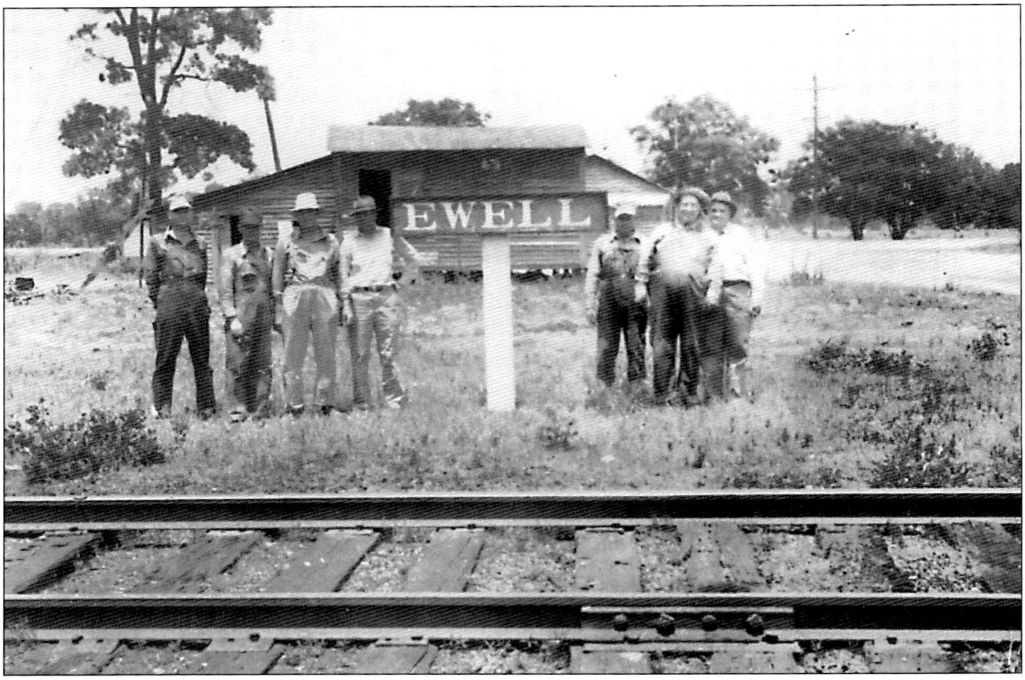

Section and train crews frequently lived in the small railroad towns that dotted the lines every five to seven miles. This ACL crew worked out of Ewell, Dale County, Alabama. They tended the main Alabama-Georgia Wiregrass line that ran from Waycross, Georgia, through Dothan, to Montgomery. (Courtesy of the Tom Solomon Collection, DLF.)

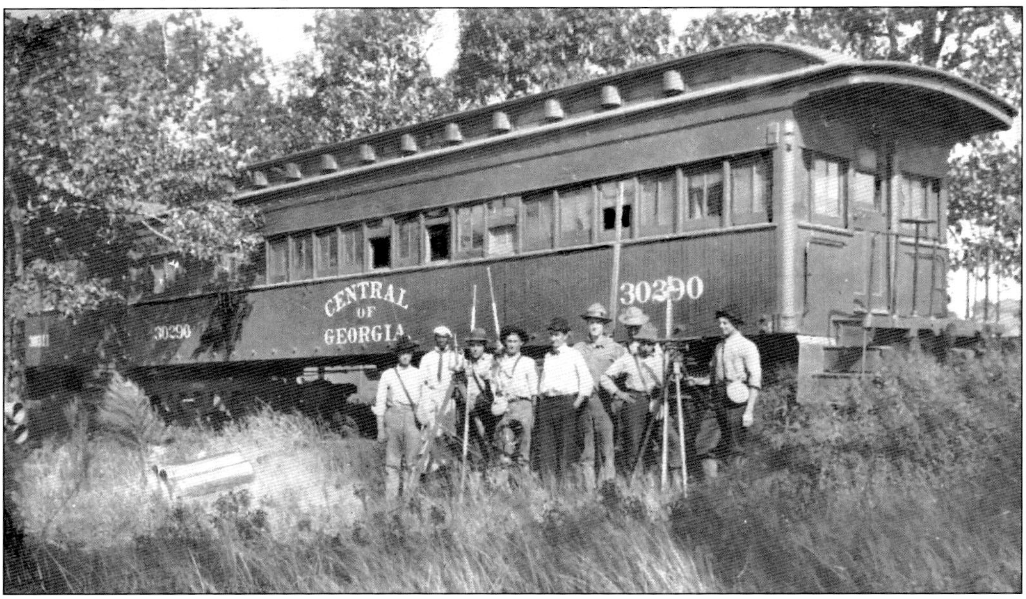

Capital costs of building rail lines were so great that companies devoted significant resources to planning routes. This photo shows a survey party at Arlington, Georgia, on the Central of Georgia line, planning the track route into Dothan. Shown in the center with hands in pockets is Chief Charles Brown. (Courtesy of Houston-Love Memorial Library, Dothan, Alabama.)

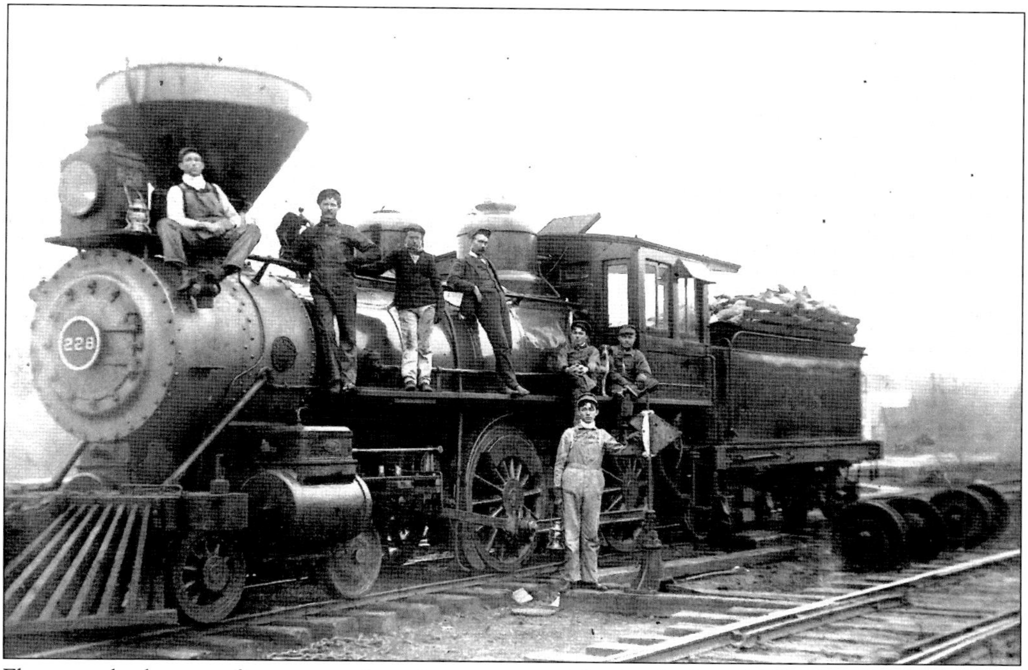

Flagmen, brakemen, firemen, and engineers pose with the Seaboard No. 228, a 4-4-0 wood-burner, at River Junction, Florida, in 1900. River Junction was also called Chattahoochee and was the intersection of the Apalachicola Northern line with the great north Florida trunk line created by Col. William D. Chipley. (Courtesy of the Tom Solomon Collection, DLF.)

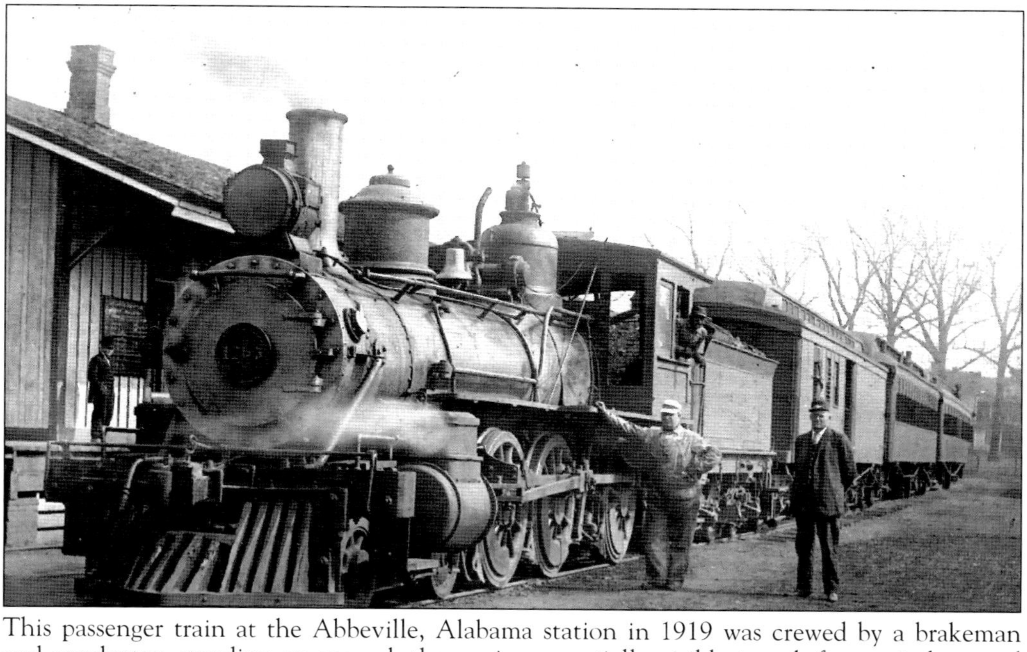

This passenger train at the Abbeville, Alabama station in 1919 was crewed by a brakeman and conductor, standing on ground; the engineer partially visible in cab front window; and the fireman hanging out of the cab side window. Note the passenger standing on the platform. (Courtesy of the Tom Solomon Collection, DLF.)

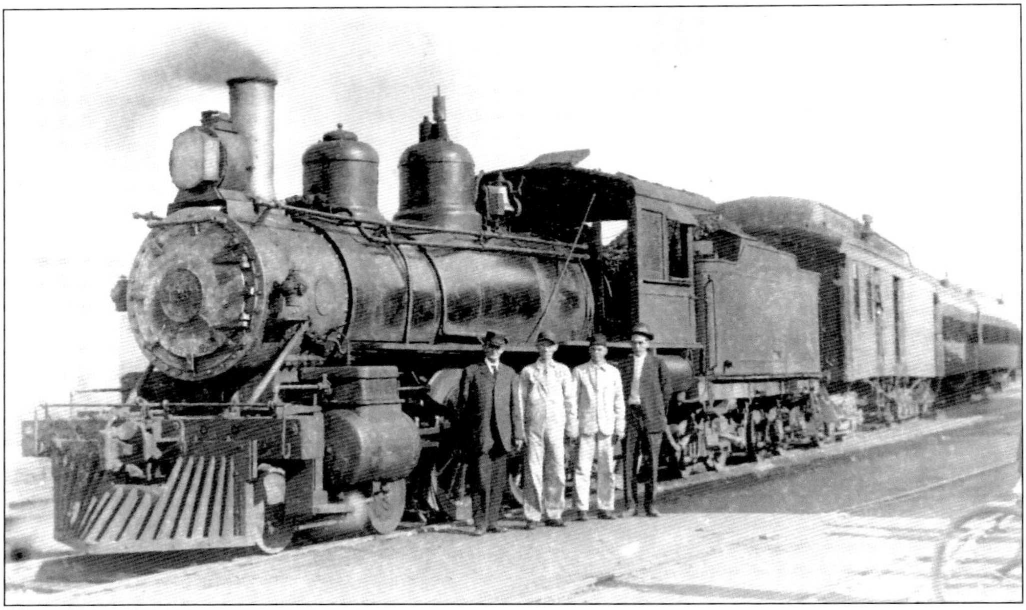

Railroading sometimes became a family affair. In the 1920s, two generations of the Dinkins family worked the Dothan-to-Abbeville run. On the far left is the patriarch, conductor Tobe Dinkins, followed by his sons, engineer Tom Dinkins, fireman Jay Dinkins, and flagman Brad Dinkins. (Courtesy of the Tom Solomon Collection, DLF.)

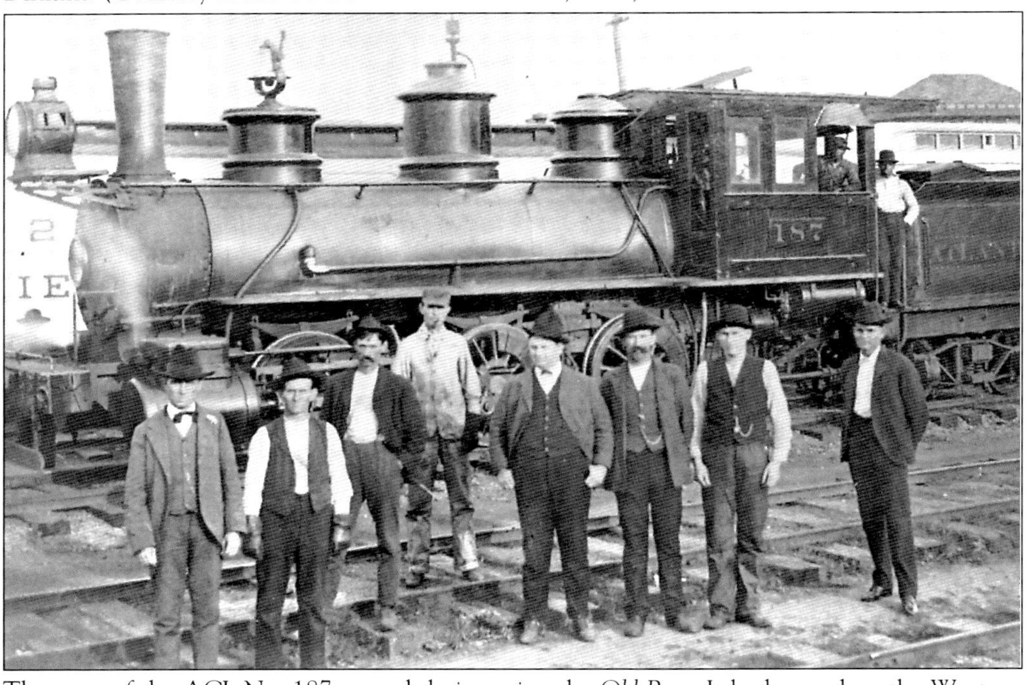

The crew of the ACL No. 187 named their engine the *Old Puss*. It had served on the Western & Atlantic line and as the Alabama Midland No. 502 before being acquired by the Atlantic Coast Line. These men are dressed according to their place in the business hierarchy. Note the two crew members in the cab. (Courtesy of Tommy Henderson.)

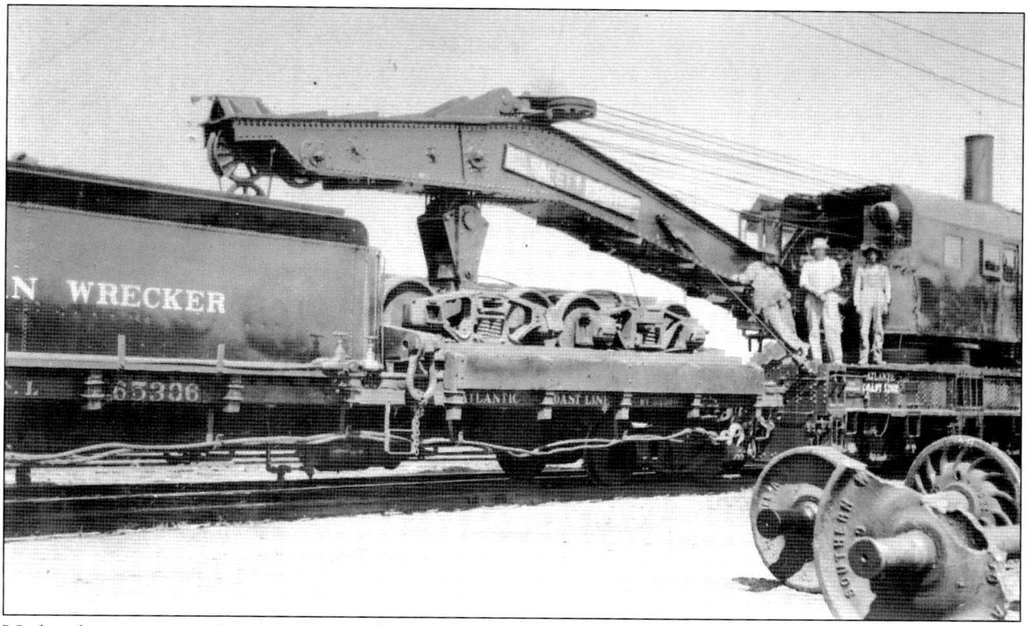

Unloading cars and righting wrecks required machine power. This crew poses on the ACL wrecker No. 65302, which has just picked up a railcar undercarriage for transport to the ACL shops. (Courtesy of the Tom Solomon Collection, DLF.)

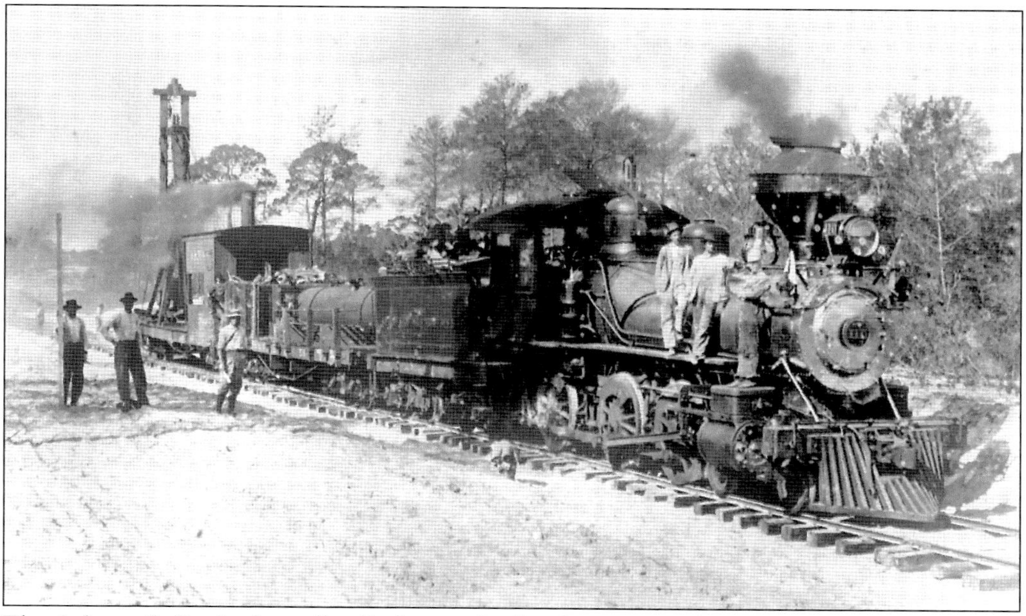

The Atlanta & St. Andrews Bay Railway—the Bay Line—runs through the Florida Panhandle from Panama City to Dothan, Alabama. Much of that terrain is boggy or cut through with ravines and creeks. Laying track there requires pylons, thousands of which were driven by this rig. (Courtesy of the Tom Solomon Collection, DLF.)

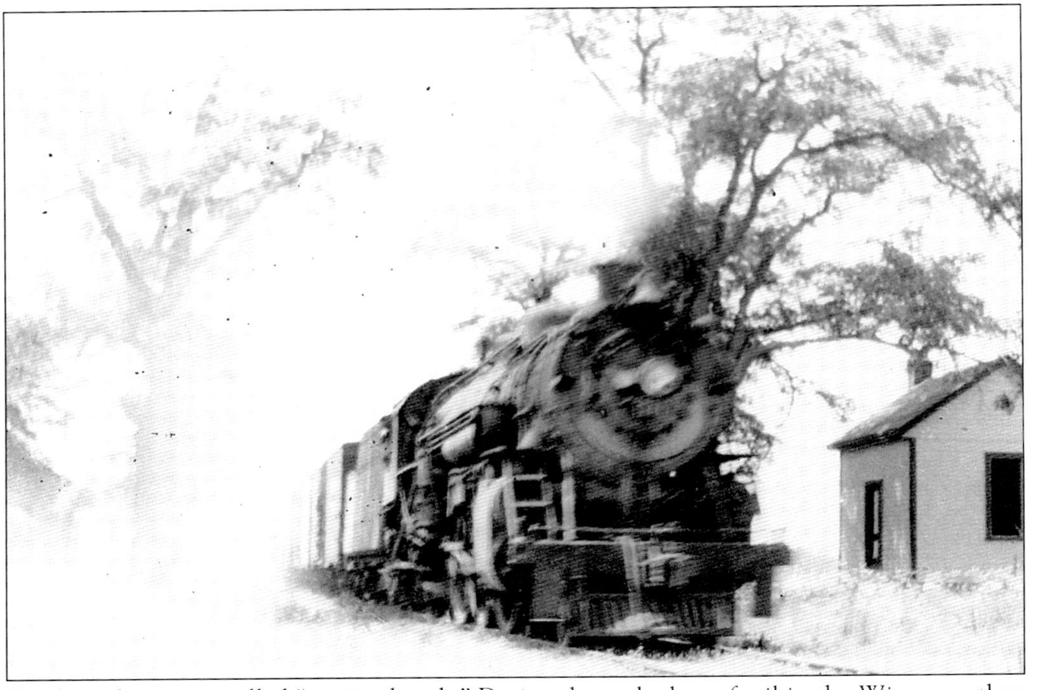

Track workers were called "section hands." During the early days of rail in the Wiregrass, they frequently lived along the tracks for which they were responsible. In June 1952, the westbound ACL No. 1517 thunders past section houses one mile west of Headland. (Courtesy of the Tom Solomon Collection, DLF.)

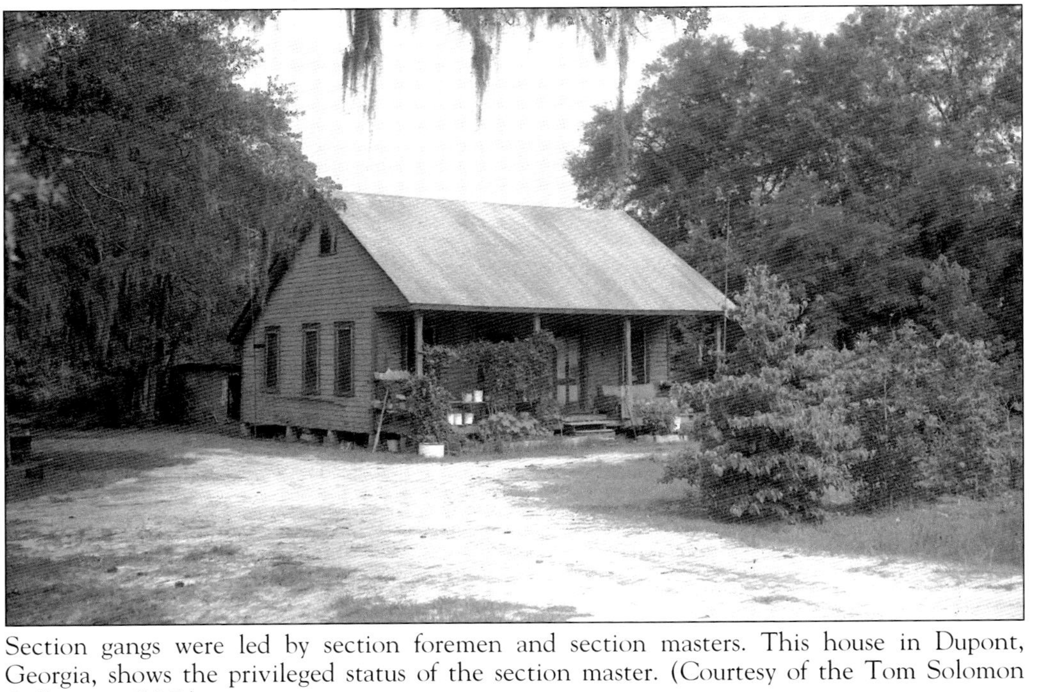

Section gangs were led by section foremen and section masters. This house in Dupont, Georgia, shows the privileged status of the section master. (Courtesy of the Tom Solomon Collection, DLF.)

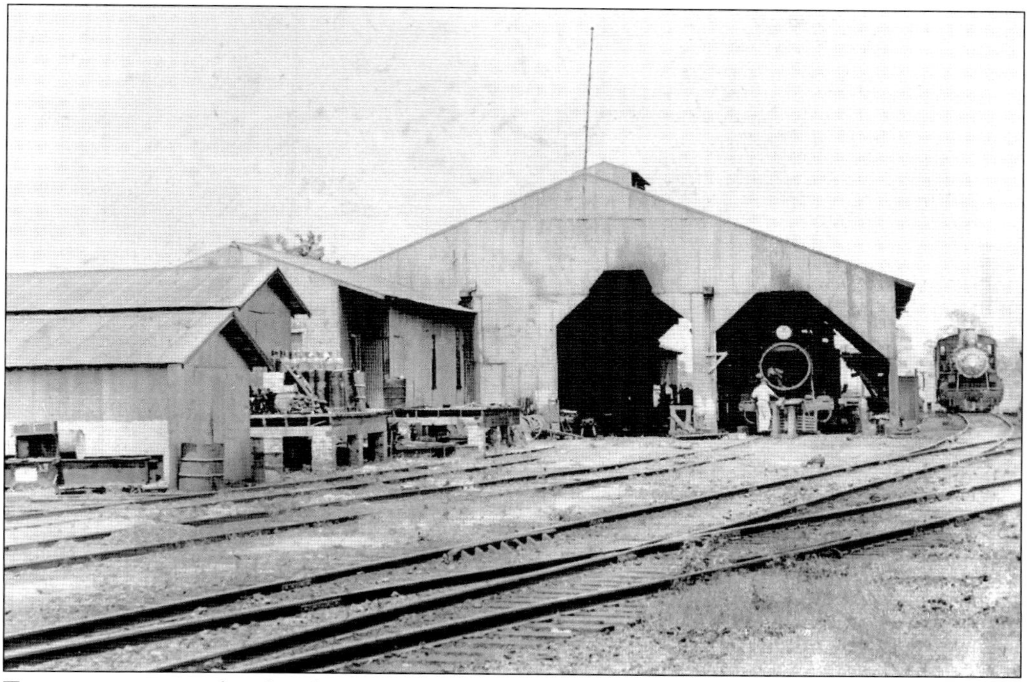

Trains were repaired, refitted, maintained, and updated in the shops built by every railroad at their terminal. These are the shops of the Apalachicola Northern in Port St. Joe, Florida, with one locomotive in a repair bay and another awaiting removal to the main line. (Courtesy of the Tom Solomon Collection, DLF.)

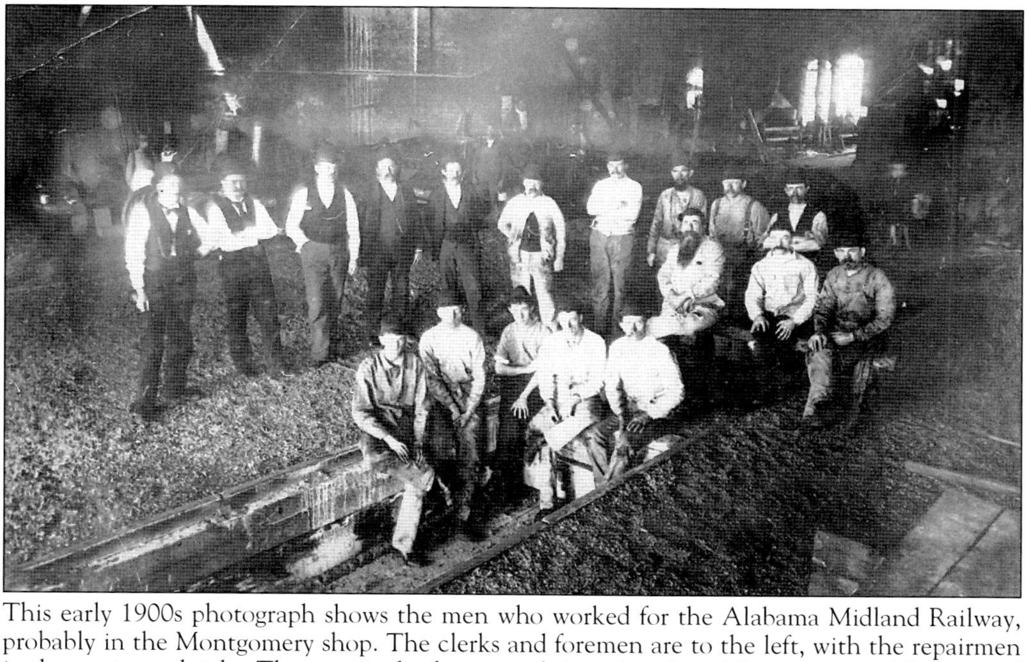

This early 1900s photograph shows the men who worked for the Alabama Midland Railway, probably in the Montgomery shop. The clerks and foremen are to the left, with the repairmen in the center and right. The men in the foreground sit at the edge of the access pit. (Courtesy of the Tom Solomon Collection, DLF.)

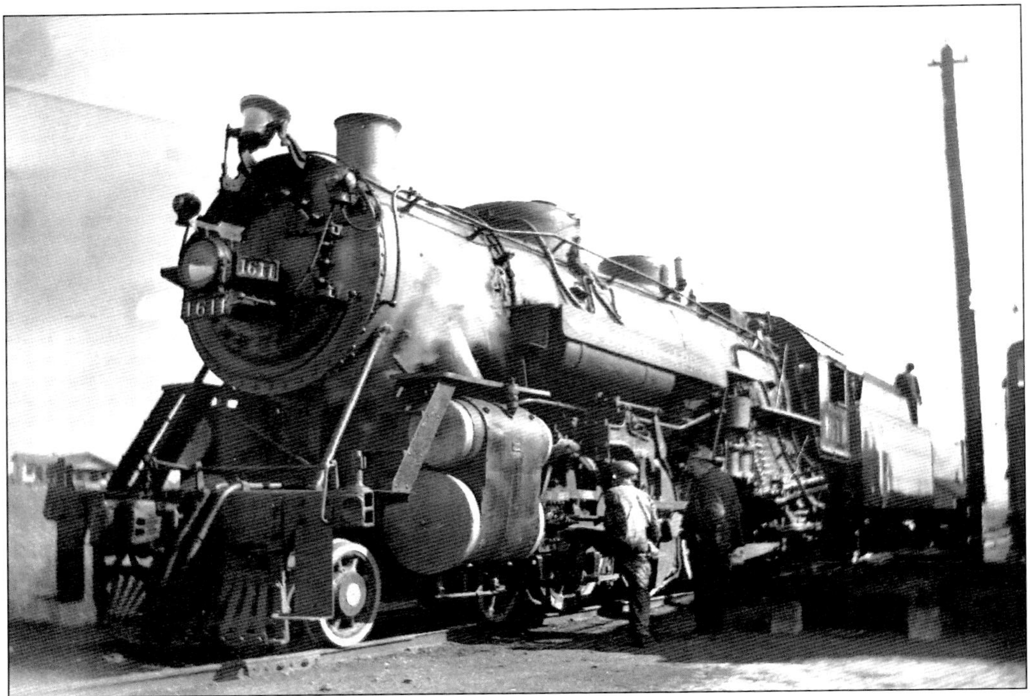

Problems frequently developed with rolling stock and engines. In February 1935, the *Florida Arrow* lost Engine No. 1611 to an overheated account guide. Alvin "Soot" Williams and J.F. Whisenant work on the problem at the Dothan, Alabama shops. (Courtesy of the Tom Solomon Collection, DLF.)

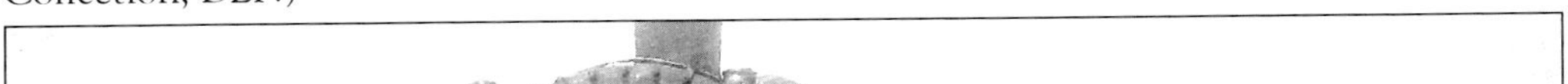

In the early 20th century, train crews were large, and jobs were very specialized. After World War I, crews became smaller, and job duties increased. In June 1934, engineer Ed Smith oils an account guide on ACL Engine No. 450 in the Dothan yards. (Courtesy of the Tom Solomon Collection, DLF.)

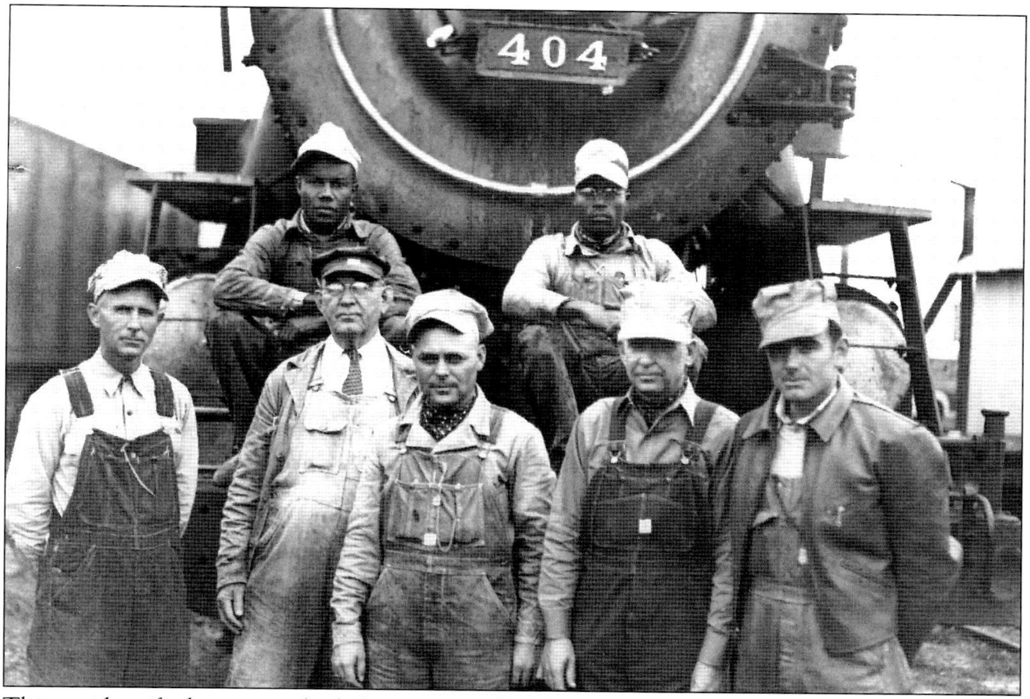

This unidentified crew worked the trains pulled by Bay Line Engine No. 404, a diesel-fired steam locomotive. Third from the left is the conductor. Like his outfit that combined overalls and a necktie, his job combined the blue- and white-collar worlds of his special place in the order of things. (Courtesy of Quinton Bruner.)

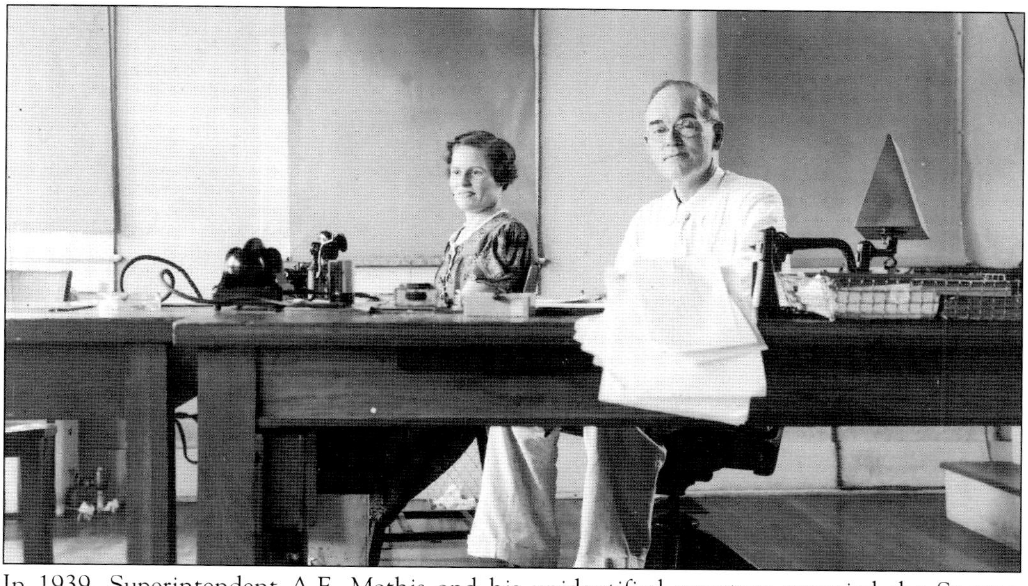

In 1939, Superintendent A.E. Mathis and his unidentified secretary occupied the Spartan general offices of the Atlanta & St. Andrews Bay Railway at 127 N. Foster Street, Dothan, Alabama. (Courtesy of Quinton Bruner.)

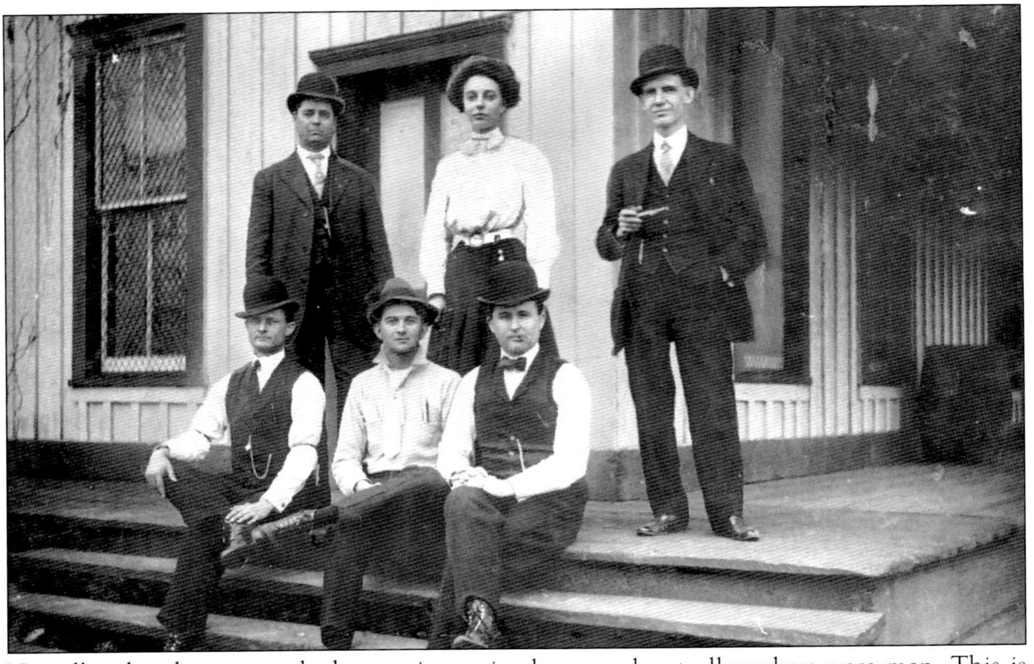

Not all railroad crews worked on trains or in shops, and not all workers were men. This is the staff of Dothan's Atlantic Coast Line freight house in 1907. Seated, from left to right, are N.S. Lisenby, warehouse clerk; Tom Appling, transfer clerk; and Barney Lisenby, ticket agent. Standing are Bob Morris, clerk; Maggie Lawson, bill clerk; and Diamond Pearson, cashier. (Courtesy of the Houston-Love Memorial Library, Dothan, Alabama.)

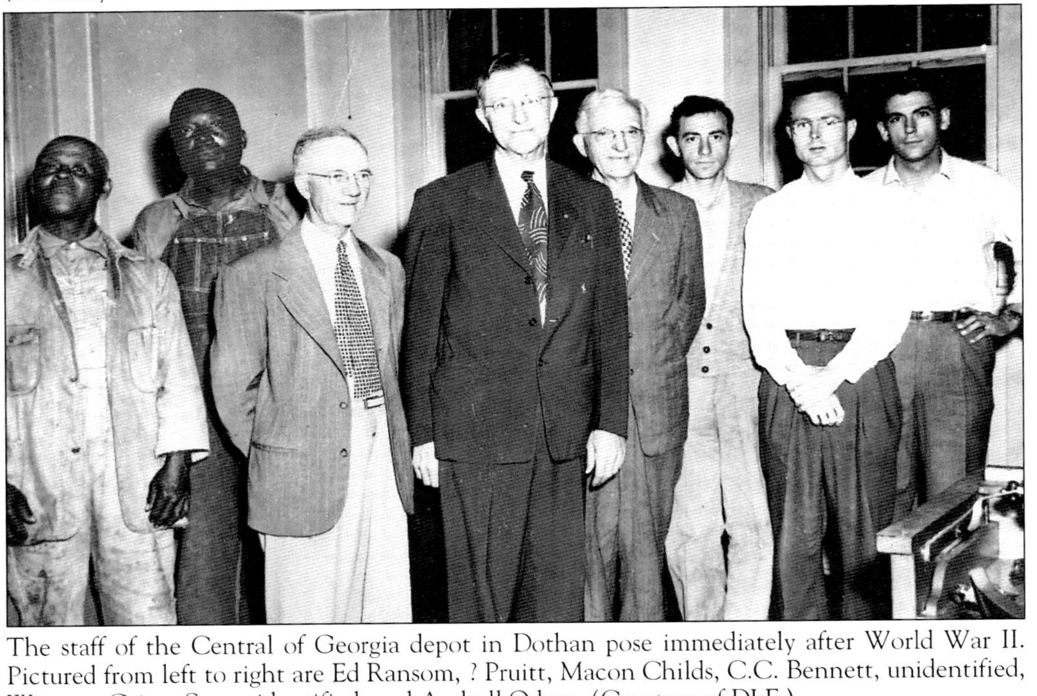

The staff of the Central of Georgia depot in Dothan pose immediately after World War II. Pictured from left to right are Ed Ransom, ? Pruitt, Macon Childs, C.C. Bennett, unidentified, Winston Griggs Sr., unidentified, and Audrell Odum. (Courtesy of DLF.)

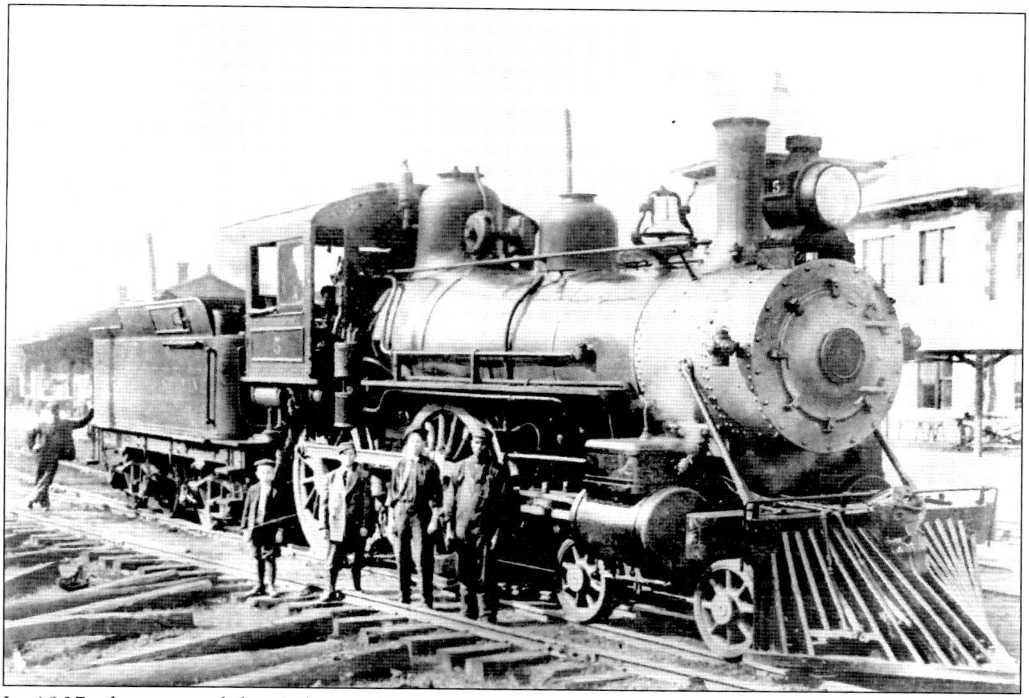

In 1907, the crew of the Atlantic Coast Line Engine No. 5 pose in Waycross, Georgia, with a pair of boys too young to wear long pants. Waycross has been an important hub for railroads in the Wiregrass since the 1880s. (Photo Courtesy of the Tom Solomon Collection, DLF.)

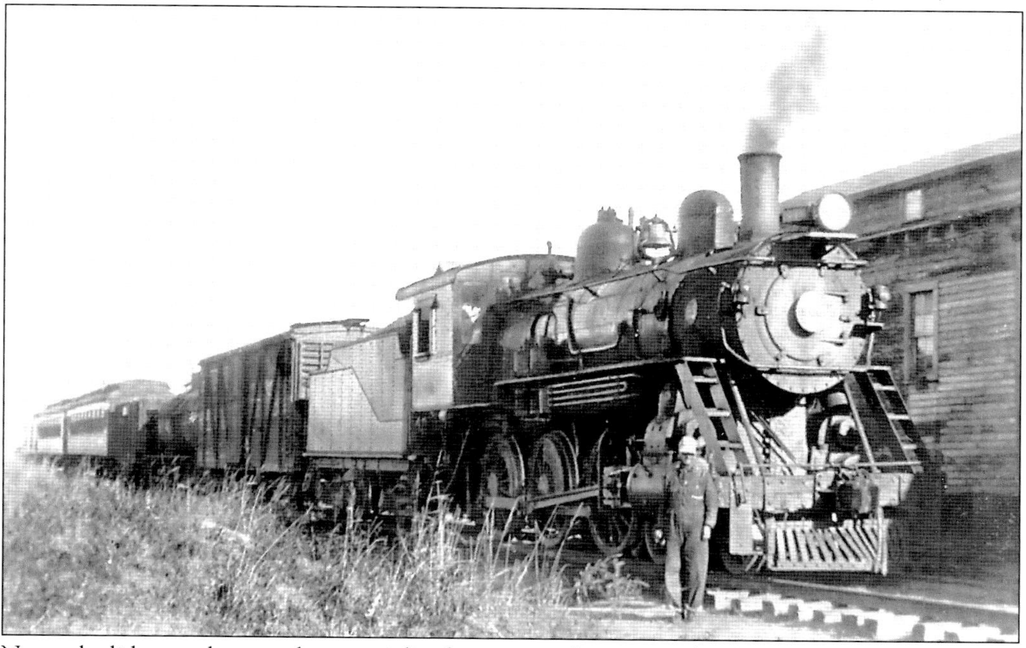

Not only did crews become less specialized over time, but trains also did general duty. This ACL train at Headland, Alabama, is "mixed," with a boxcar, tanker, and passenger cars. (Courtesy of the Abbeville [Alabama] Memorial Library.)

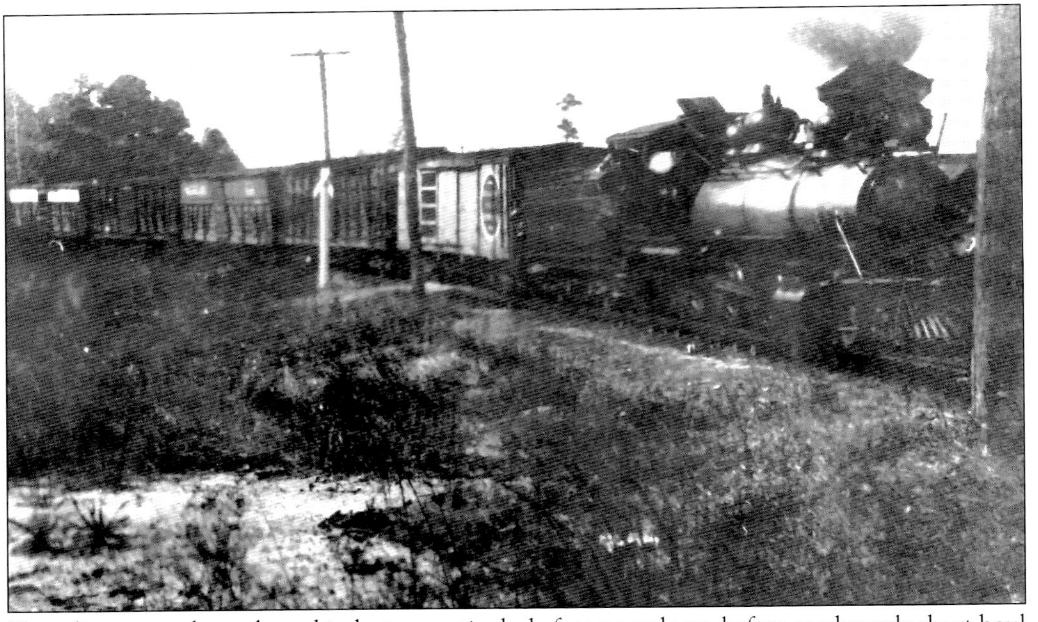

Short lines served people and industry, particularly forest products, before roads made short haul trucking and passenger cars usable. In 1921, W.S. Wilson Sr. of Dothan built the Alabama, Florida, & Gulf (AF & G) Railroad from the old Marbury Lumber Company line running from Gordon, Alabama, to Malone, Florida. (Courtesy of Harry and Leslie Summerford.)

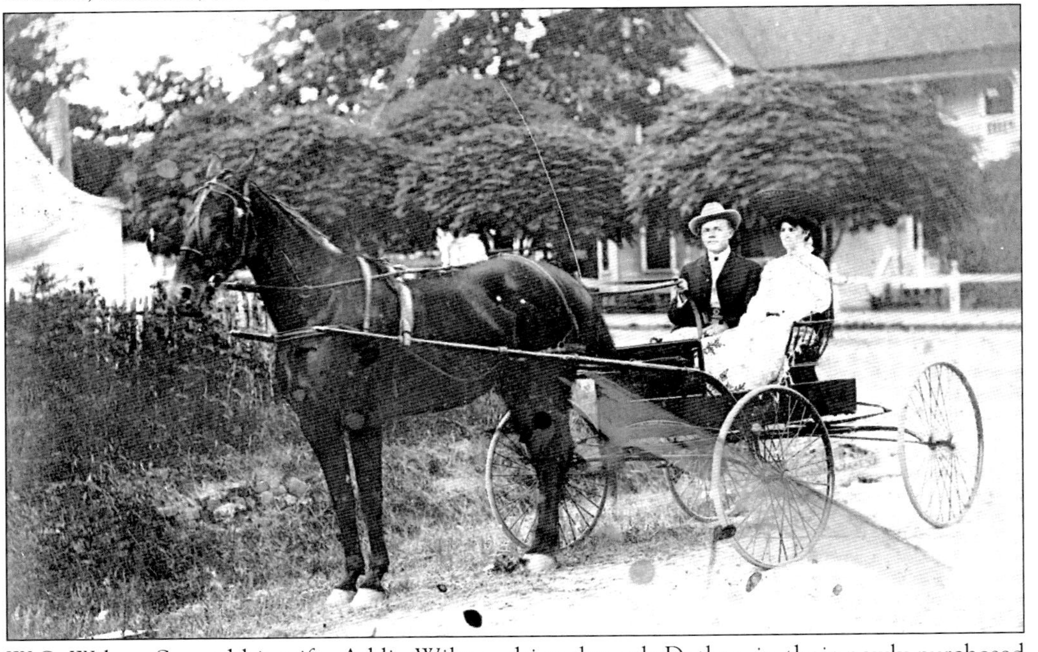

W.S. Wilson Sr. and his wife, Addie Wilson, drive through Dothan in their newly purchased buggy. A man of means, Wilson created the AF & G Railroad in 1921 by combining the Marbury Lumber Company line from Gordon, Alabama, to Malone, Florida, with the old AF & G Railway line from Cowarts, Alabama, to the Florida state line. (Courtesy of Harry and Leslie Summerford.)

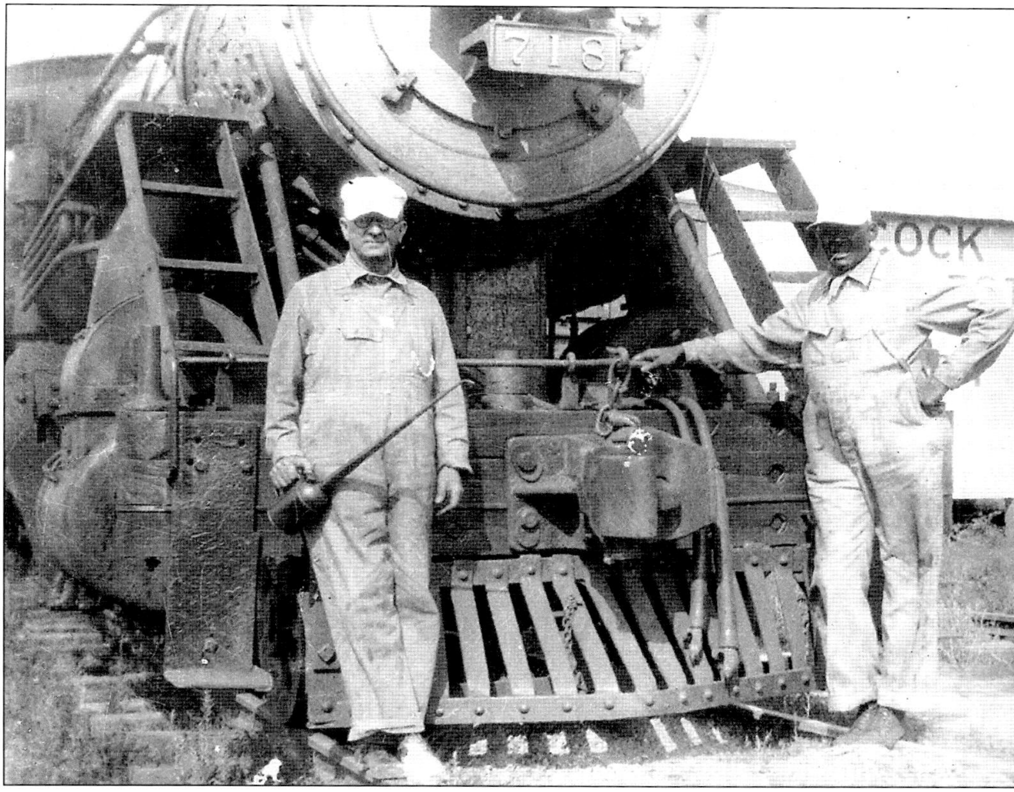

Engineer Calvin (C.V.) Oliver (with oil can) and fireman Robert "Bud Buck" Culver stand with the ACL Engine No. 718 in 1932 in front of the "Cock of the Walk" Fertilizer Co. in Headland. Both of these men worked the Abbeville branch for over 35 years. (Courtesy of the Tom Solomon Collection, DLF.)

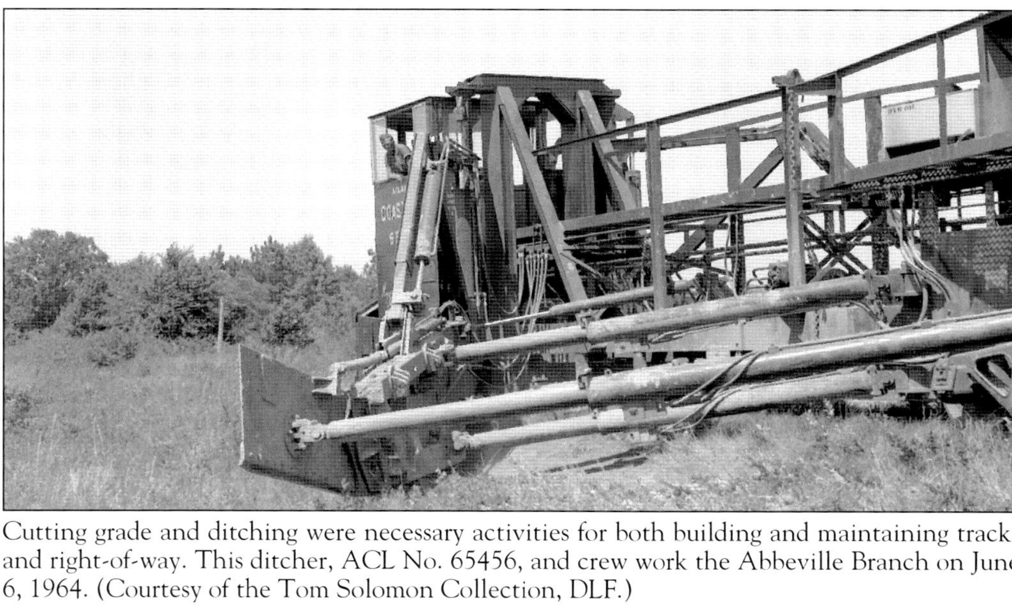

Cutting grade and ditching were necessary activities for both building and maintaining tracks and right-of-way. This ditcher, ACL No. 65456, and crew work the Abbeville Branch on June 6, 1964. (Courtesy of the Tom Solomon Collection, DLF.)

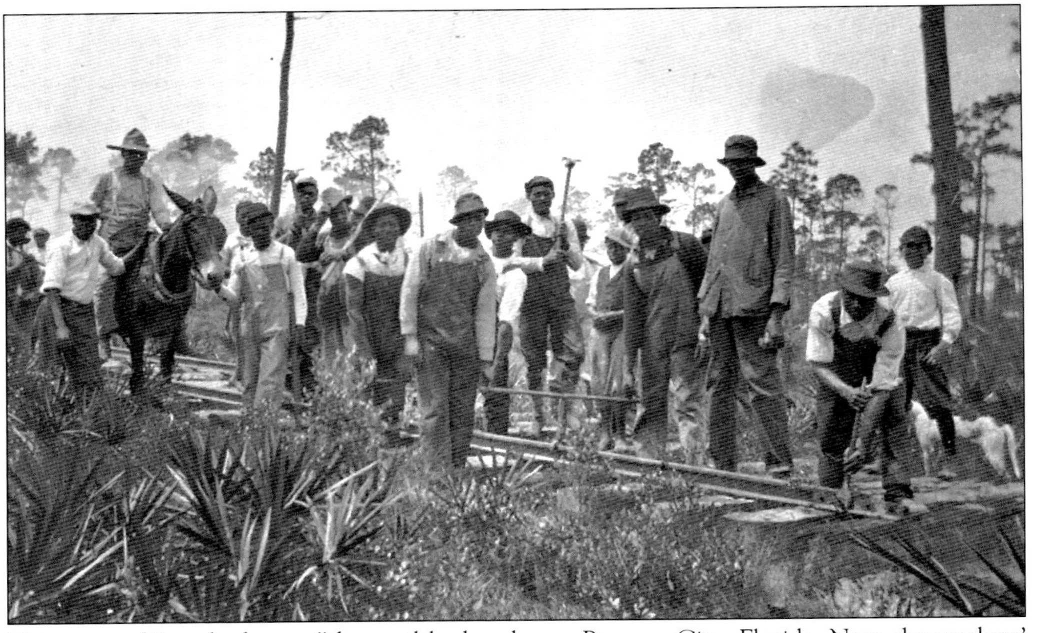

This gang of "gandy dancers" lays rail by hand near Panama City, Florida. Note the workers' tools—to the right, the long wrench for tightening connections; in the center, the rail clamp held by two men and the sledgehammer by the man behind; and at left, the pick across a man's shoulder. (Courtesy of the Bay County [Florida] Public Library.)

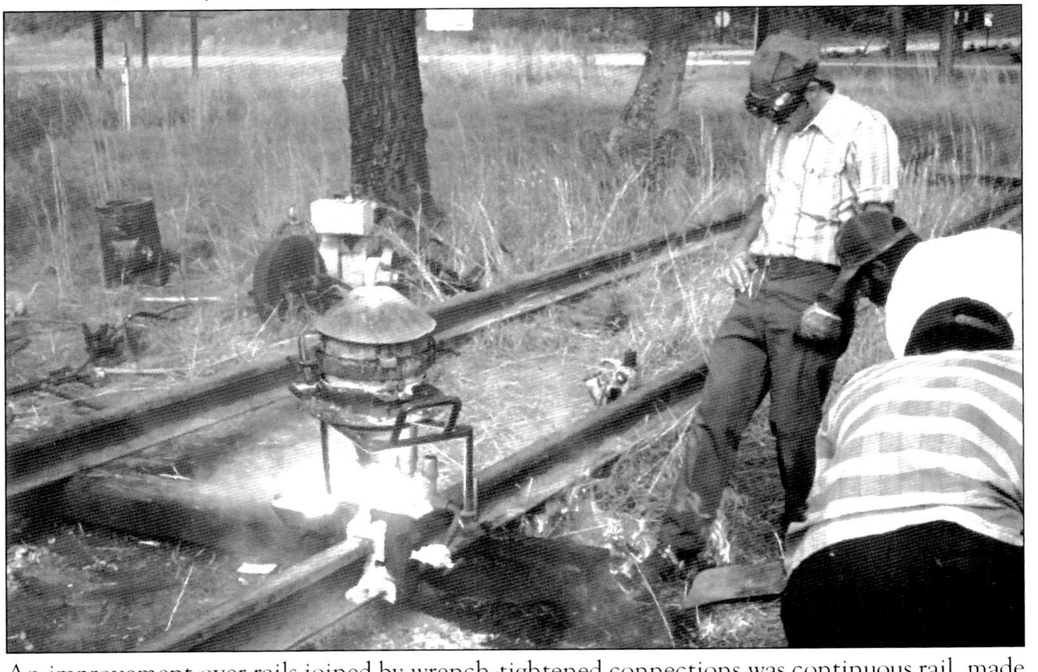

An improvement over rails joined by wrench-tightened connections was continuous rail, made possible by the "Thermfit" rail welder. In 1978, this Chattahoochee Industrial Railroad (CIRR) crew created continuous welded rail at the crossing of Georgia Highway 363. The worker in goggles is stomping out a small grass fire. (Courtesy of the CIRR.)

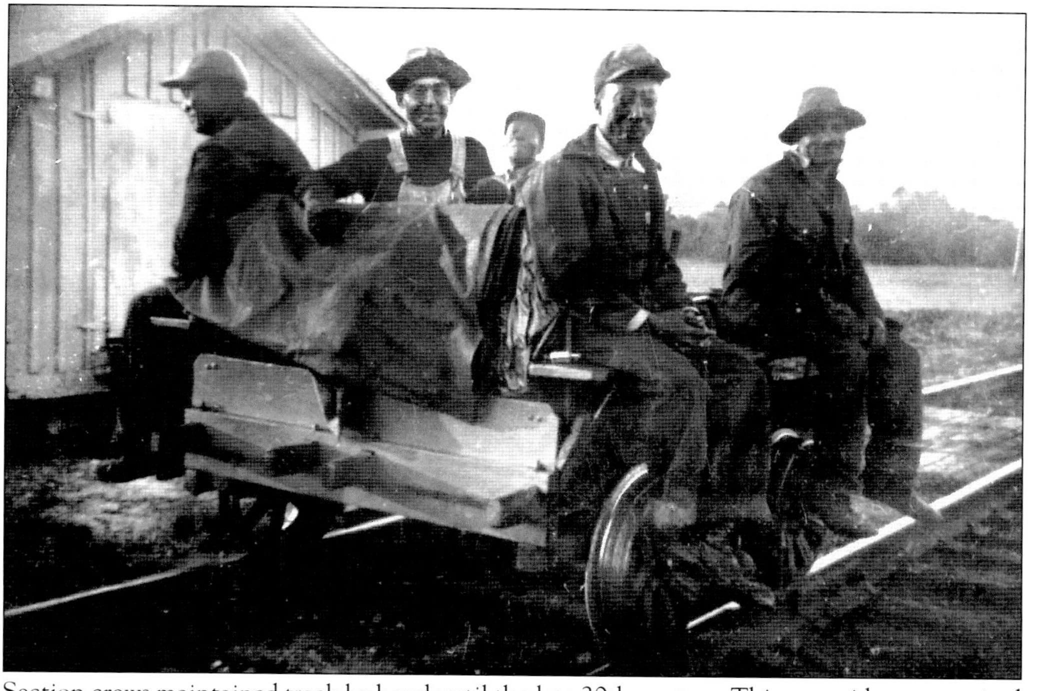

Section crews maintained track by hand until the late 20th century. This crew rides a motorized car to its work assignment on the ACL tracks in Dothan in 1949. From left to right are section hand Mr. ? Booth, foreman Dewey Benton, unidentified hand, section hand Rabe Jackson, and unidentified hand. (Courtesy of Billy Benton.)

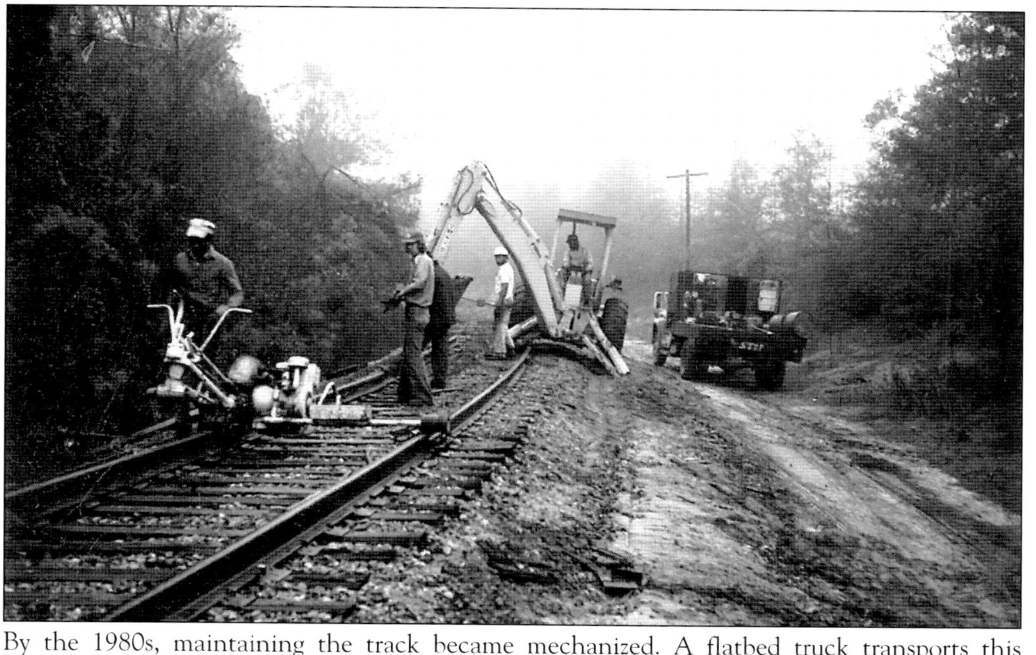

By the 1980s, maintaining the track became mechanized. A flatbed truck transports this Chattahoochee Industrial Railroad section crew and its equipment to their work site. (Courtesy of the CIRR.)

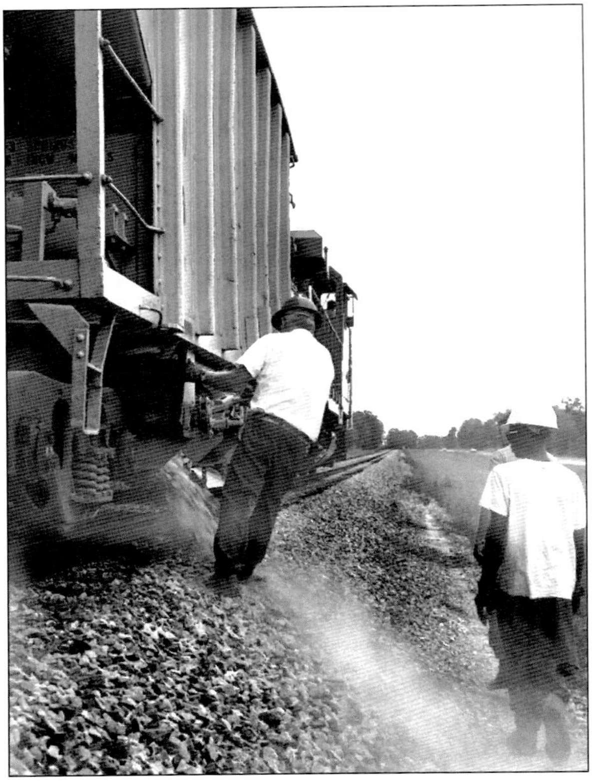

The Chattahoochee Industrial Railroad spends enormous effort to keep their heavily-used tracks in tip-top shape. This 1999 photograph shows Emmett Yoemens and crew adding crushed-rock ballast to the CIRR track from a hopper car. (Courtesy of the CIRR.)

This CIRR employee sprays the tracks with herbicide to prevent weed and grass growth. His sprayer is attached to a "high-rider" dump truck equipped with a custom hydraulic system to lower the flanged wheels that allow it to ride on the rail tracks. (Courtesy of the CIRR.)

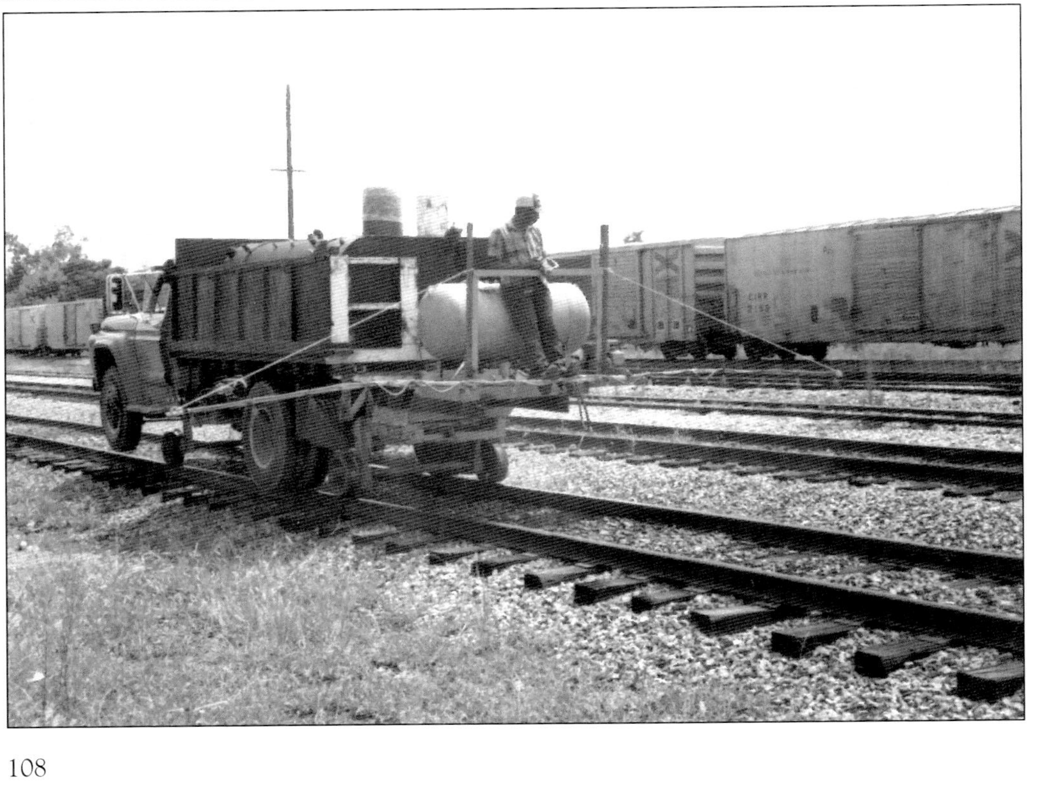

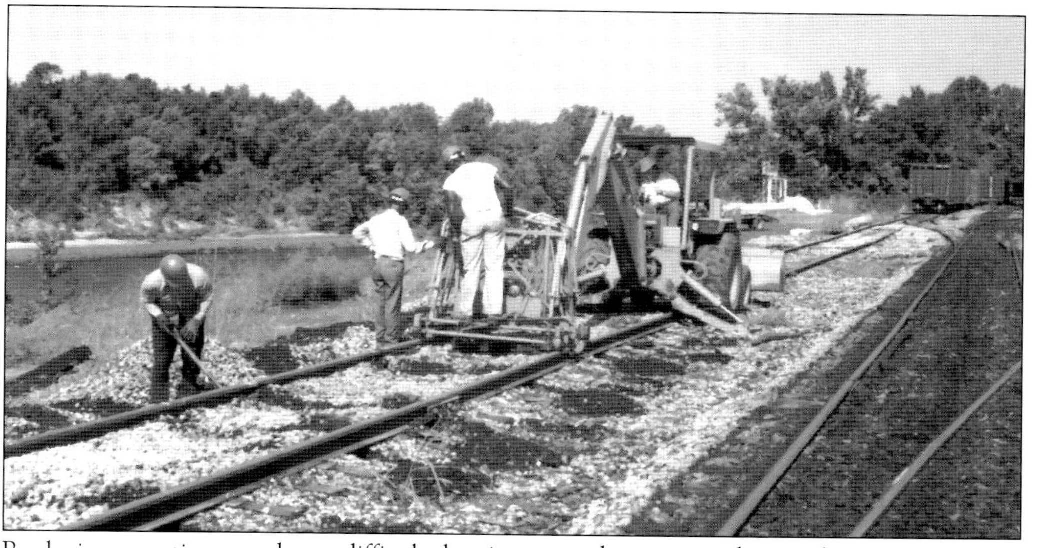

Replacing crossties was always difficult, but it was made easier in this mechanized era. Here, workmen on the Chattahoochee Industrial Railroad use a specialized tool attached to a backhoe to remove, reset, and align crossties. (Courtesy of the CIRR.)

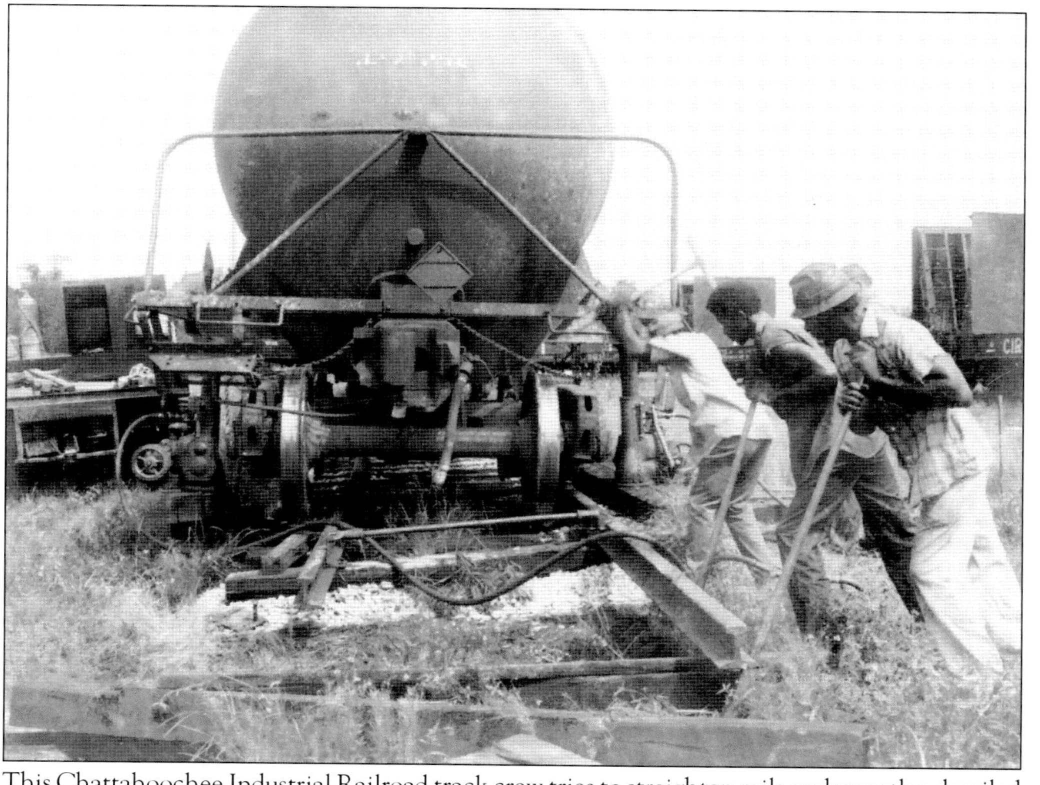

This Chattahoochee Industrial Railroad track crew tries to straighten rails underneath a derailed tanker car. Note the rail spacer holding the rails to gauge. This crew does the perennial work of the "gandy dancers," setting rails by hand and straightening track by pry bar and raw muscle. (Courtesy of the CIRR.)

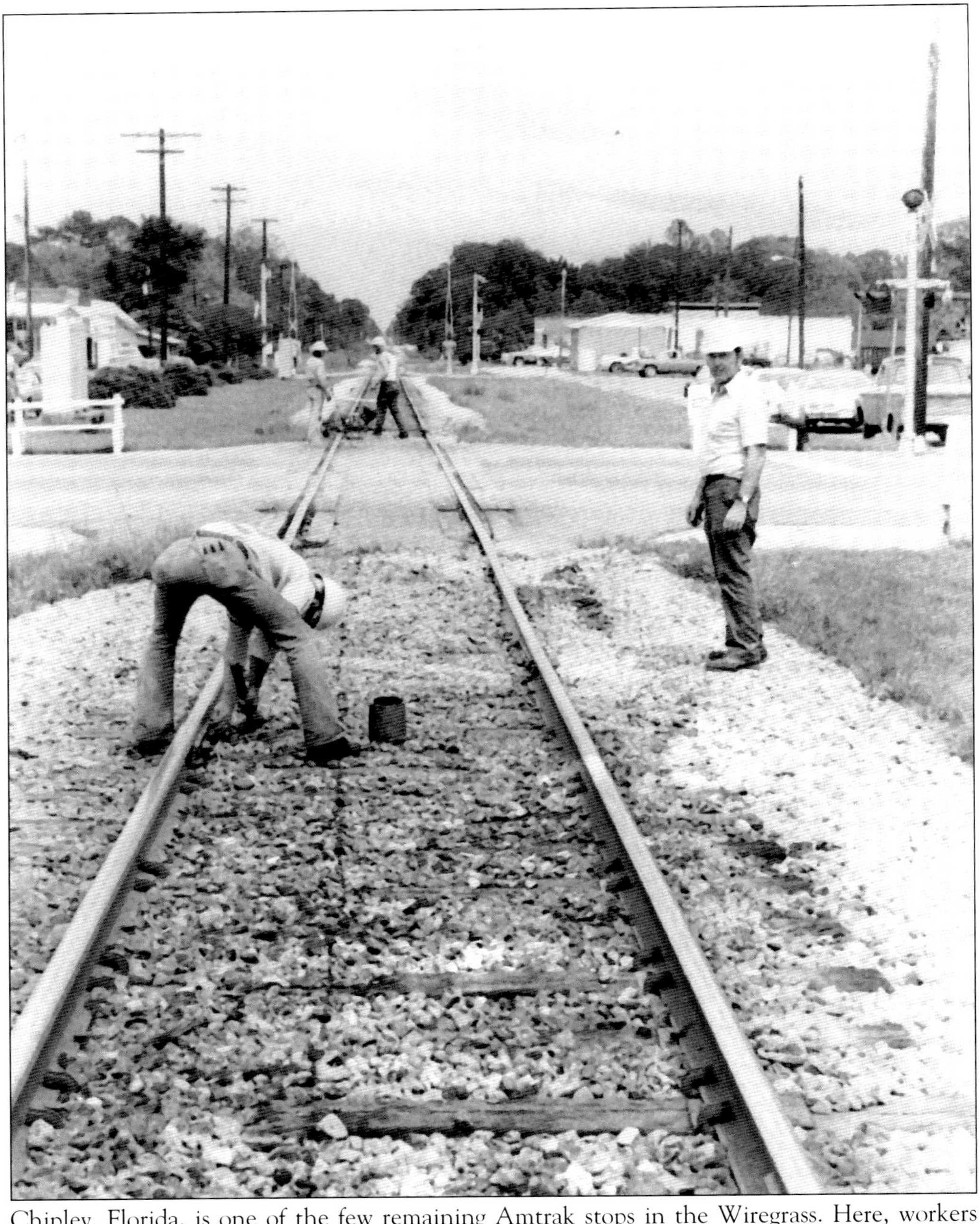

Chipley, Florida, is one of the few remaining Amtrak stops in the Wiregrass. Here, workers maintain the tracks at a downtown Chipley crossing for both passenger and freight service across north Florida. (Courtesy of the Washington County [Florida] Historical Society.)

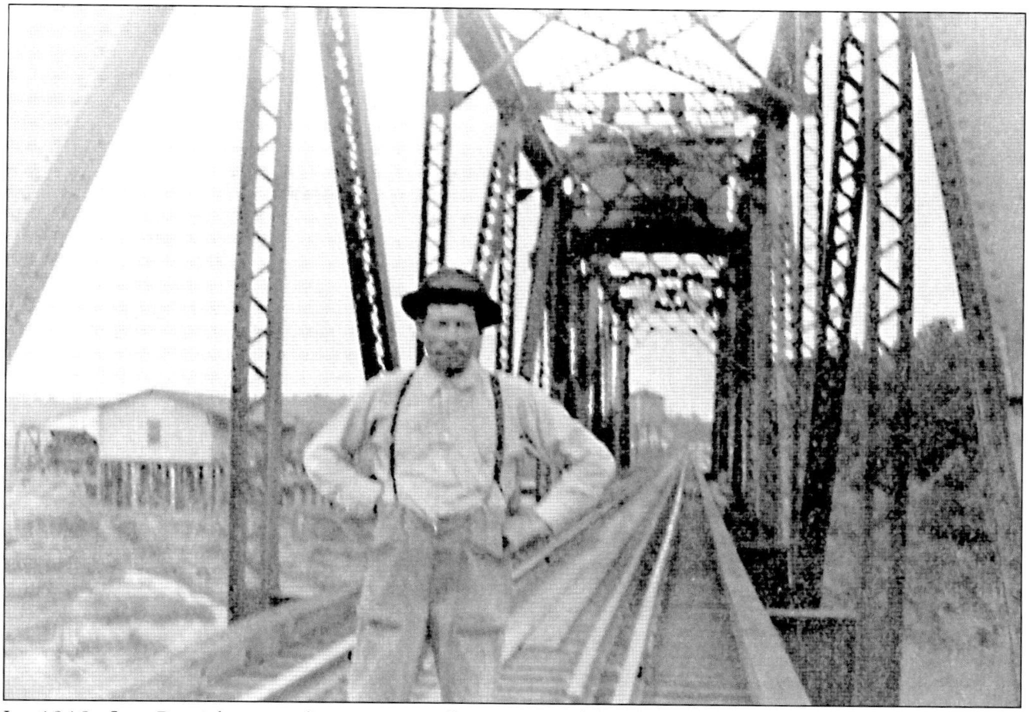

In 1918, Joe Parrish served as section foreman and bridge tender for this span across the Chattahoochee River at Alaga, Alabama. Steamboats unloaded their freight into the warehouses to the left, and train crews transferred the goods onto railcars. (Courtesy of the Tom Solomon Collection, DLF.)

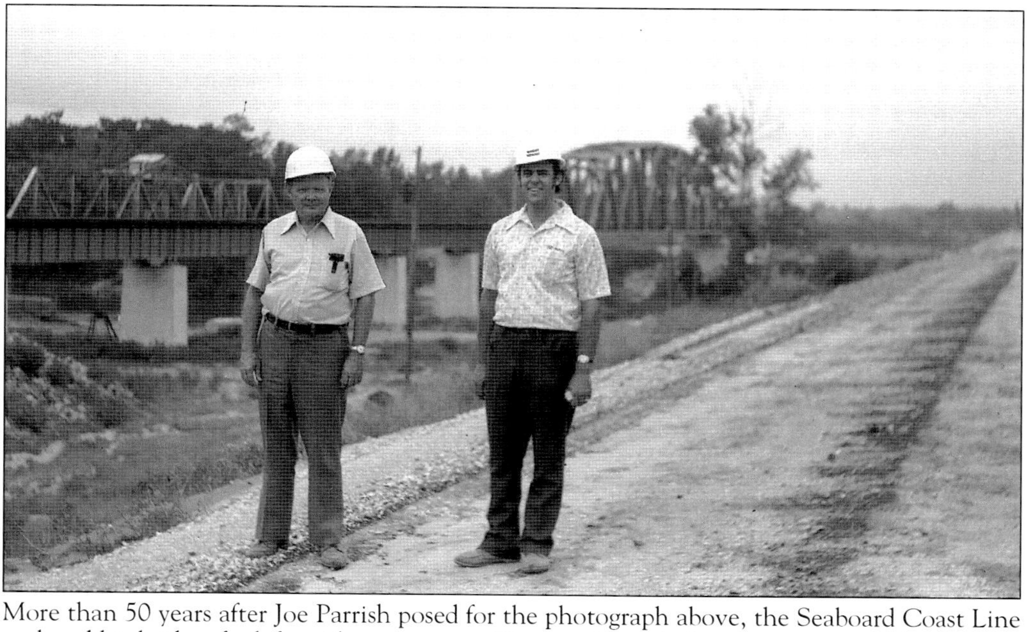

More than 50 years after Joe Parrish posed for the photograph above, the Seaboard Coast Line replaced his bridge, far left, with a new span. These unidentified engineers pose in front of the modern structure they built. (Courtesy of the Tom Solomon Collection, DLF.)

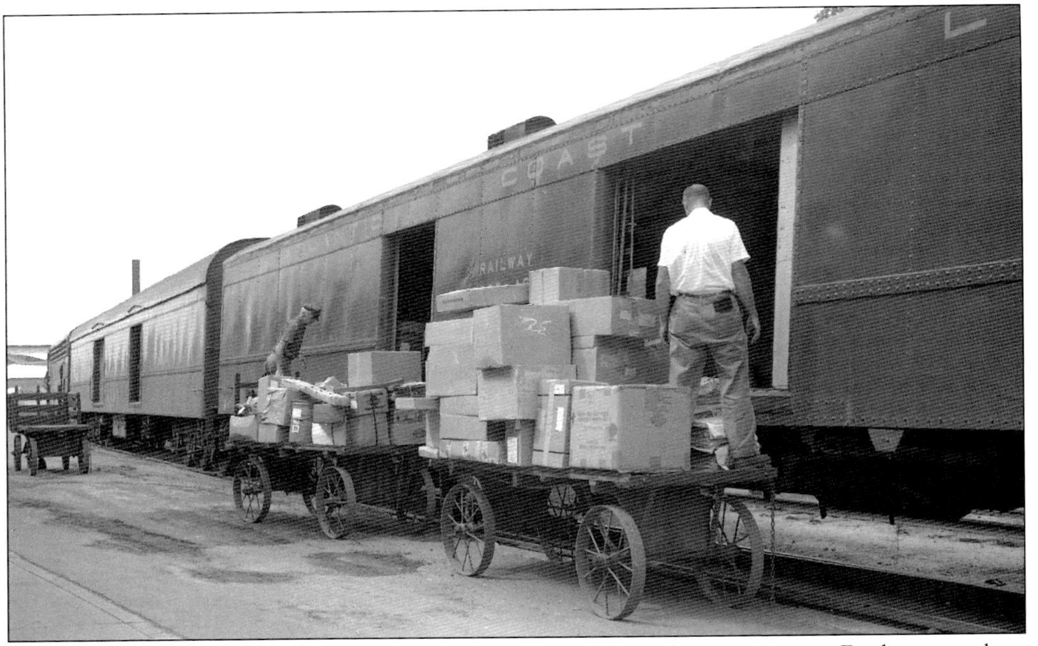

On September 3, 1965, ACL trains No. 180 and No. 189 ran late, arriving at Dothan together. These station workers scurry to unload baggage and parcels from one train and then the other. Note the old but still sturdy and usable baggage carts. (Courtesy of the Tom Solomon Collection, DLF.)

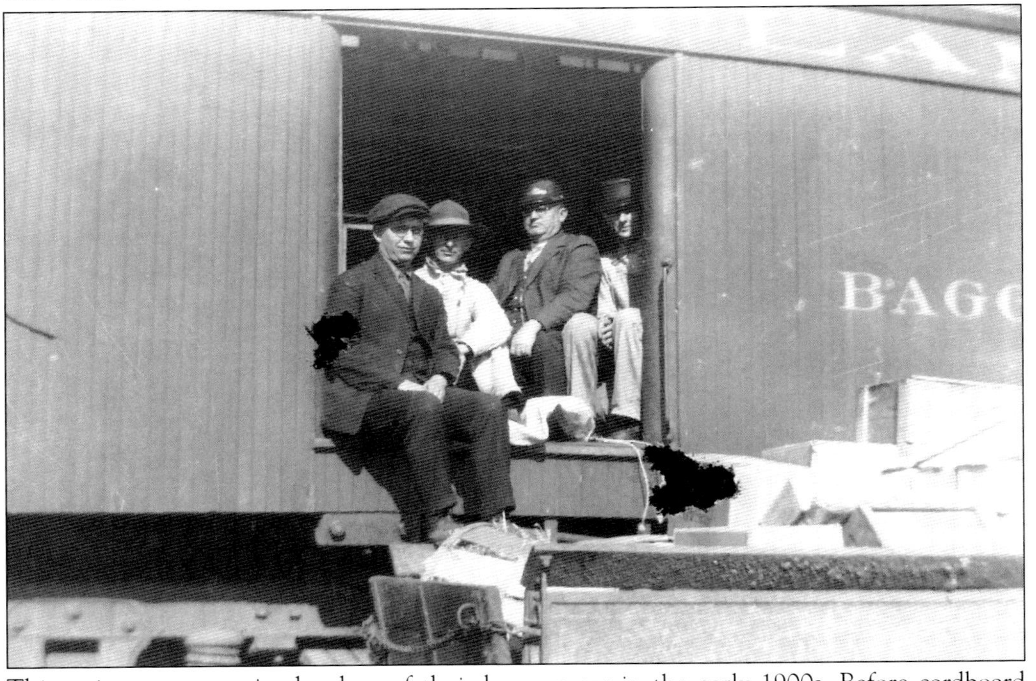

This train crew poses in the door of their baggage car in the early 1900s. Before cardboard became the preferred packaging medium, goods were packed in wooden crates. Nevertheless, baggage handling never really changes. (Courtesy of the Tom Solomon Collection, DLF.)

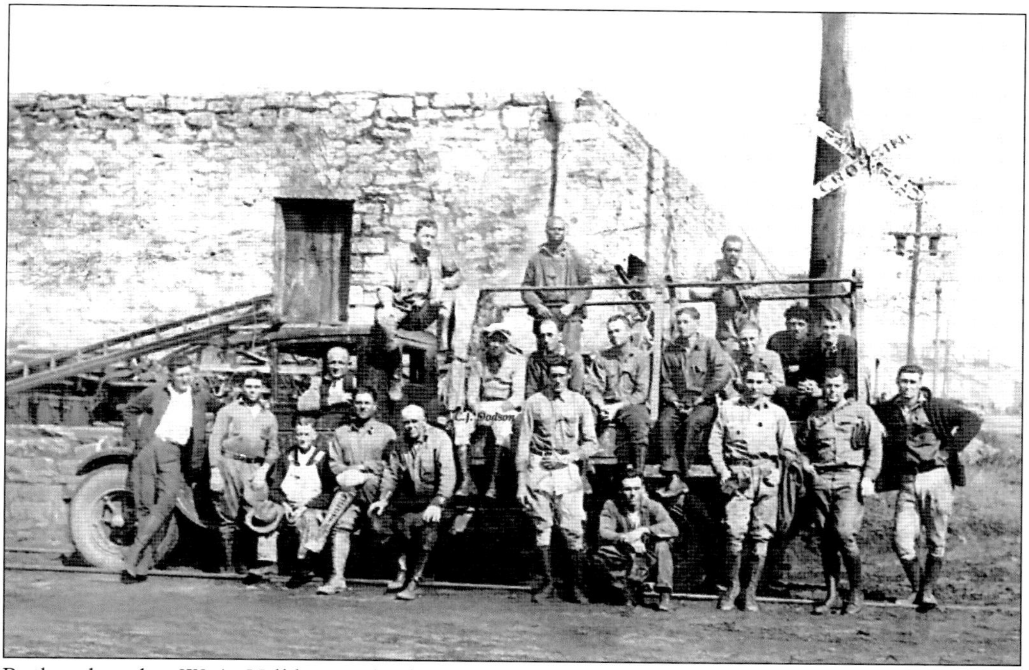

Railroad worker W.A. Hill began the first telephone service in Ozark, Alabama, when he strung a line between his home and the rail depot about 1900. He opened a local phone company in 1903. Phone companies, like telegraph companies before them, used crews like this to construct lines along rail routes. (Courtesy of Gordon Dodson.)

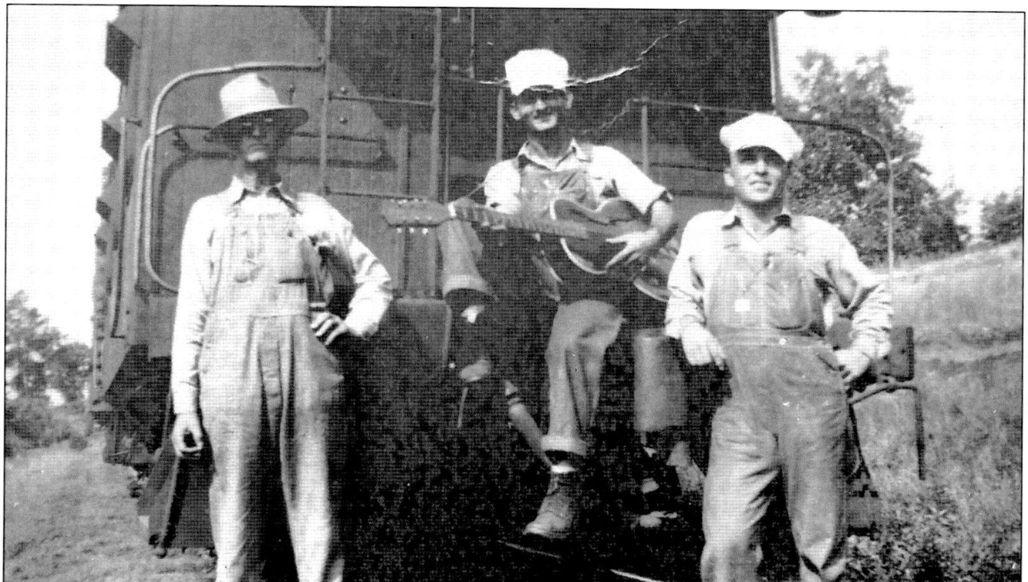

This photo of a train crew is unusual because of their jauntiness and the photo site—the rear of the train rather than the engine. The man with the guitar is probably the rear brakeman, who would have had space and time to play the instrument in the caboose. (Courtesy of the Tom Solomon Collection, DLF.)

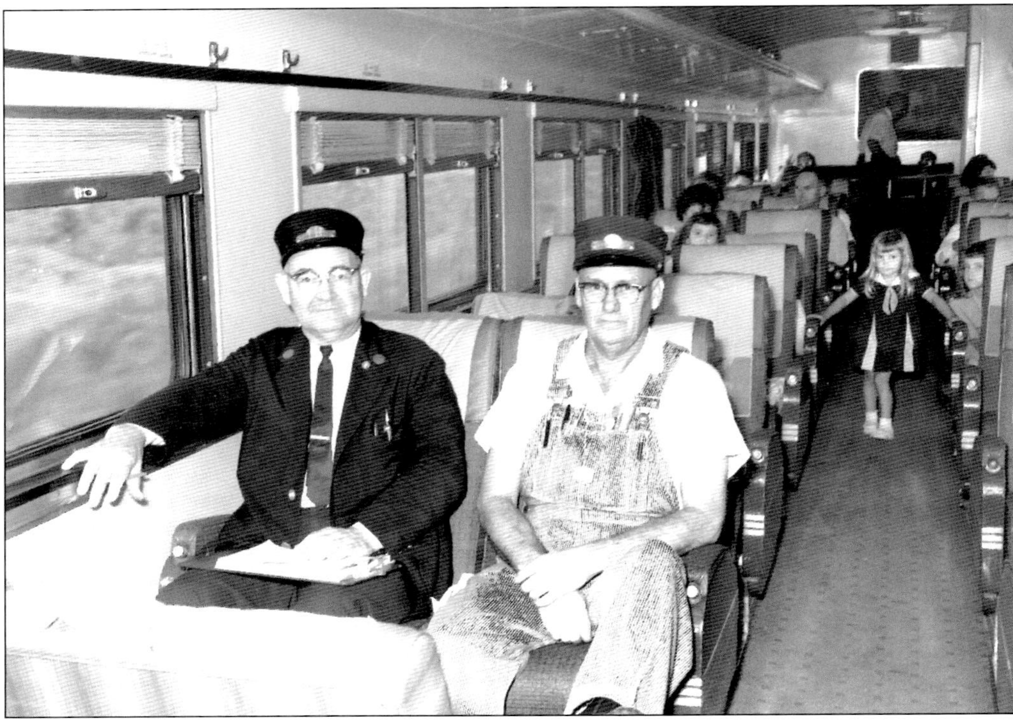

After the 1950s, passenger trains stopped using cabooses, leaving train crews without an office and without separate travel accommodations. In this June 28, 1964 photograph, conductor D.W. Davidson and baggage master Mr. Whitehead ride in a passenger car. (Courtesy of the Tom Solomon Collection, DLF.)

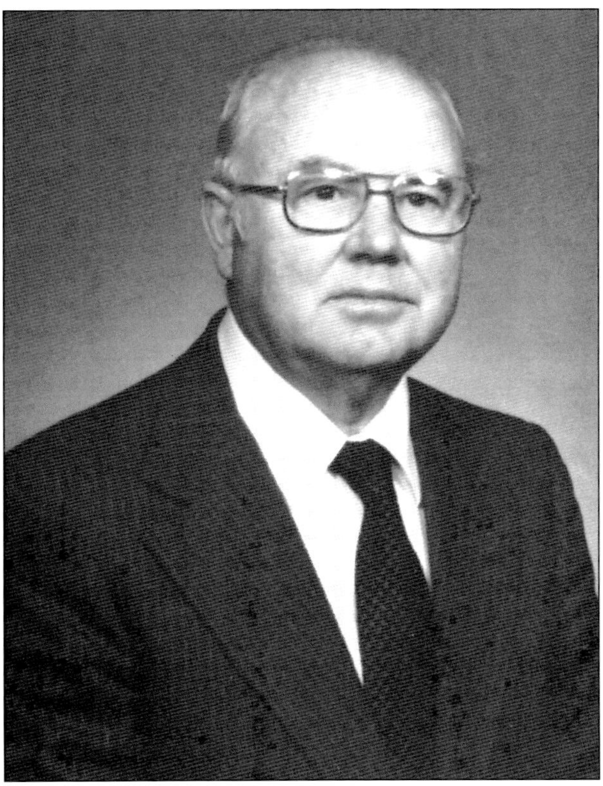

Conductors and engineers held the most powerful positions on moving trains, but when they stopped at a depot, the station master was in charge. Tommy Henderson, a third-generation railroad man born in an Alaga, Alabama section house, served as the ACL station master in Ashford, Alabama, from 1950 to 1966. He worked in the Dothan ACL depot until his retirement. (Courtesy of the Ashford Depot Restoration Foundation.)

Railroaders usually worked long careers. Here, conductor ? McIntosh boards his train for Ben Harper's final run as engineer on February 28, 1964. Harper worked the railroad for 45 years. (Courtesy of the Tom Solomon Collection, DLF.)

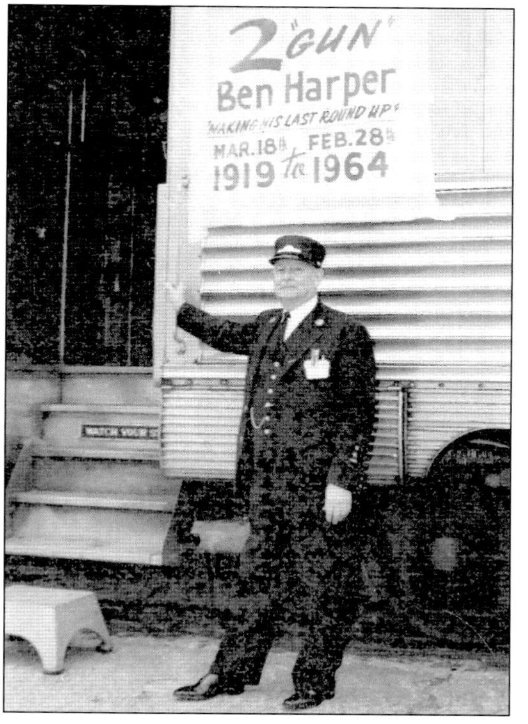

The happy fellow in the center of this photo is Jack Siglar, retiring engineer on the ACL. Mrs. Siglar affixes a service pin to her husband's lapel in the Dothan yard. The engine in the background is an ALCO RS-1, ACL No. 665, and is probably Siglar's last assignment. (Courtesy of the Tom Solomon Collection, DLF.)

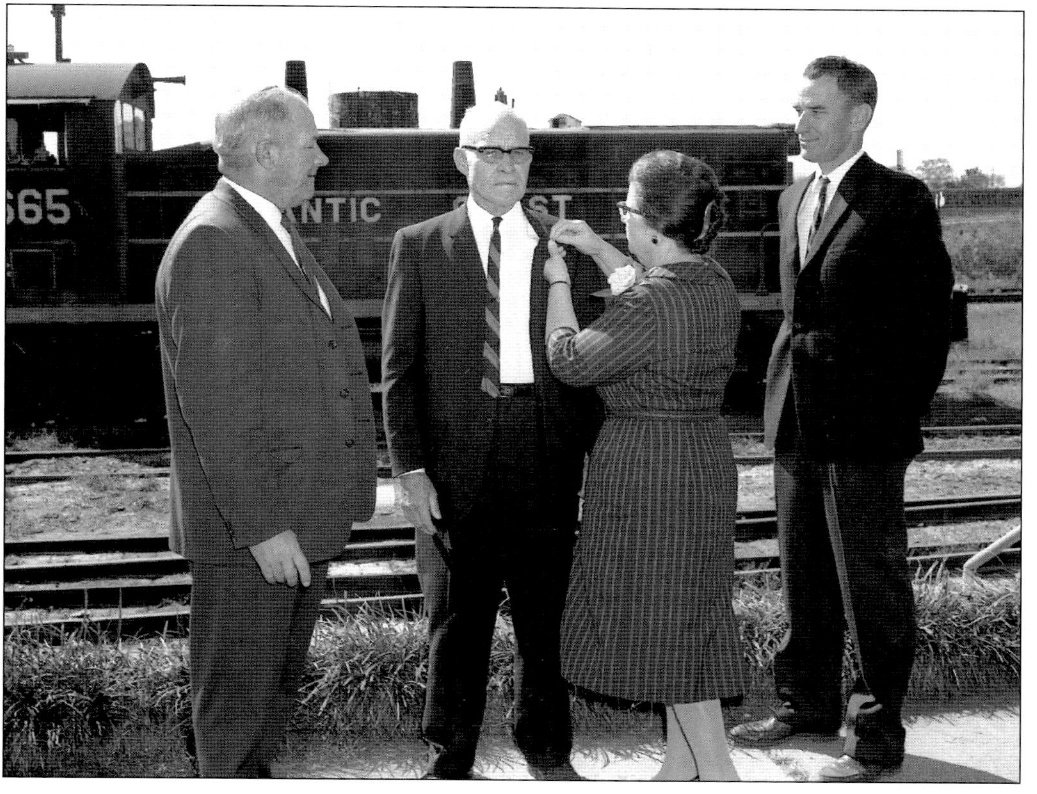

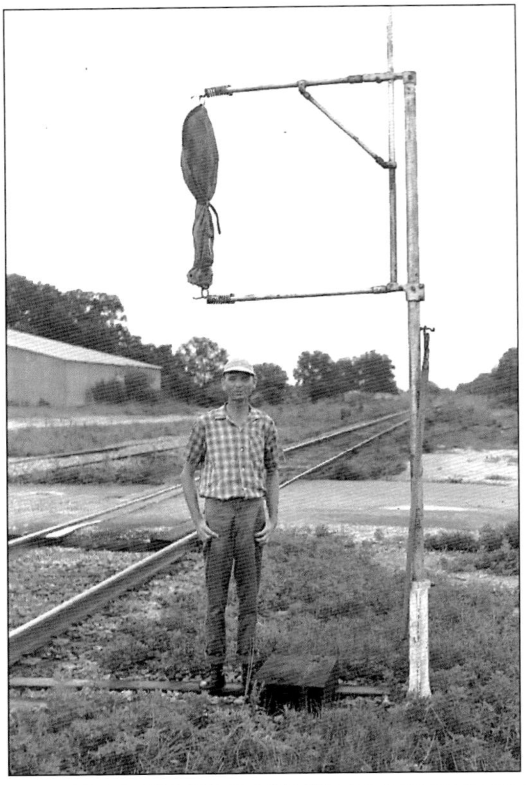

Trains carried the mail, so postal employees worked at the depots. Julius Boreland waits at the mail crane in Pinckard, Alabama, on July 3, 1964. The following business day, the United States Postal Service halted use of mail cranes at whistle stops like Pinckard, thus sending Mr. Boreland into retirement. (Courtesy of the Tom Solomon Collection, DLF.)

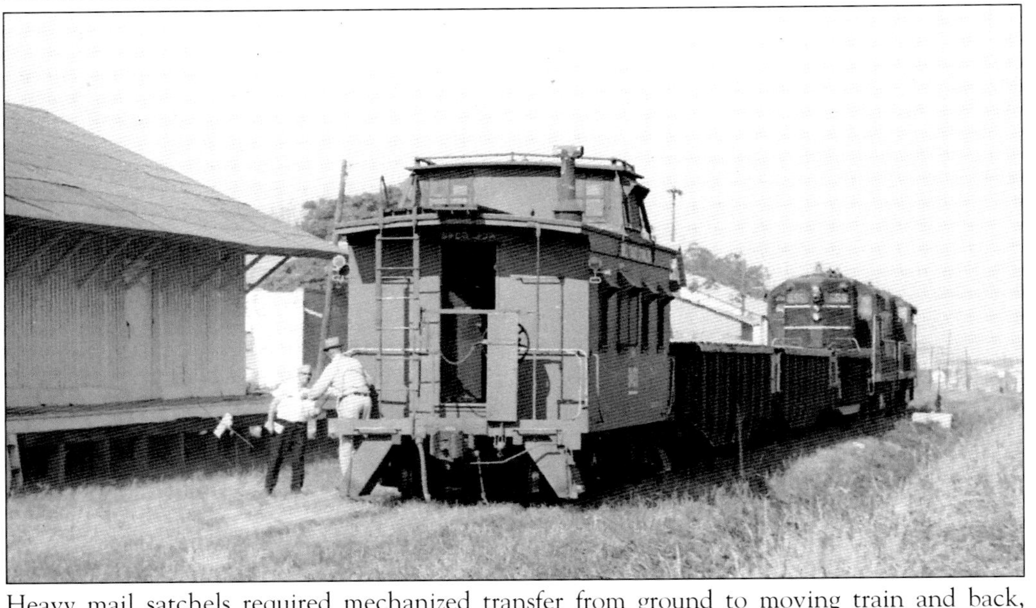

Heavy mail satchels required mechanized transfer from ground to moving train and back, but the lighter interoffice communications could be transferred by hand. Here, conductor ? McIntosh catches the order hoop from ACL station agent H.H. McAilily on the Abbeville, Alabama branch. McAilily was Headland's last depot agent. (Courtesy of the Tom Solomon Collection, DLF.)

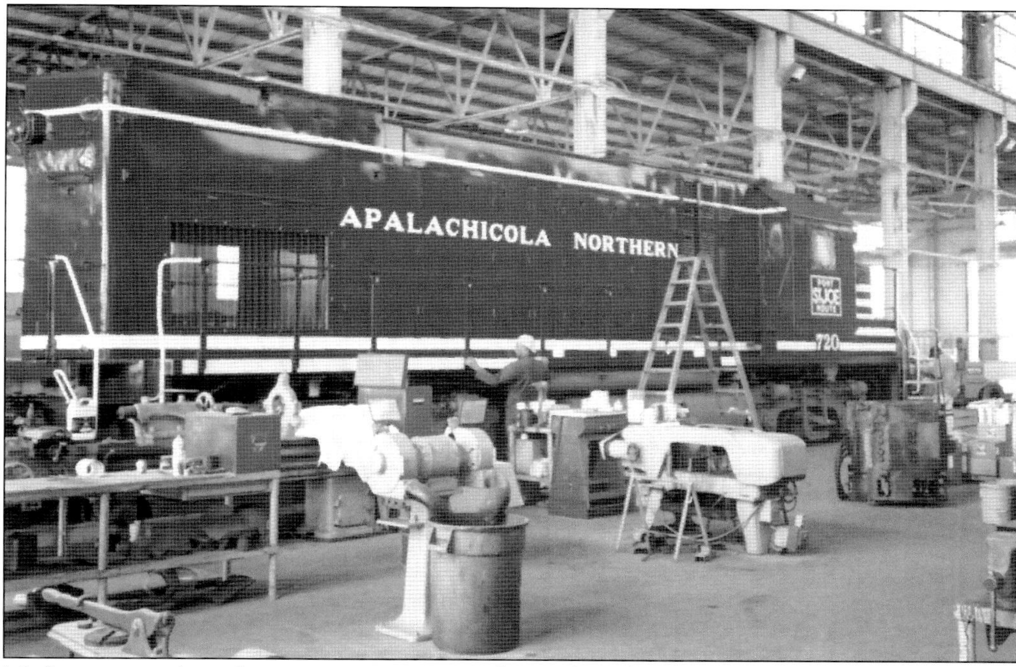

Modern repair shops have grown more complex with technological advances in locomotives and rail cars. In this c. 2000 photograph, the Apalachicola Northern No. 720 receives routine maintenance. (Courtesy of David Kirkland.)

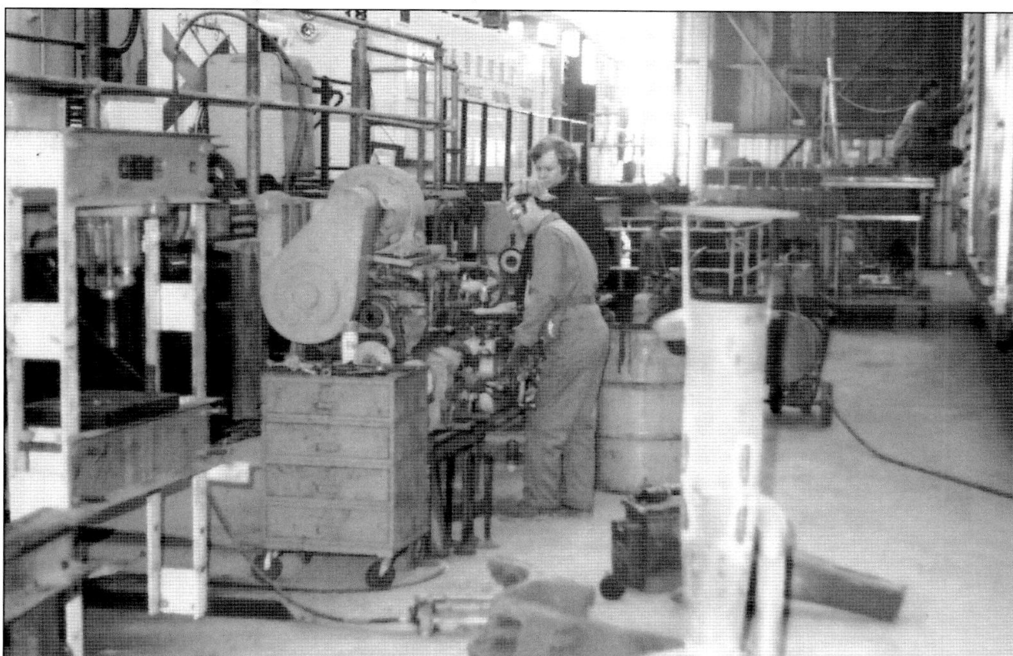

Even busy modern shops required substantially fewer workers than their older counterparts. In the Chattahoochee Industrial Railroad shop at Cedar Springs, Georgia, Tony Douglas, Bobby Shelley, and Lemuel Ross work on two locomotives and a box car. (Courtesy of the CIRR.)

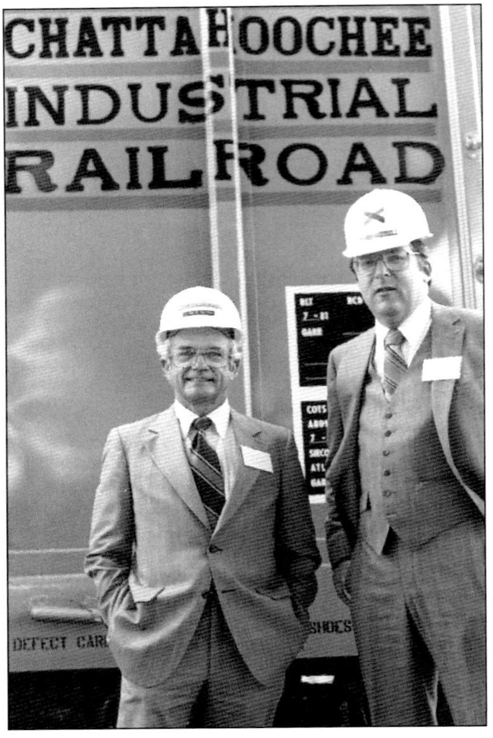

Although the Chattahoochee Industrial Railroad hauled freight for a variety of manufacturing companies in Early County, Georgia, its largest customer was and is the Great Southern Paper mill. In 1981, Great Southern traffic manager Reid Smith (left) and Paul Angelhoff pose with a new Plate C boxcar designed to haul extra large paper loads. (Courtesy of the CIRR.)

This set of drawings accompanied the new national standard for Plate C boxcars carrying rolls of kraft paper in 1980. Using this system developed by Reid Smith of Great Southern Paper and implemented on the CIRR, railroads used 20 percent fewer cars, and the paper mill saved over $2 million in shipping costs per year. (Courtesy of Reid Smith.)

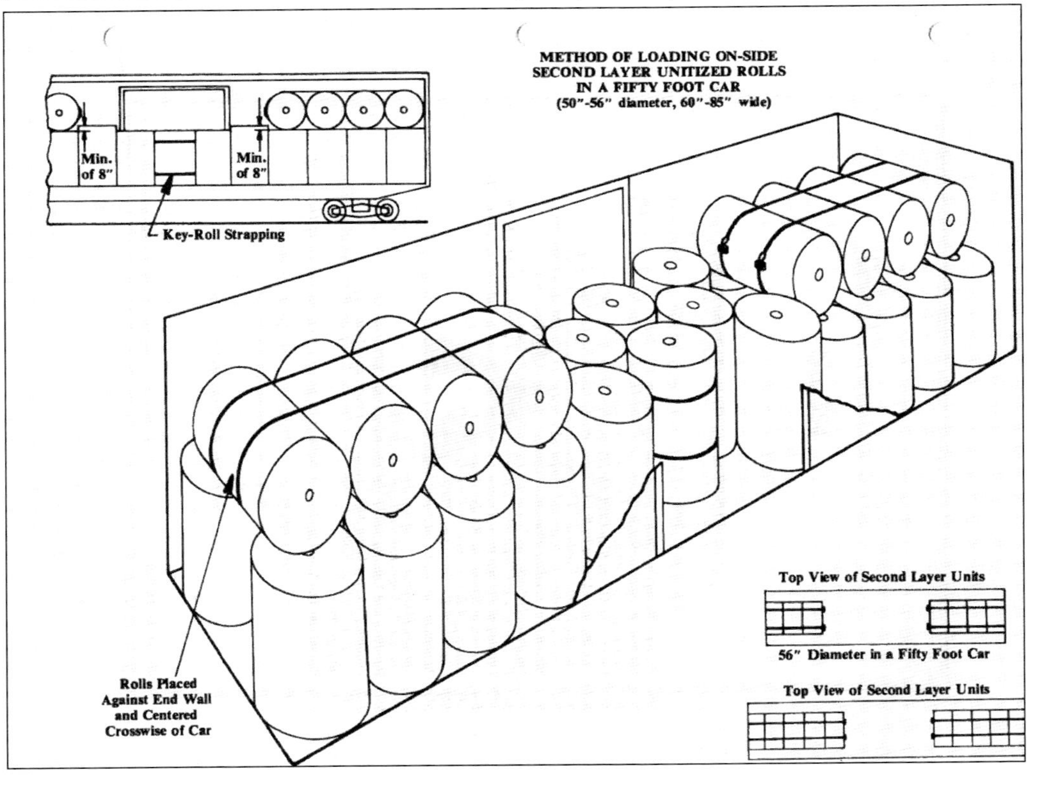

Six

Railroad Reflections

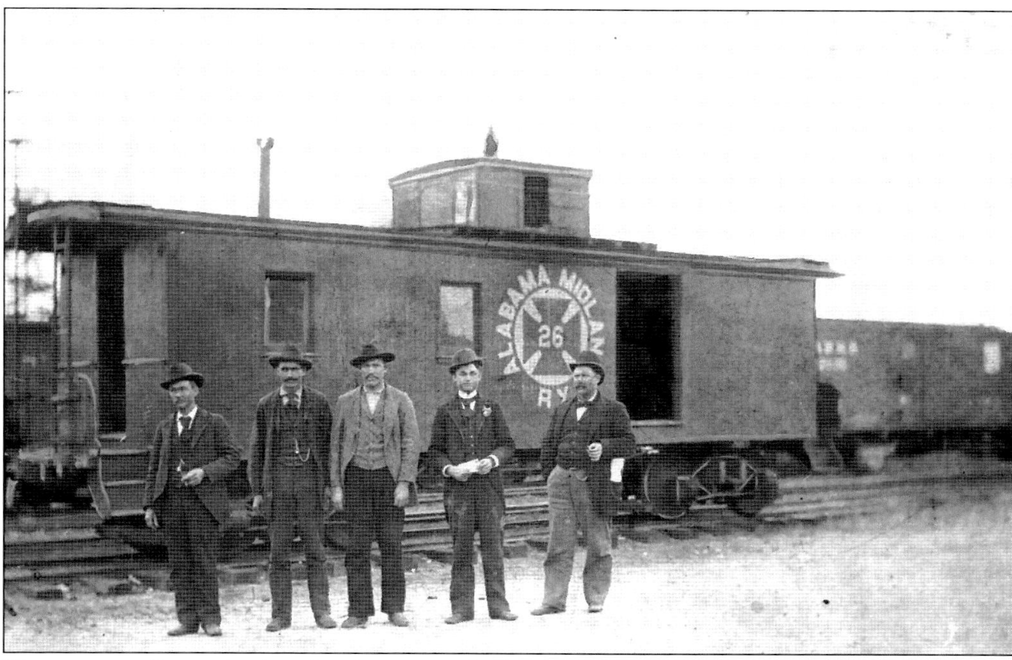

This, reportedly, is the first freight run to Dothan on the Bainbridge-to-Montgomery route of the Alabama Midland Railway. Note the AM logo for Caboose No. 26 immediately behind this gallery. Everett Crawford stands in the center. (Courtesy of the Houston-Love Memorial Library, Dothan, Alabama.)

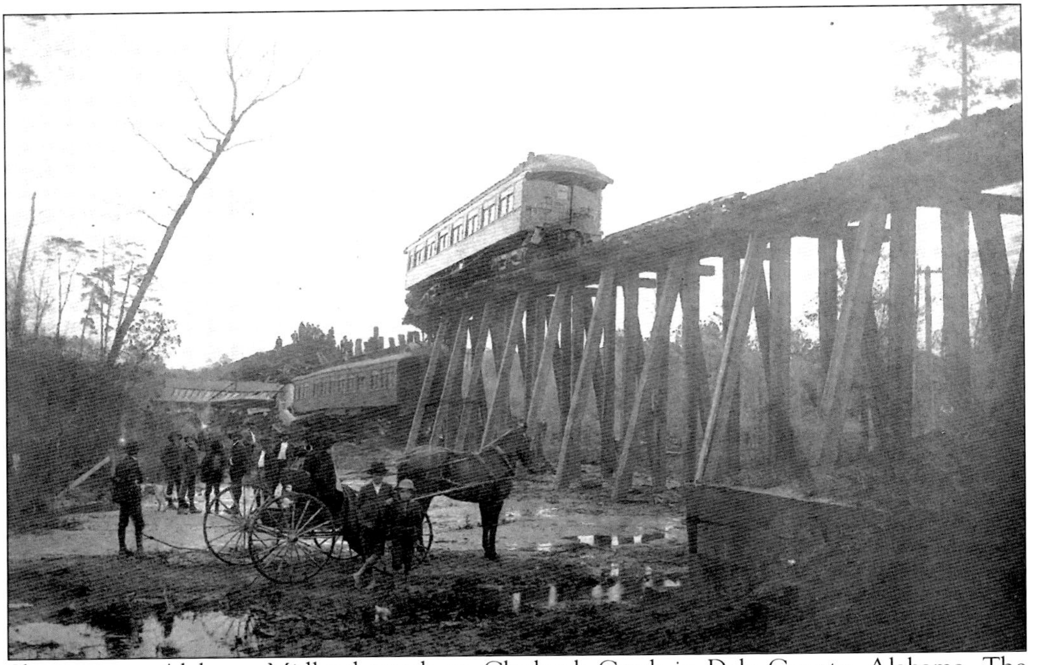

Shown is an Alabama Midland wreck on Claybank Creek in Dale County, Alabama. The train later became ACL No. 58. Facing east, this photo shows coaches and a narrow-vestibule Pullman car. (Courtesy of the Tom Solomon Collection, DLF.)

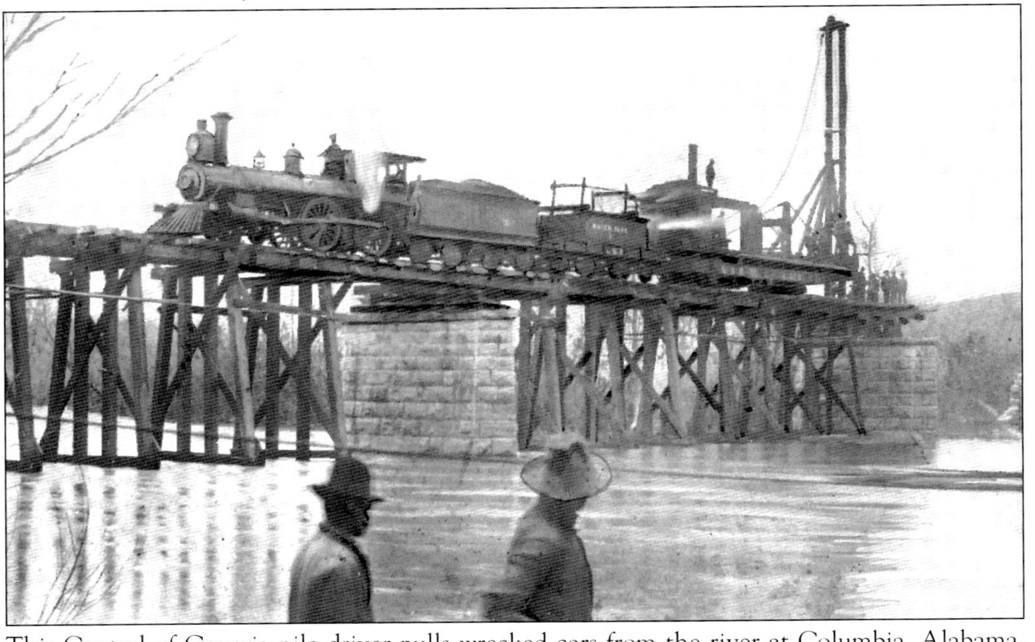

This Central of Georgia pile driver pulls wrecked cars from the river at Columbia, Alabama, after crossed signals led a train to cross while the bridge was still open. A passenger rescued his dog from the mail car after it caught fire. The railroad suspended the baggage clerk because he did not rescue the United States mail from that same car. (Courtesy of the Houston-Love Memorial Library, Dothan, Alabama.)

This image depicts a wreck near Youngstown, Florida, of an early excursion on the Bay Line Railroad. (Courtesy of the Houston-Love Memorial Library, Dothan, Alabama.)

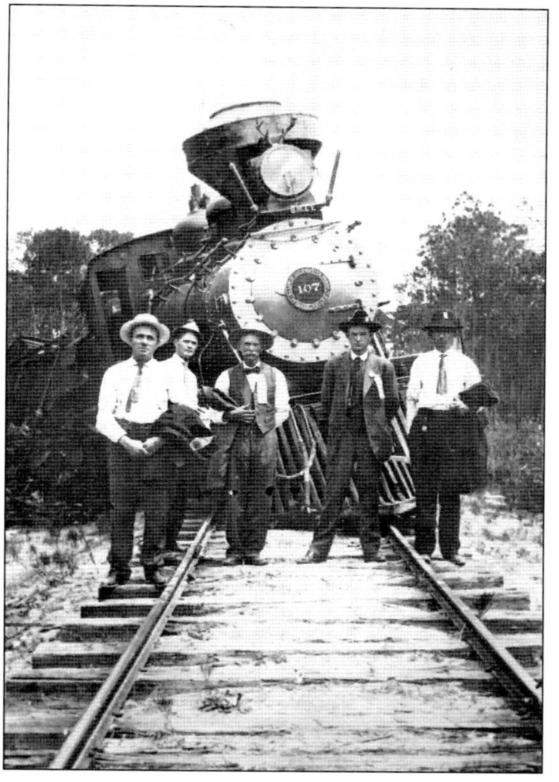

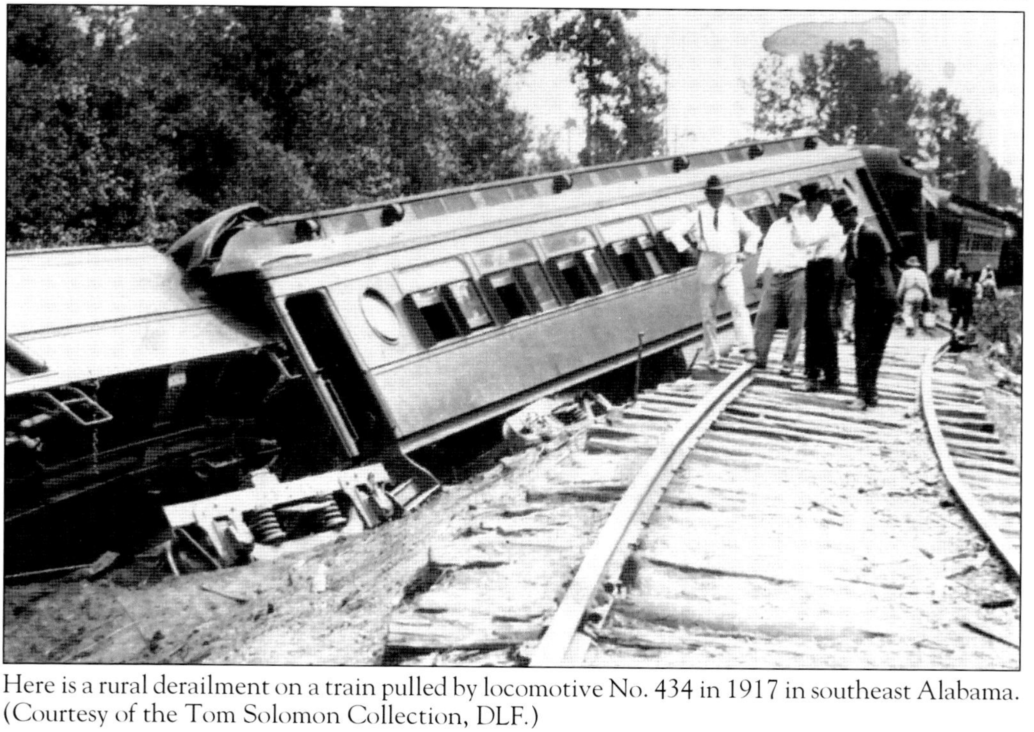

Here is a rural derailment on a train pulled by locomotive No. 434 in 1917 in southeast Alabama. (Courtesy of the Tom Solomon Collection, DLF.)

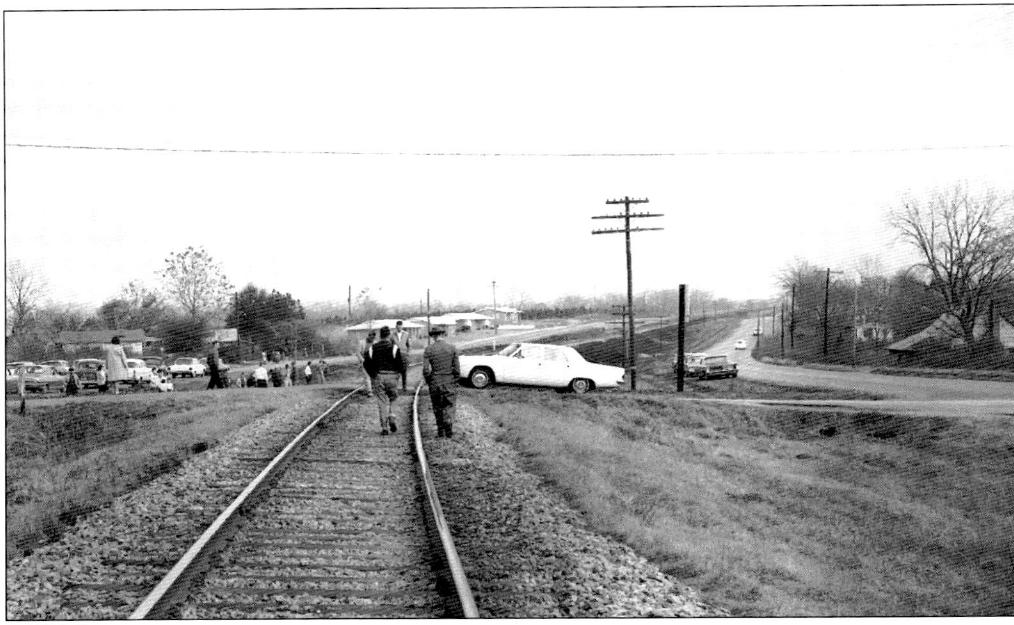

This photo was taken shortly after a tragic wreck at a railroad crossing in Midland City in Dale County, Alabama, on December 7, 1963. This accident killed 12 members of the Henry Langford family who were riding in a station wagon. Only a one year-old child survived the wreck. This scene is looking toward Dothan. (Courtesy of the Tom Solomon Collection, DLF.)

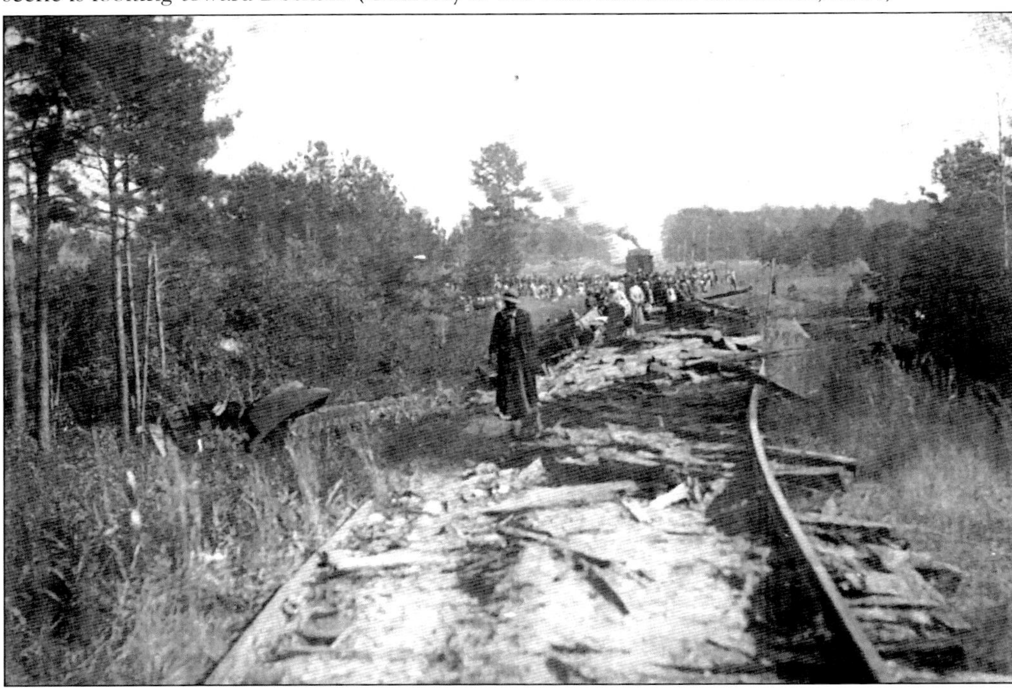

This November 13, 1913 derailment between Clayton and Eufaula in Barbour County, Alabama, devastated the tracks, but it was worse for train passengers. Thirteen, including prominent citizen Monroe Floyd, died. (Courtesy of the Henry County Historical Group.)

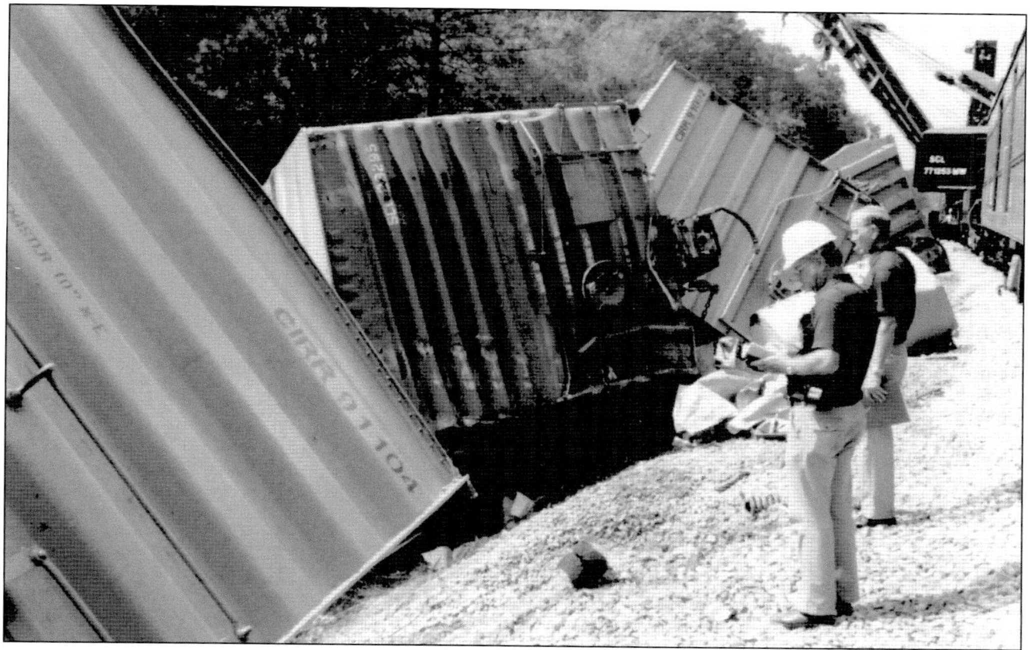

Freight accidents usually cause fewer deaths than passenger accidents, but they can damage expensive rolling stock and goods. These boxcars of the Chattahoochee Industrial Railroad are being hauled out of a ditch by a Seaboard Coast Line crane and wrecker. (Courtesy of the CIRR.)

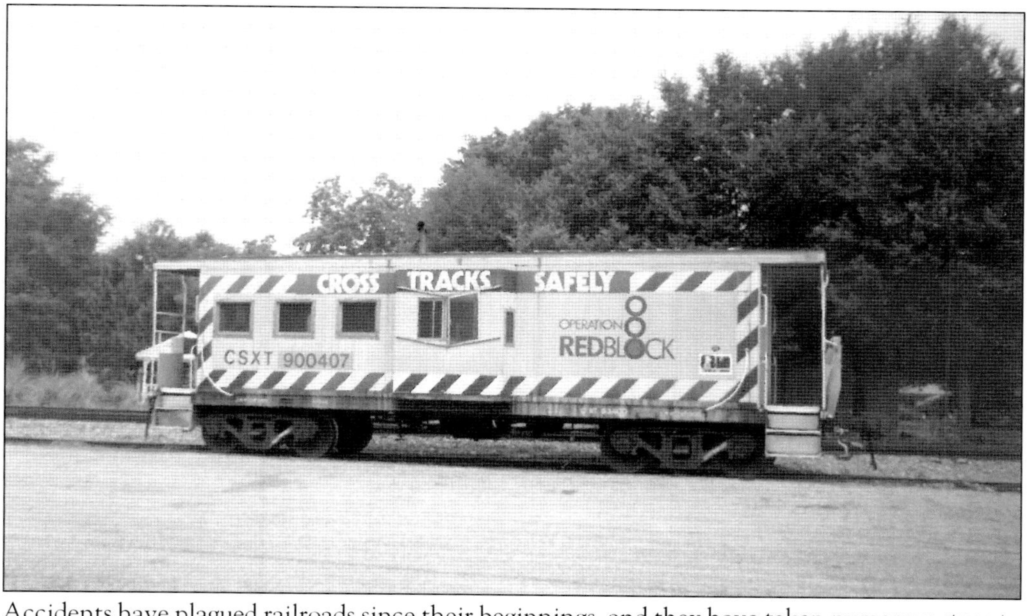

Accidents have plagued railroads since their beginnings, and they have taken numerous steps to make themselves safer. In the 19th century, railroads established time zones across the country to coordinate train schedules and prevent wrecks. In the 1980s, they began a multi-million dollar campaign to halt fatalities from drivers and pedestrians unsafely crossing tracks. (Courtesy of David Kirkland.)

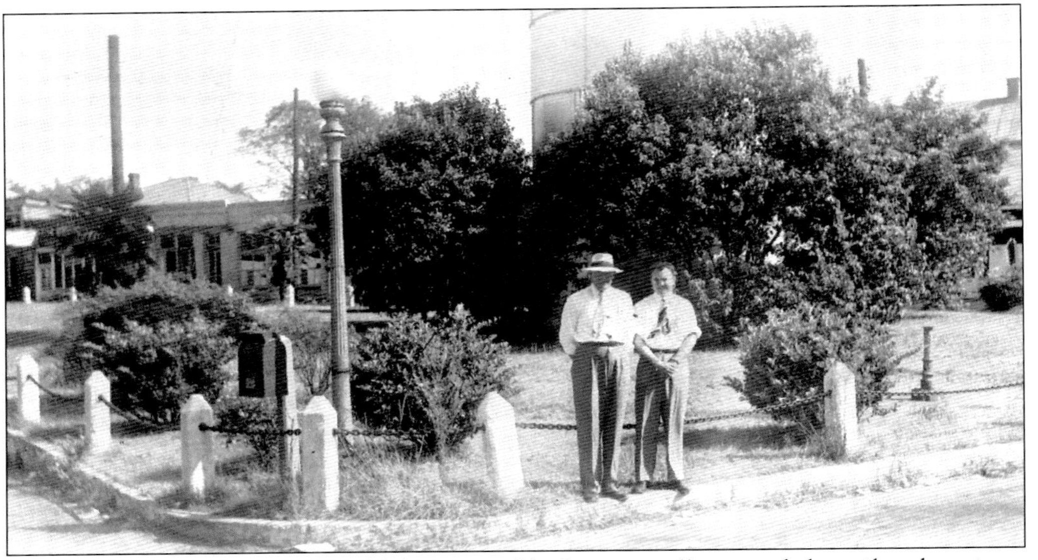

Urban blight has ruined many old downtown blocks, especially around the railroad stations. Standing in the park that once graced Dothan's "Standpipe" and the ACL depot are Tommy Henderson and J.T. Weeks. The City of Dothan plans to restore this park, which has become just a slab of asphalt. (Courtesy of the Tom Solomon Collection, DLF.)

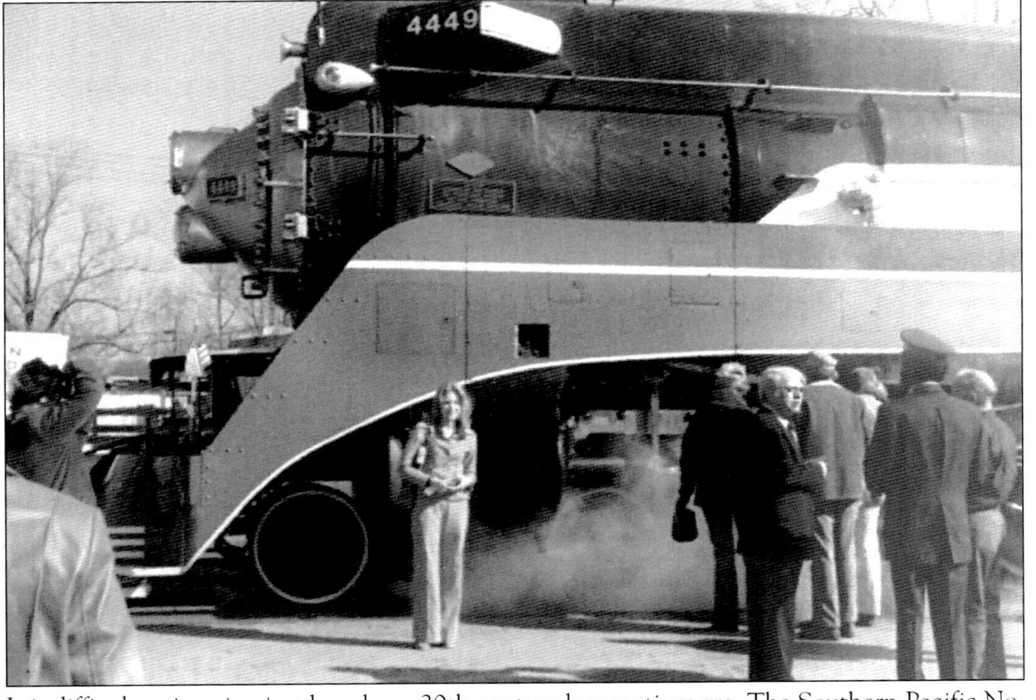

It is difficult to imagine just how large 20th century locomotives are. The Southern Pacific No. 4449 was built in 1941 at the Lima Locomotive Works in Ohio and is shown in this Dothan photograph after it was restored to pull the 26-car *American Freedom Train* in 1976–1977. The massive engine truly dominates everyone in the foreground. The No. 4449 is retired in Portland, Oregon. (Courtesy of Gordon Dodson.)

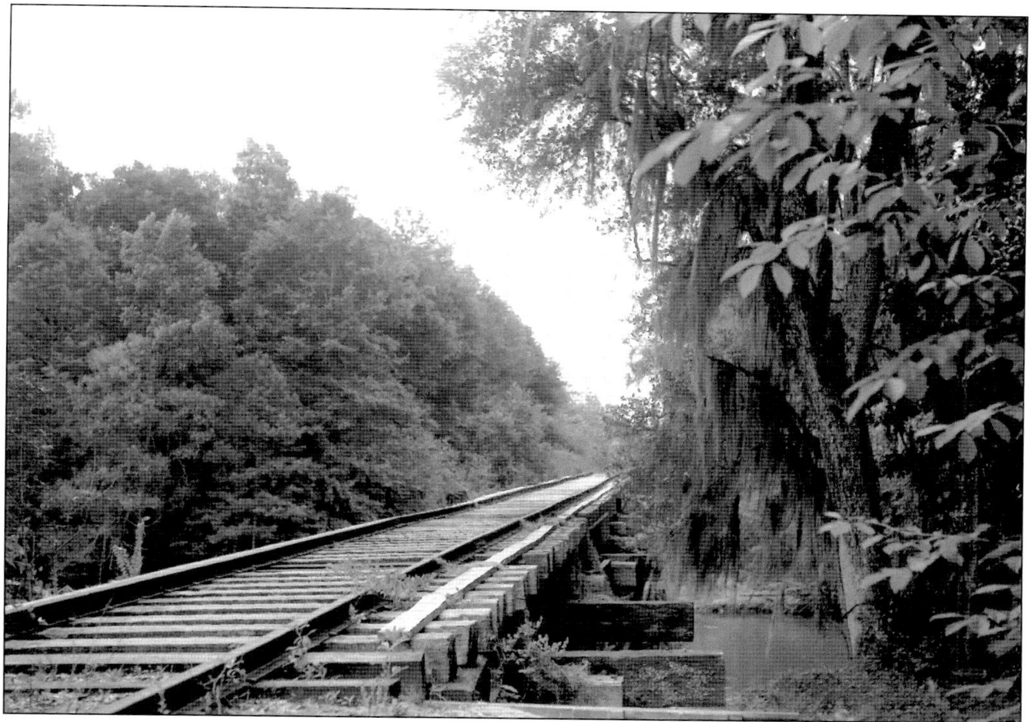

Nature slowly reclaims the abandoned tracks of the Marianna & Blountstown Railroad as they cross the trestle over the Chipola River in Florida. (Courtesy of the Tom Solomon Collection, DLF.)

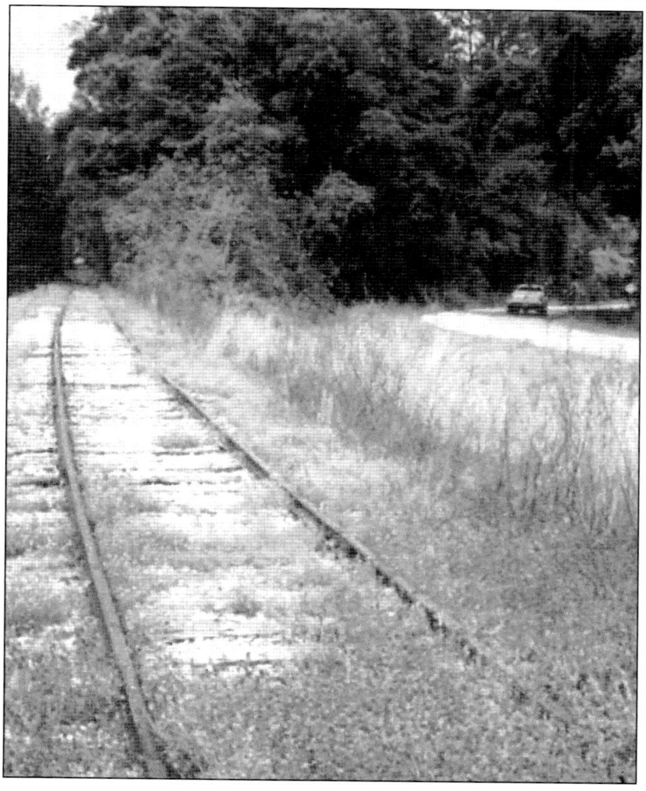

This abandoned track at Dozier in Crenshaw County, Alabama, is being engulfed by vegetation. The Central of Georgia established the railroad village of Dozier when it extended its line from Troy to Andalusia. Landscape reminders of the railroads' impact on the Wiregrass region is slowly being diminished by the loss of railroad tracks, depots, and other buildings that made small places an important element in the Wiregrass. (Courtesy of Dr. Larry Brown.)

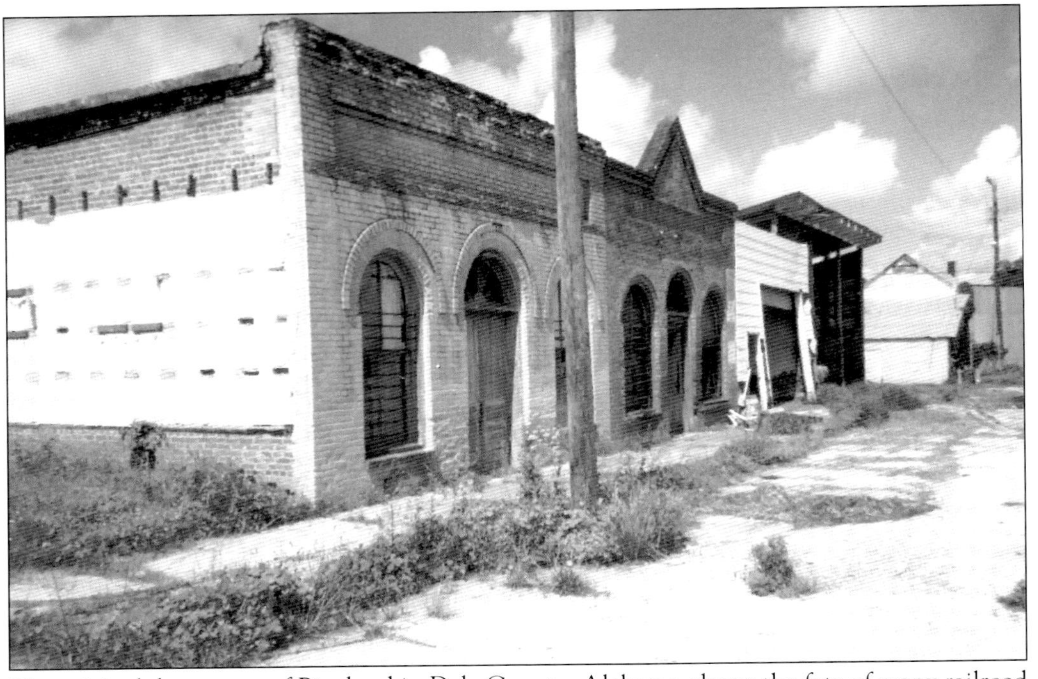

The original downtown of Pinckard in Dale County, Alabama, shows the fate of many railroad towns in the Wiregrass as highways replaced rails. These buildings face the railroad tracks, while a block behind them, traffic moves through the newer section of town on Alabama Highway 134. (Courtesy of Dr. Larry Brown.)

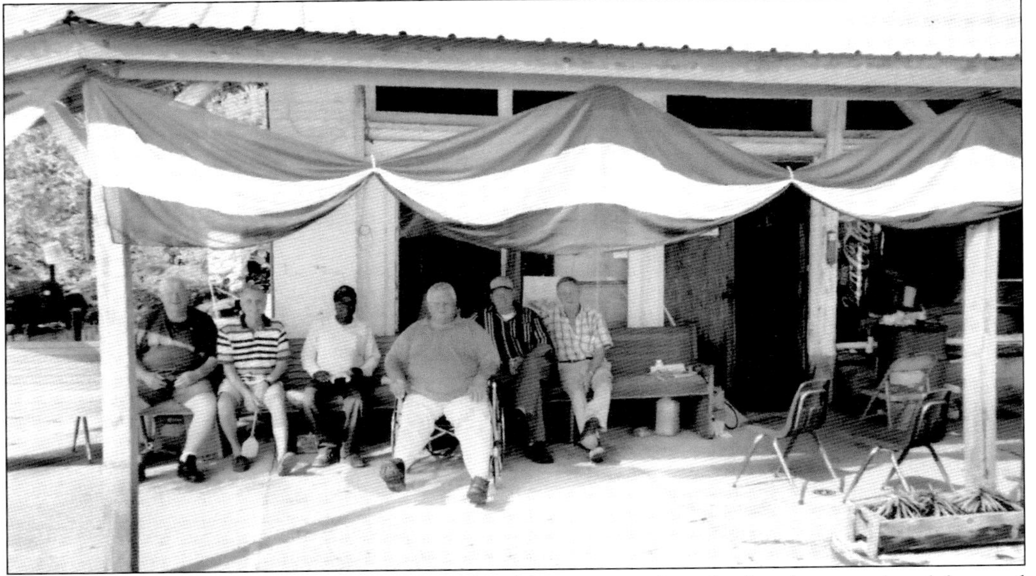

The original C.L. Berry store, in Glenwood, Alabama, is a place for locals to eat breakfast and swap stories. Glenwood formerly had several mercantile stores, a barber shop, a café, a cotton gin, a drug store, a bank, and other establishments. The town jail once housed Hank Williams, who was said to have been a guest of many sheriffs in this part of the state. (Courtesy of Dr. Larry Brown.)

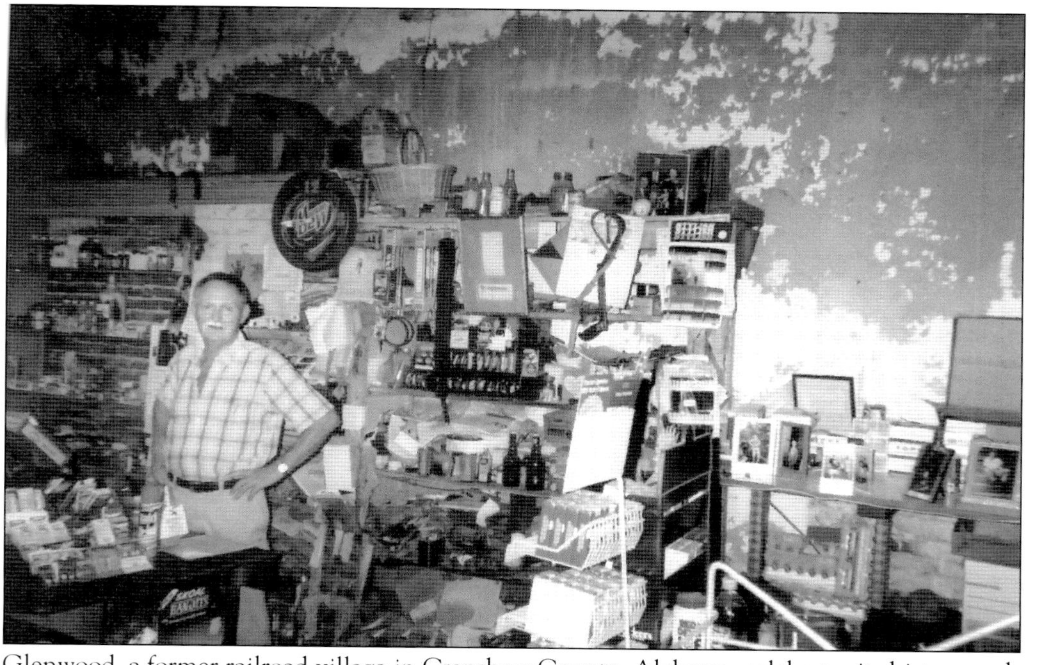

Glenwood, a former railroad village in Crenshaw County, Alabama, celebrates its history each May with "The Festival at the Well." Across from the well is the C.L. Berry Store, which has been operated continuously since 1935 by C.L. Berry and his son Boyd (pictured). C.L. Berry has ordered that nothing be changed in the store including the masses of cobwebs that hug the corners of the ceiling. (Courtesy of Dr. Larry Brown.)

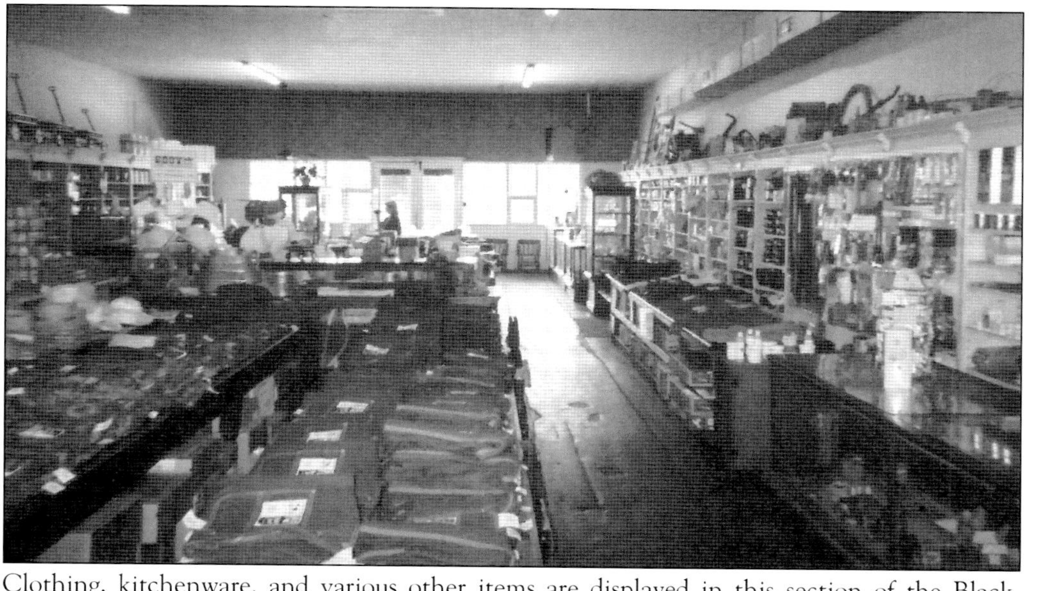

Clothing, kitchenware, and various other items are displayed in this section of the Black, Henderson, and Merrill Store in Dozier, Crenshaw County, Alabama. Today, the store stocks auto parts, paint, hardware, feed and seed, lumber, and building materials. In an earlier period, the store provided financial functions as well as the sale of mules to local farmers. Dozier remains a "working village." (Courtesy of Dr. Larry Brown.)

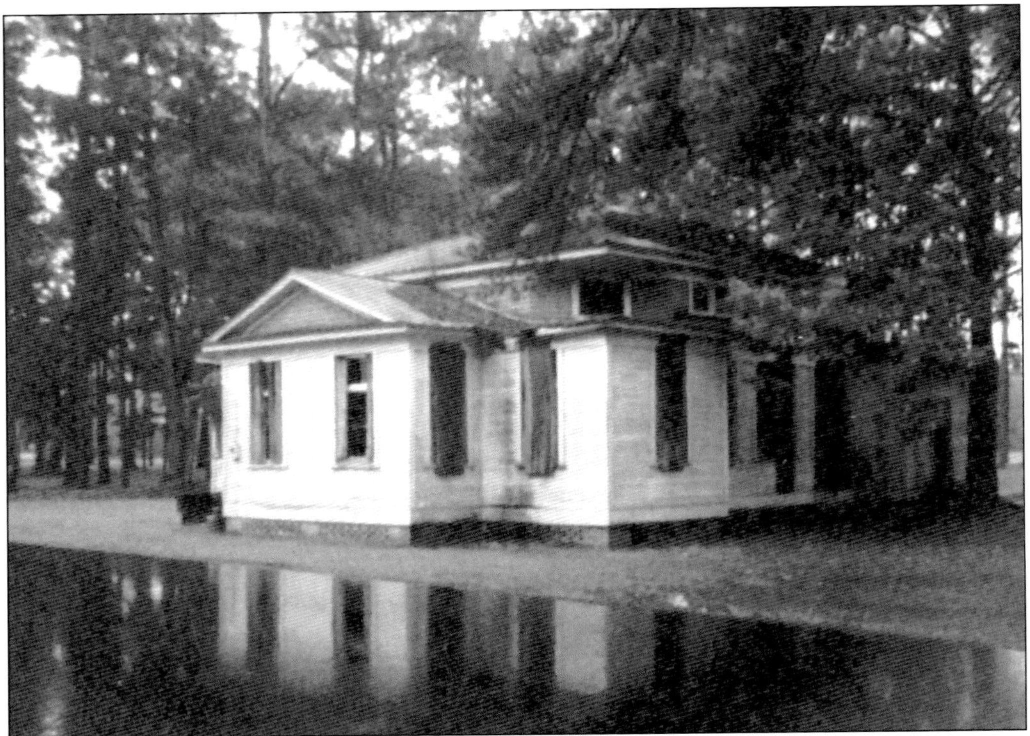

Although most of the functions of railroad villages have been lost to larger places, churches reflect the strong spiritual base of these communities. This unusual building, the former Baptist Church in Pollard, Escambia County, Alabama, awaits restoration and possible use as a community library. Pollard has three active churches for a population of about 100. (Courtesy of Dr. Larry Brown.)

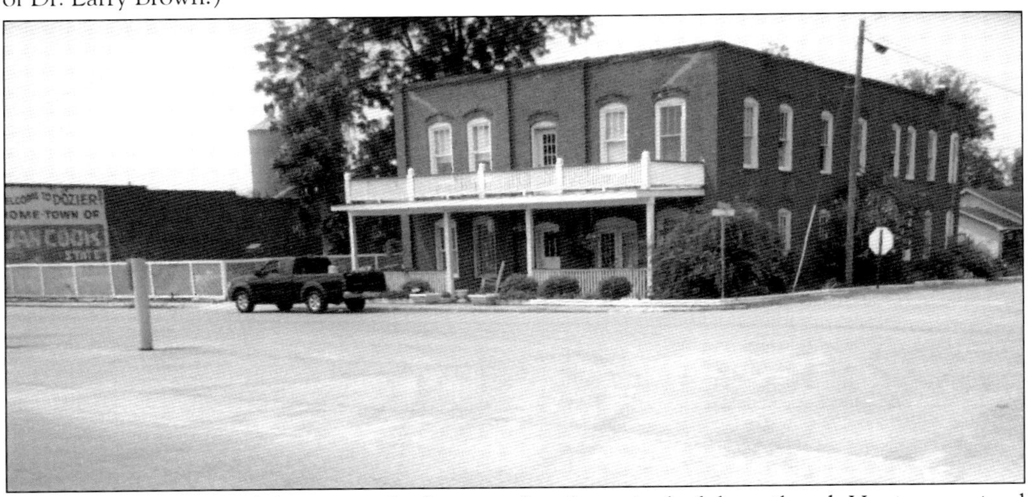

The hotel in Dozier, Alabama, was built soon after the arrival of the railroad. Having survived fire and other calamities such as abandonment for long periods, the hotel now serves as a private residence. The new owner is gradually restoring the building and is seeking to have the structure included in the National Register of Historical Places. Most railroad village hotels were constructed of wood and have long since been lost to time. (Courtesy of Dr. Larry Brown.)